THE CATHOLIC UNIVERSITY OF AMERICA
CANON LAW STUDIES
NO. 382

Canonical Relations Between the Bishops and Abbots at the Beginning of the Tenth Century

A DISSERTATION

SUBMITTED TO THE FACULTY OF THE SCHOOL OF CANON LAW OF THE CATHOLIC UNIVERSITY OF AMERICA IN PARTIAL FULFILLMENT OF THE REQUIREMENTS FOR THE DEGREE OF DOCTOR OF CANON LAW

BY

REV. CHARLES W. HENRY, O.S.B., A.B., S.T.L., J.C.L.
MONK OF ST. JOHN'S ABBEY, COLLEGEVILLE, MINNESOTA

THE CATHOLIC UNIVERSITY OF AMERICA PRESS
WASHINGTON, D.C.
1957

IMPRIMI POTEST:

✠BALDWIN DWORSCHAK, O.S.B.
Abbot of St. John's Abbey

NIHIL OBSTAT:

CLEMENS V. BASTNAGEL, S.T.L., J.U.D.
Censor deputatus

IMPRIMATUR:

✠PETER BARTHOLOME, D.D.
Bishop of St. Cloud

St. Cloud, Minnesota
Aug. 26, 1957

Printed by St. John's University Press, Collegeville, Minn., U.S.A.

Dilecto Patri
Meo

TABLE OF CONTENTS

FOREWORD

It would be difficult to grasp the significance of the canonical relations between bishops and abbots in the tenth century without a familiarization with canonical developments between the same in the centuries prior to this one. Rather than assume an arbitrary date from which to begin, and confuse the reader with references to past legal developments not included in the substance of this work, it seems only logical to begin with the first legislation covering the point, which necessitates a return to the fifth century, and the Council of Chalcedon. A brief introduction covering the coming-to-life of the monastic movement also seems necessary for the sake of casting more light on the import of the first ecclesiastical legislation regarding monasteries.

It is the purpose of this survey, then, to open to the reader a sketch of the historical development of canonical relations between bishops and abbots from the beginning of Christian monasticism until the middle of the tenth century, when Cluny had seen its first successes. If much historical matter is included herein, it is done designedly, since "the student of the Middle Ages finds himself confronted with a world in which canonical institutions were an integral part of the social and political structure; with an intellectual framework for which canonical doctrines were living realities in the realm of thought and learning."[1] Pursuant, therefore, to discovering the actual state of canon law in the tenth century, the writer has had recourse to the historical atmosphere in which that law was formed, and from which, in a large manner, it must be educed.

Knowing these underlying facts, one will regard the tenth century scene more as a logical outcome of a sequence of canonical and historical stages than merely as the precipitate mushrooming of privileges—although these latter are by no means ignored. It is hoped that the work will likewise prove

[1] Stephan Kuttner, "The Scientific Investigation of Medieval Canon Law: The Need and Opportunity," *Speculum*, XXIV (1949), p. 493.

a useful link in establishing a better understanding of present day relations between bishops and abbots through a fuller evaluation of those which obtained in other periods in the past.

The writer acknowledges with deep gratitude the assistance given him by Dr. Kuttner, Dr. Bastnagel, and the Faculty of the School of Canon Law at the Catholic University of America. He likewise wishes to thank his superior, the Rt. Rev. Baldwin Dworschak, O.S.B., who saw fit to send him on for higher studies, his parents and confreres, the members of his family, relatives, classmates and friends, and all who in any way have aided in bringing this work to its conclusion.

CHAPTER I

THE CANONICAL INCORPORATION OF MONASTICISM INTO THE CHURCH

ARTICLE 1. EASTERN MONACHISM BEFORE CHALCEDON

The first church legislation respecting monks and their relation to diocesan bishops was enacted in the Council of Chalcedon in the year 451.[1] Norms set by this Council formed the basis for many of the developments in later centuries regarding the position of monks in the Church.

One should bear in mind that "in the matter of conciliar decrees and canons, . . . that refer to discipline . . . their content or subject matter is dependent not only on circumstances of persons, places, and times, but also on considerations of expediency or temporal necessity."[2] Therefore, it seems advisable, not only to investigate the pronouncements of the Council, but also the conditions, whether proximate or remote, which prompted its disciplinary legislation concerning monks, and finally to trace briefly the inclusion of Chalcedon's canons about monks in later legislation. First of all, a cursory survey of early monastic life will set the stage remotely for the council's enactments.

The earliest type of Christian monasticism was eremitical. It was solitary life in the strictest sense, and in the beginning the manner of life of the recluse gave him the name Μόναχος, one who lives a solitary life.[3] He was motivated to pursue his

[1] Lafontaine, *L'Evêque d'Ordination des Religieux, Etude Historico-Juridique* (Ottawa: Editions de l'Université d'Ottawa, 1951), p. 43; Bittermann, "The Council of Chalcedon and Episcopal Jurisdiction," *Speculum*, XIII (1938), 198; Kurtscheid, *Historia Iuris Canonici, Historia Institutionum*, Vol. I (ab Ecclesiae Fundatione usque ad Gratianum), (2.ed., Romae: Catholic Book Agency, 1951), pp. 185-186; Pöschl, *Bischofsgut und MENSA EPISCOPALIS* (3 vols., Vol. I, Bonn, 1908), I, 81.

[2] Schroeder, *Disciplinary Decrees of the General Councils* (St. Louis: Herder Book Co., 1937), p. 5 (hereafter cited *Disciplinary Decrees*).

[3] Creusen, *De Juridica Status Religiosi Evolutione, Synopsis Historica*

isolated life by a desire for evangelical perfection through the means of recollection, protracted prayer, strict poverty and perfect chastity. The origin of this type of Christian monasticism is roughly set at *circa* 341, the death of St. Paul the Hermit. His disciple, St. Anthony the Abbot (d. 356), called the Father of Monasticism,[4] popularized this type of life throughout northern Egypt.

A contemporary of Anthony, St. Pachomius (d. 347), initiated another variety of monasticism in southern Egypt, the cenobitical type (*κοινὸς βίος*-common-life)[5] and was the first legislator for this Pachomian type of monasticism.[6] The fame and sanctity of these holy men at the outset gave to monasticism its first great impetus, which was to be continued and extended by others.[7]

The name of St. Basil (d. 379) is usually associated with the spread of monasticism into Asia Minor and other parts of the East. He likewise wrote for his monks several rules based upon careful inquiries into many contemporary rules.[8] Canons of the Council of Chalcedon, therefore, bore a relation to the cenobitical monasticism principally, although their application could also extend to other forms.

The monastic movement in its origins was strictly a lay

(Romae: Apud Aedes Pont. Univ. Gregorianae, 1948), p. 14; Kurtscheid, *op. cit.*, pp. 180-183.

[4] Butler, *Benedictine Monachism* (London, 1919), p. 12; Lévy-Bruhl, *Elections Abbatiales en France* (Paris, 1913), pp. 6-7.

[5] Beste, *Introductio in Codicem* (3. ed., Collegeville: St. John's Abbey Press, 1946), p. 311; Schaefer, *De Religiosis* (4.ed., Romae: Editrice Apostolato Cattolico, 1947), p. 21.

[6] Butler, *op. cit.*, p. 12; Creusen, *op. cit.*, p. 14.

[7] Creusen, *op. cit.*, p. 15; McLaughlin, *Le très ancien droit monastique de l'Occident* (Ligugé, 1935), p. 112.

[8] Butler, *op. cit.*, p. 12: "St. Basil's construction of the monastic life was fully cenobitical, being an advance in this line of that of St. Pachomius. (He)...established a common roof, a common table, common work, and common prayer daily; so that we meet here for the first time in Christian monastic legislation the fully realized idea of the *cenobium* and common life, properly so-called. From St. Basil is derived the monasticism of Eastern Europe."

movement,[9] and this by design rather than accident.[10] As individuals baptized into the Church's membership, the monks were in spiritual things subject to their spiritual father, the bishop,[11] yet as a community the monks were outside the jurisdiction of the bishop.[12] His only grounds for interfering with monastic life was to correct flagrant lapses from the true Christian principles.[13] He could not touch the temporal goods of the monastery, nor disturb the internal discipline of the community. The not altogether rare case of the bishop who was also abbot or founder is excepted here, for in this case it was not by virtue of his episcopal consecration but rather by virtue of another right that he exercised such a power.[14]

[9] Schmitz, *Histoire de l'Ordre de Saint Benoît* (7 vols., Vol. I, Les Editions de Maredsous, 1942), II, 347; Lévy-Bruhl, *op. cit.*, p. 65; Creusen, *op. cit.*, p. 14; Lafontaine, *op. cit.*, p. 41.

[10] Lafontaine, *op. cit.* p. 19.

[11] Hefele-Leclercq, *Histoire des Conciles* (11 vols. in 21, Paris: Letouzey et Ané, 1907-1952), Tom. II, 782.

[12] Lévy-Bruhl, *op. cit.*, p. 21: "Les conciles reconnaissent d'ailleurs pour la plupart, qu'au sein du monastère il n'y a place que pour une seule autorité, celle de l'abbé. L'évêque n'a d'autorité que sur ce dernier, mais cette autorité elle-même, considérable en théorie, est restreinte, en pratique, par cette considération que l'abbé tient son pouvoir non point de l'évêque, ou de l'église, mais de la communauté monastique, et, par son intermédiaire, du Saint-Esprit, c'est-à-dire d'un pouvoir indépendant, et égal en dignité a celui de l'évêque lui-même. L'évêque ne pouvait, en outre, lutter contre l'abbé sans lutter par là même contre la congrégation dont celui-ci était l'élu et qu'il incarnait en quelque sorte;" cf., McLaughlin, *op. cit.*, p. 129; Pöschl, *op. cit.*, I, 81.

[13] "Natürlich konnten sie (the bishops) (auch früher schon) in die Verwaltung der Klöster eingreifen, wenn durch eine schlechte, das heisst unklösterliche verweltlichte Art des ökonomischen Betriebs die Reinheit des Klosterlebens geschädigt oder unmöglich gemacht wurde, wenn das Kloster zum Aergernis der Christen wurde. Das war dann ein Eingreifen RATIONE SCANDALI oder PECCATI. Das gehört auch weiterhin vor allem zu dem neuen und erweiterten Aufsichtsrecht;"—Ueding, "Die Kanones von Chalkedon in ihrer Bedeutung für Mönchtum und Klerus;" from Grillmeier-Bacht, *Das Konzil von Chalkedon* (3 vols., Würzburg: Echter Verlag, 1951-1953), II (*Die Entscheidung um Chalkedon*), p. 609.

[14] Creusen, *De Jur. Status Rel. Ev.*, p. 17, "In monasteriis quorum episcopus fundator et superior est, nulla quaestio de dependentia oritur." Ueding, "Die Kanones von Chalkedon," p. 596; also p. 589. In some other

The monastic life of these communities was therefore independent of the bishop.[15] Their position in the Church was not entirely clear, however, for although they were as individuals (by baptism) surely members of the Church, their type of life had no canonical status. They could be legally characterized as existing and operating alongside rather than *outside of* and *opposed to* the Church.[16] The bishop frequently sent a priest to administer to the monks' spiritual needs in virtue of their spiritual relationship to him, since, as was indicated above, in the earliest times there was a marked antipathy among the monks themselves toward the promotion of any of their number to the clerical state. But gradually clerics were admitted to the communities in the capacity of members, and many monasteries, for convenience' sake, had some of their own monks ordained.[17] These last named clerics remained under the jurisdiction of the bishop with regard to the exercise of their ministry by virtue of their ordination, and yet as monks they were independent of him in everything which pertained strictly to monastic life.

Some question could be raised concerning such independence in the case of the founding of monasteries, but there too the bishop seems to have had little to say.[18] Since the monasteries had absolutely no juridical character,[19] whether with respect

cases the author shows that some monks, such as Pachomius, acknowledge the bishop as being head of the diocese with some jurisdiction over the monastic community, for Pachomius (e.g.) sends a thief to the bishop to be judged, "since he is a monk."

[15] Ueding, *art. cit.*, p. 576.

[16] McLaughlin, *Le très ancien droit*, p. 130: "Le monachisme... était un pouvoir dans l'Eglise, et l'on peut dire, pendant un certain moment, à côté de l'Eglise. Ce serait une exagération de dire, opposé à l'Eglise."

[17] Heimbucher, *Die Orden und Kongregationen der katholischen Kirche*, (2 vols, Paderborn, 1933), I, 93: "Während Pachomius den Empfang der Priesterweihe verbot, schreibt Basilius vor, dass jedes Kloster einige Priester haben soll."

[18] Ueding, *art. cit.*, p. 581: "Der einzige bekannte Fall, dass ein Bischof gegen eine Klostergründung protestiert, liegt in Kapitel 58 der *Vita bohair* ("Vita Pachomii bohairice scripta," LeFort, *Les Vies Coptes de Saint Pachome et de ses premiers successeurs* (Louvain, 1943)." Cf. also *ibid.*, p. 579.

[19] *Ibidem*, (Note), p. 579,... da die Gründung eines Klosters vor der Zeit

to Church or State, their erection was independent of either bishop or emperor. Visits made by either of these dignitaries to monasteries were not undertaken by them for the purpose of manifesting their jurisdictional rights, but for some other reason, of whatever sort.[20] But the right to interfere in case of scandal always was acknowledged.[21]

On the whole, the early history of monasticism shows that it promoted the best interests of the Church,[22] and that friendly relations existed between bishops and monasteries.[23] However as monasticism expanded its influence and numbers, it took on a semi-clerical nature, both from the attitude of the faithful toward it, and on the part of the monks themselves.[24]

Chalkedons gar keinen juridischen Charakter hatte, da die Klöster weder vor der Kirche noch vor dem Staat "*de jure*" anerkannte Institutionen waren. Es gab zwischen Klöstern und Aussenwelt keine juridischen, sondern nur tatsächliche Beziehungen."

[20] Ueding, *art. cit.* p. 591.

[21] Ueding, *art. cit.*, p. 609: "Freilich darf man nicht vergessen, dass auch in der früheren Zeit ein Recht der Bischöfe, "*ratione peccati,*" in die Klöster einzugreifen, wie bei jedem öffentlichen Ärgernis der Diözese, nicht zu leugnen ist."

[22] Bacht-Cramer, "Die Rolle des Orientalischen Mönchtums in den kirchenpolitischen Auseinandersetzungen um Chalkedon (431-519)," from Grillmeier-Bacht, *Das Konzil von Chalkedon* (3 vols., Würzburg: Echter Verlag, 1951-1954), II (*Die Entscheidung um Chalkedon*), p. 313: "Heute wissen wir, dass das Mönchtum sich nicht nur *in* der Kirche und aus den genuinen Kräften der Kirche entwickelt hat, insofern es die authentische Fortsetzung des urchristlichen, evangelischen Asketentums ist, sondern dass es auch von Anfang an um seine Verpflichtung gegenüber der Kirche gewusst hat, mag auch die Art und Weise, wie dieses Wissen in die Tat umgesetzt wurde, sehr mannigfach sein. Auch im einsamsten Gebetsringen und im erbitterten Kampf mit den Dämonen der Wüste stand der Mönch nicht nur für sich und sein Heil ein, sondern zugleich. . . für die ganze Kirche." Hauck (*Kirchengeschichte Deutschlands* [2 Bände, Leipzig, 1887], I, 221-222) noted that several authors spoke of continual strife between bishops and abbots in this early period, but he proved the point to be inaccurate.

[23] McLaughlin, *Le très ancien droit*, p. 129: "Les rapports entre les monastères et les évêques furent, en règle générale, très cordiaux, exception faite pour une période de brève durée". Cf. also Lafontaine, *L'Evêque d'Ordination*, p. 41; Ueding, "Die Kanones von Chalkedon," p. 575. But there were exceptions; cf., e.g., Ueding, "art. cit.," p. 575.

[24] McLaughlin, *Le très ancien droit*, p. 129: "Les choses ne restèrent pas

Moreover, monks began to mix in the affairs of Church and State, to preach, to take part in the theological discussions, to criticize the clergy.[25] Some became heretical.[26] Since the Church was feeling the impact of this army of monks, it had no other choice than to recognize them in a canonical manner, although the necessity to do so certainly arose only shortly before the Council of Chalcedon, otherwise there would surely have been legislation enacted prior to it.[27]

ARTICLE 2. THE COUNCIL OF CHALCEDON (451)

Legislation concerning monks was introduced in the sixth session of Chalcedon, in which the Emperor Marcian and the Empress Pulcheria appeared with full solemnity.[28] The Emperor presented the most important basic desiderata regarding monastic legislation, which specific suggestions were later incorporated under canons 3, 4 and 20 of the Council. The Fathers of the Council were to elaborate upon these points in the other sessions.

longtemps ainsi, car les moines, par leur but et par leur genre de vie, acquirent bientôt, aux yeux des fidèles, un caractère au moins semi-clérical. Le pouvoir ecclésiastique, reconnaissant ce fait, et pour d'autres raisons encore chercha à faire entrer le monachisme dans ses propres cadres."

[25] Lafontaine, *op. cit.*, p. 43: "Mais les moines se mêlaient au peuple et à ses querelles, soulevaient des émeutes, causaient des désordres. Ils erraient de ville en ville et promenaient partout le scandale de leur vie désorbitée. Ills s'immisçaient dans les questions de théologie, alors qu'ils n'avaient ni la formation ni le savoir requis. Ils se révoltaient contre les évêques, faisaient la vie dure aux fonctionnaires, et ne manqaient pas d'embarrasser, par leur conduit, jusqu'à l'empereur." Cf. Hefele-Leclercq, *op. cit.*, Tom. IIb, p. 780, (note 1).

[26] Cf. Bacht-Cramer, "Die Rolle des Orientalischen Mönchtums," pp. 313-338.

[27] Lafontaine, *L'Evêque d'Ordination*, p. 42: "...Il semble bien, qu'avant le milieu du IV siècle...les conciles de l'époque n'ont pas senti le besoin de légiférer sur ce point."

[28] Hefele, *A History of the Councils of the Church* (5 vols., Edinburgh, 1876-1896), III, 353-354; Mansi, *Sacrorum Conciliorum Nova et Amplissima Collectio* (53 vols. in 60, Parisiis, 1901-1927), VII, col. 458-491 (hereafter cited as Mansi).

Canon 4, easily the most noteworthy canon with regard to the regulation of monastic life, stated:[29]

> Those who lead a true and sincere monastic life ought to enjoy due honor. Since, however, there are some who, using the monastic state as a pretext, disturb the churches and the affairs of the state, roam about aimlessly in the cities, and even undertake to establish monasteries for themselves, it is decided that no one shall build or found a monastery or a house of prayer without the consent of the bishop of the city. It is decided, furthermore, that all monks in every city and country place shall be subject to the bishop, that they love silence and attend only to fasting and prayer, remaining in the places in which they renounced the world; that they shall not leave their monasteries and burden themselves either with ecclesiastical or worldly affairs or take part in them unless they are commissioned to do so for some necessary purpose by the bishop of the city; that no slave shall be received into the monasteries and become a monk without the consent of his master. Whosoever transgresses this decision of ours shall be excommunicated, in order that the name of God be not blasphemed. The bishop of the city, moreover, shall exercise a strict supervision over the monasteries.

The canon is clear. It obviously affected both the civil and ecclesiastical sphere, for in the East the two were quite intimately intertwined. Although history evidences[30] that quite generally monks had been most peace-loving, there was a group of them which disturbed the public order and had to

[29] Schroeder, *Disciplinary Decrees*, p. 92; Mansi, VII, col. 359-360; Bruns, *Canones Apostolorum et Conciliorum Veterum Selecti* (2 vols., Berolini, 1839), I, 26; Hefele-Leclercq, *Histoire des Conciles*, II, 779. For the Greek text of the Council, the best edition is that of Schwartz, *Acta Conciliorum Oecumenicorum* (4 vols. in 15 parts, Berolini et Lipsiae, 1914-1927), Vol. III, *Concilium Chalcedonense* (1927), p. 179.

[30] Cf. *supra*, art. 1.

be quelled.[31] This group of monks was headed by Barsumas, (d. 489) the Archimandrite, and was Monophysite in tendency. It was this proximate circumstance which set off the spark of reaction from the Emperor and the Council against monasticism as a whole, although[32] one might look for a more remote preparation in the Robber Council of Ephesus, when Dioscurus of Alexandria (444-451, d. 454) was supported both by military strength and over a thousand monks led by the same Barsumas.[33]

The way was paved for such demonstrations by the gradual evolution of monasticism first from eremetical to cenobitical life, and thence to the "semi-clerical"[34] and frankly secular interests.[35] Since many of these last named were unable to adequately adjust themselves to these nuances in their way of life, it was the purpose of the first part of this canon to coerce them to do so. Its end was ostensibly to restore monasticism to its pristine purity, although one reads into the canon that such a measure would relieve the bishop and secular clergy of much discomfiture, caused not a little by the lack of monastic discipline.

The next part of the canon limited the founding of new

[31] Ueding, "Die Kanones von Chalkedon," p. 578: "Höchstens kann man annehmen, dass die Mönche als öffentliche Ruhestörer angesehen wurden, als Fanatiker, die eben deshalb der Bischof zur Rede stellen musste, weil sie als Skandalum in seiner Gemeinde galten."

[32] Cf. Schroeder, *Disciplinary Decrees*, pp. 92-94; Hefele-Leclercq, *Histoire des Conciles*, II, 780 (note).

[33] Schroeder, *op. cit.*, p. 93: "The disgraceful part they (Barsumas and the thousand illiterate monks) had in that council [the Robber Council of Ephesus] is well-known. . . The restrictions of this canon did not, however, moderate the irrepressible and misdirected zeal of the Eastern monks."

[34] McLaughlin, *Le très ancien droit*, p. 112: "L'état du moine devient semi-clérical vis-a-vis de la législation séculière qui l'excepte de certaines lois. De son côté, la législation ecclésiastique considère les obligations spéciales du moine comme des obligations ecclésiastiques et l'assimile sur certains points au clerc."

[35] Lafontaine, *L'Evêque d' Ordination*, p. 43: "Les moines de cette dernière catégorie commencèrent à nourrir des préoccupations cléricales ou séculières. Le monachisme oriental se vit bientôt entaché de plusieurs éléments médiocres ou même franchement mauvais."

monasteries to such as received the permission of the local bishop. These monasteries were also to be subject to the bishop, but just which bishop was meant and how they were to be subject to him is not accurately defined. Later on, those who fell under this precept could circumvent it by picking the bishop to whom they wished to be subject. Unable to suppress the monastic institution, which was already so strongly ensconced in the Church's life, and which satisfied the mystical needs of the age and local environment, the Fathers of the Council sought to bend it to the Church's needs. They were able to do this only by first admitting it into the Church canonically, which this canon initially undertook to do, and then by immediately subjecting it to the Church's authority.

The section treating of the slaves need not be a matter of grave concern here. In passing, one may simply note that the spirit which prompted it was a justifiable and unselfish one, meaning to prevent the abbeys from becoming havens for runaway slaves who could seek to join the communities for unworthy motives.[36]

Outside of this most important canon 4, other canons of the Council also touched monks, and monastic discipline. Canon 2 forbade the practice of simony, the delinquent monk suffering an anathema.

> If any bishop has conferred sacred orders for money and put to sale the grace that cannot be sold, and for money ordained a bishop, *chorepiscopus*, priest, deacon, or any other cleric, or for money, for the gratification of his own base greed, appointed a steward, advocate, sacristan or any other servant in the church, he shall if convicted imperil his rank; but the person so ordained or promoted shall gain nothing, but shall be deprived of the dignity of office thus obtained. Should anyone be proved to have been an intermediary in these disgraceful and unlawful transactions, he shall, if he be a cleric, be deposed from his rank; if a layman or a monk, anathematized.[37]

[36] Hefele-Leclercq, *Histoire des Conciles*, II, 780.

[37] Schroeder, *Disciplinary Canons*, p. 86. Cf. also Hefele-Leclercq, *His-*

Canon 3 spoke of clerics being too enmeshed in secular affairs.

> It has come to the knowledge of the holy council that some members of the clergy for sordid gain become tenants of the estates of others and engage in secular occupations, neglecting the service of God, insinuating themselves into the houses of the people of the world, and from covetous motives undertake the administration of their property. The holy and great council has decreed, therefore, that in the future no bishop, cleric, or monk shall be engaged in farming estates or in business, or undertake secular administrations, unless he be summoned by law to assume the guardianship of minors and cannot escape that charge, or the bishop of the city should commission him, because of the fear of the Lord, to manage ecclesiastical affairs, or the affairs of orphans and widows not otherwise provided for, and of such persons as especially need the aid of the church. If anyone in the future transgresses this ordinance, he shall undergo the ecclesiastical penalties.[38]

The religious clerics likewise fell under this reprobation, although there is no evidence from the words of the canon that the Emperor or the delegates had directed it especially at them rather than at the secular clerics.

Canon 7 prohibited monks from army service and forbade them the acceptance of secular dignities.

> We have decreed that those who have once been numbered among the clergy or have chosen the monastic state shall not enter the military service or accept any secular dignity. Those who dare act thus, and do not so repent that they return to the vocation

toire des Conciles, II, 772; Bruns, *Canones Apostolorum et Conciliorum Veterum Selecti*, I, 25 (hereafter cited as Bruns); Mansi, VII, col. 358.

[38] Schroeder, *Disciplinary Canons*, p. 90. Cf. also Hefele-Leclercq, *Histoire des Conciles*, II, 775; Bruns, I, 26; Mansi, VII, col. 359-360.

> they once chose for God's sake, shall be anathematized.[39]

The 8th canon forbade clerics to exercise their orders in the churches and oratories without the permission of the bishops. It certainly applied to religious as well as to secular clerics, but was to cause not a little difficulty in its application.

> Clerics of poorhouses, monasteries, and oratories shall remain under the jurisdiction of their respective bishop in each city, in accordance with the tradition of the holy fathers, and shall not indulge in self-will or rebel against their bishop. Those who dare in any manner to transgress this ordinance and refuse submission to their bishop are, if clerics, to incur canonical censure (deposition), if monks or laymen, to be excommunicated.[40]

In the 16th canon, monks or virgins consecrated to God were forbidden to marry, but the bishops had power to mitigate the penalty of excommunication for just reasons.

> A virgin who has consecrated herself to the Lord God, and also a monk, are not allowed to marry; if they do so, they are to be excommunicated. The local bishop, however, shall have the authority to mitigate the severity of the punishment.[41]

It was the first such legislation for monks, but not for virgins, for obvious reasons.

The 18th canon condemned the malpractice whereby clerics and monks conspired against bishops. This precept seems to have been directed pointedly against the subjects of Bishop

[39] Schroeder, *Disciplinary Decrees*, p. 96. Cf. also Hefele-Leclercq, *Histoire des Conciles*, II, 788; Bruns, I, 27; Mansi, VII, col. 361-362.

[40] Schroeder, *Disciplinary Decrees*, p. 97. Cf. also Hefele-Leclercq, *Histoire des Conciles*, II, 789; Bruns, I, 27; Mansi, VII, col. 361-362; McLaughlin, *Le très ancien droit*, p. 131; Ueding, "Die Kanones von Chalkedon," p. 616.

[41] Schroeder, *Disciplinary Decrees*, p. 114; Hefele-Leclercq, *Histoire des Conciles*, II, 804; Bruns, I, 29; Ueding, "Die Kanones von Chalkedon," p. 615; Mansi, VII, col. 365-366.

Ibas of Edessa (435-457), who had plotted against him.

> The crime of conspiracy or faction has been absolutely prohibited even by the secular laws, much more ought it be forbidden in the Church of God. If, therefore, any clerics or monks be found forming a conspiracy or plot or concocting plans against bishops or fellow-clerics, they shall be completely deposed from their rank.[42]

This canon seemed to exclude from its consideration the ordinary monk, but it contained special threats against the clerics and the dignitaries of the monastery.[43]

Canon 23 was directed against those fanatical monks and clerics who, though lacking the permission of their bishop, spent too much time in the capital city of Constantinople.

> It has come to the ears of the holy council, that some clerics and monks, without having received any commission from their bishop, and sometimes even under sentence of excommunication by him, betake themselves to Constantinople and remain there a long time, causing disturbances and creating disorders in the affairs of the Church, even turning over the houses of some people. The holy council has decided, therefore, that such persons shall first be notified by the advocate of the most holy Church of Constantinople to depart from the imperial city; but if they imprudently persist in the same practices, they are to be expelled by the same advocate even against their will and must betake themselves to their own places.[44]

It gave the prelate of Constantinople the right to expel such persons. This was but an extension and particular application

[42] Schroeder, *Disciplinary Decrees*, p. 117. Cf. also Hefele-Leclercq, *Histoire des Conciles*, II, 806; Bruns, I, 30; Mansi, VII, col. 365-366.

[43] Ueding, "Die Kanones von Chalkedon," p. 611.

[44] Schroeder, *Disciplinary Decrees*, p. 121. Cf. also Hefele-Leclercq, *Histoire des Conciles*, II, 809; Bruns, I, 31; Mansi, VII, col. 367-368; Marin, *Les Moines de Constantinople depuis la fondation de la ville jusqu'à la mort de Photius* (Paris, 1897), p. 253. The author shows how formidable a power the monks could be when congregated together.

of the ecclesiastical legislation that forbade the cleric to abandon his parish or diocese without the permission of the bishop, and thereby implicitly presupposed the quasi-clerical status of monks.

The very important canon 24 finally granted perpetuity to monasteries legally established as well as to all possessions attached to the monastery, and forbade these from being converted into secular dwellings.

> Monasteries which have once been consecrated with the consent of the bishop shall remain monasteries in perpetuity, and all the property belonging to them shall be preserved to them and no longer shall they be permitted to become secular dwellings. Those who permit this to be done shall be subject to the canonical penalties.[45]

They were, then, "*res sacrae*," and as such were untouchable for other than the monastic purposes. Not even the bishop could exert any property or fiscal right over them.

What then, in brief, was accomplished by the Council regarding the monks? First of all, by taking cognizance of the monastic state, the Council officially made monasticism a canonical organ of the Church,[46] and the monasteries became "juridic persons."[47] Secondly, it strove to control this canonical neophyte lest it endanger the traditional doctrinal belief. Thirdly, to protect the external order of the Church, it regulated by precept, but in the broadest terms, the discipline of monasteries, by making their founding depend upon the con-

[45] Schroeder, *Disciplinary Decrees*, p. 121. Cf. also Hefele-Leclercq, *Histoire des Conciles*, II, 810; Bruns, I, 31; Mansi, VII, col. 367-368.

[46] Ueding, "Die Kanones von Chalkedon," p. 616.

[47] Ueding, *art. cit.*, p. 617. Cf. McLaughlin, *Le très ancien droit*, p. 81: "...à l'origine, l'évêque ne possède aucun droit sur la société monastique en tant que société. C'est un groupement laïque, dont tous les membres y compris l'abbé appartiennent à l'état laïque. Chrétien, chaque moine a certains devoirs envers le chef de l'Eglise locale mais le groupement comme tel ne lui est pas directement soumis. A partir du moment où le monachisme est reconnu comme une société religieuse, l'évêque y aura un droit de contrôle."

sent of the bishop, and, once they were founded, by making them "subject" to the surveillance of the bishop. On the positive side this subjection protected the monasteries from arbitrary abuse from the secular powers.

The few words taken from canon 4, *τοὺς δὲ καθ' ἑκάστην πόλιν καὶ χώραν μονάζοντας ὑποτετάχθαι τῷ ἐπισκόπῳ*[48] effected perhaps the greatest precedent regarding monasticism, particularly with respect to its passion for autonomy. It was mentioned above that the subjection of the monastery to the bishop was certainly of a spiritual nature, for the circumstances of the Council and the conduct of the delegates convinces one of this. However, was this subjection inclusive of the temporal sphere also?[49]

It is certainly true that the bishops were using their opportunity to assure themselves a position of complete hegemony in their own spheres, since they did not restrict themselves to the few suggestions of the Emperor, but subjected the monks by conciliar legislation to as many of the general disciplinary acts as they were able.[50] Yet, since the innovation was to be of such a radical nature, and so contrary to tradition, and since there was no evidence of a positive nature to urge the point, many believe that the Fathers had never envisioned submitting the temporal control of the monasteries to themselves. Helen Bittermann presents this latter view, in forming a basis for her opinion on later developments in the West with regard to such temporal control.[51]

[48] Mansi, VII, col. 359; Bruns, I, 26; Hefele-Leclercq, *Histoire des Conciles*, II, 779.

[49] Schmitz, *Histoire de l'Ordre*, I, 307: "Mais les limites des pouvoirs de l'Ordinaire n'avaient pas été fixées par le concile, d'où la tendance chez certains évêques à abuser de leur autorité, et les efforts des moines pour s'y soustraire. Des conflits devaient naître. L'enjeu était important: il s'agissait de droits spirituels et temporels considérables, d'intérêts moraux et politiques qui pouvaient être décisifs dans certaines occasions. Laisser la question indéterminée, c'était abandonner la solution au plus fort, au plus puissant."

[50] Hefele-Leclercq, *Histoire des Conciles*, II, 781: "La législation canonique (in the council) marque en Occident comme en Orient une tendance soutenue à maintenir les privilèges épiscopaux."

[51] Bittermann, "The Council of Chalcedon and Episcopal Jurisdiction,"

It is the opinion of some that the point does not rest on what later councils and bishop-abbot relations can prove, but rather upon the non-approbation of the disciplinary canons of Chalcedon by the pope, and hence their restriction to the Eastern Church exclusively.[52] *De facto*, as will be seen in later chapters, either interpretation was adopted in the period after Chalcedon to support those whose interests it best served.[53] However, the opinion that the discipline imposed by the Council did not apply to the whole Church rests upon shaky ground indeed, for the pope had doubtless read the canons, and considered them, and passed judgment also upon them, for he

Speculum, XIII (1938), 198: "Of the Bishop's spiritual jurdisdiction, there is no question... The question is whether, in addition, he was also granted the right to interfere in the administration of monastic properties and in the general internal economy of monasteries in his dioceses... If by virtue of the fourth canon of Chalcedon, bishops were granted temporal as well as spiritual jurisdiction over monasteries in their diocese, then the behavior of the Merovingian episcopate with respect to monasteries was only a logical development of their former powers, (This is the opinion of most scholars. Cf. August Hufner, "Das Rechtsinstitut der klösterlichen Exemption in der abendländischen Kirche," *Archiv für katholisches Kirchenrecht*, LXXXVI [1906], 304-305; F. K. Weiss, *Die kirchlichen Exemptionen der Klöster von ihrer Enstehung bis zur Gregorianisch-Cluniacensischen Zeit* [Basel, 1894], p. 10; etc.) and the episcopal charters amounted to exemptions from the bishop's authority. If, on the other hand, the Council of Chalcedon restricted episcopal authority to the spiritual sphere, then the high-handed treatment which most Merovingian bishops seem to have accorded monasteries was an encroachment on the rights of the monks, and the episcopal charters were not exemptions from episcopal power but merely attempts to restrain bishops to the bounds set in 451." She holds to this latter view, saying shortly after: "Limitation of the jurisdiction conferred upon bishops at Chalcedon to the spiritual realm would seem to be borne out by the proceedings of those later councils which are thought to have been based on Chalcedon."

[52] Lafontaine, *L'Evêque d'Ordination*, p. 45.

[53] Lafontaine, *op. cit.*, p. 41: "Du milieu du Ve siècle au concile de Trente, comme un flux et reflux perpétuel l'exemption monastique subit progrès et reculs. Les évêques, coupables parfois d'abus intolérables mais souvent dans leurs droits, revendiquèrent la reconnaissance de leur autorité sur les religieux. Ceux-ci, soit par un désir peu chrétien d'indépendance, soit très souvent afin de remplir plus saintement leur mission, tentèrent d'échapper au contrôle du diocésain."

expunged from his approval the 28th canon. It seems little likely that he would not have struck out others which, he believed, would not benefit the Church.

Yet, since there is too little evidence that the Fathers wished to extend the monks' subjection to the temporal sphere, one certainly cannot do so, and accordingly one must conclude that had they intended to bind the monks also in this other sphere, their language would have been sufficiently clear to indicate it. "*In dubio,*" says canon law, "*nulla est lex.*"

On this point one may conclude with a double observation: 1) spiritual subjection to the bishop was defined only in the most general terms, and 2) the monks' subjection in temporal matters was not contemplated by the Council.

ARTICLE 3. THE EFFECTS OF CHALCEDON—EAST AND WEST

A dearth of positive data prevents a thoroughgoing investigation of the immediate consequences of Chalcedon's canons in the East. Where similarities exist between canons of Chalcedon and those of later councils, one cannot point to Chalcedon as the certain original source unless it is cited explicitly. Yet, it seems almost certain that at least three later legislative councils looked to Chalcedon for inspiration in a few points. For example, the Synod which was held in Constantinople in 627 hearkened to Chalcedon's second canon with respect to simony. The Trullan Synod in 692, in its 34th canon, took over the substance of the 18th canon of Chalcedon, while its 49th canon repeated the 24th of Chalcedon. The Council of Nicea in 787 has a canon (10) which embodies the 3rd and 23rd canons of Chalcedon. These last two councils did not wish to legislate, but only to restate the ancient enactments and to relate them to problems current during the period in which the councils were held. Further references, however, even though difficult to find, are actually not absolutely necessary in proof of the influence of Chalcedon, since Justinian's thorough adoption of Chalcedon's legislation in the *Codex* and *Novellae* made it a matter of everyday knowledge.[54]

[54] Ueding, "Die Kanones von Chalkedon," from Grillmeier-Bacht, *Das Konzil von Chalkedon*, II, 622.

The same problem obtains in attempting to trace the effects of Chalcedon in the West. It seems that Chalcedon, for a short interval following its conclusion, was little known, or better, badly observed although known.[55] The West actually was not particularly interested in the legislation of the East, since the synodal apparatus in Gaul, Spain, and Italy was functioning satisfactorily.[56] In addition there were the papal decretals and the legislation from earlier African synods, all of which circulated throughout the West with a great deal more facility than the Eastern legislation, even though the latter was ecumenical in character.[57]

A first hint of recognition of the monastic legislation of Chalcedon in the West appears in a provincial council held in 540 in Barcelona under the presidency of Sergius, archbishop of Tarragon.[58] The 10th canon of the council reads: "*De monachis vero id observari praecipimus, quod synodus Chalcedonensis constituit.*" In the Spanish canonical collections, however, it is ignored until the end of the 6th century, when the *Epitome Conciliorum et Decretalium* mentions it. Martin of Braga did not use the canons of Chalcedon in his collection. The canons of the II Council of Seville made frequent mention of Chalcedon. The collection *Hispana*, most important of the Spanish collections, redacted in 633, contained all the canons of Chalcedon discussed above. Some authors mention another collection, the *Arlesian*, which was, however, simply another version of the *Hispana*, hence containing like matter.

Sixth century Gaul had certain knowledge of Chalcedon from the dissemination of the *Quesnelliana* collection. Of more importance, however, was the *Dionysiana*, since it received wider acknowledgment and was, in its enlarged *Hadriana* form, made the official code of the Frankish lands under Charlemagne, and the Papal Chancery used it as a handbook of reference for Canon Law.[59]

[55] Ueding, *loc. cit.*; McLaughlin, *Le très ancien droit*, p. 133.

[56] Ueding, *art. cit.*, p. 619.

[57] Ueding, *loc. cit.*

[58] McLaughlin, *Le très ancien droit*, p. 132 (note.)

[59] Fournier-LeBras, *Histoire des Collections canoniques en Occident depuis*

It offered a faithful recording of Chalcedon's canons. The *Pithou* collection from Western France, appearing about 580, contained many of the canons pertinent to monks. Another very important collection was that of *Angers*, which found great favor in France and contained the 2nd, 3rd, 4th, 7th, 16th, and 24th canons of Chalcedon. The 8th and 23rd, it is to be noted, were not included. Another edition of this collection mentioned by LeBras[60] has the same omissions and concludes the 4th canon after the first sentence, thus omitting all the sections prejudicial to monks. Still another version of the *Angers* collection has most of the canons of Chalcedon, most important for us being the 3rd, 4th, 7th, 10th, 23rd, and 24th. The *Dacheriana* contains the same, but with this collection one is already almost four hundred years removed from Chalcedon, and other councils had in the meantime made themselves felt with tendencies not entirely in harmony with that which earlier obtained in 451.

les fausses décrétales jusqu'au Décret de Gratien (2 tomes, Paris, 1931-1932), Tom. I, p. 36.

[60] *Op cit.*, I, 83-84.

CHAPTER II

EARLY MONASTICISM IN THE WEST[1]

The year 339 marked the debut of monachism in Europe. It was then that St. Athanasius (297-376) and two Oriental monks in a visit to Rome called the attention of the West to monastic life. St. Jerome's (342-420) translation of parts of the Rule of St. Pachomius, and St. Ambrose's (d. 397) monastic foundation in Milan, did much to assure for the monastic way of life a permanent berth in the West. The bishop of Vercelli Eusebius, (d. 371), deserves to be noted also for being the first to combine the monastic and clerical states and to prescribe a community life under a monastic rule for the clergy of his cathedral church.

In Gaul, however, there was even a more fruitful field for the birth and growth of monachism, for it was blessed with the energetic labors of St. Martin (317-397) to promote it. In 360 the saint founded ancient Gaul's first Christian monastery at Ligugé near Poitiers, and later the famous Marmoutier outside of Tours, both following the Antonian type of monachism, which emphasized the eremitical life and bodily austerities. Further south, on the Mediterranean coast, two other famous monasteries sprang up within a few years, at Lérins in 400-410 under St. Honoratus, (d. 429) and at Marseilles in c.415 under Cassian (360-430/5). The latter is the renowned author of the *Institutes* and *Collations*, for the guidance of the first abbots of Lérins. These two monasteries adapted Egyptian monachism to the western climate and racial temperament, following by preference the Pachomian plan for monastic life.

St. Augustine as Bishop of Hippo (396-430) adopted Eusebius' way of life for his monastery at Hippo in northern Africa, but his must be considered the exception to the more common lay monachism which prevailed at the time. St. Patrick (385-461), monastically formed in the French foundations, instituted

[1] Cf. Schmitz, *Histoire de l'Ordre de St. Benoît*, Tom. I; Butler, *op. cit.*; Montalembert, *Monks of the West* (7 vols., Edinburgh, 1861-1879); Heimbucher, *op. cit.*; etc.

an eremitical type of monachism in Ireland about 450. Records are too rare to indicate any well-developed monastic life in Spain before the advent of the Benedictine monks.

Monasticism's greatest advance in the West was made through the efforts of the Patriarch of Occidental monachism, St. Benedict of Nursia (480-ca.547). He was the founder of the monastery of Monte Cassino and the author of the well-known Rule for monks. Since the Rule had such a tremendous impact upon Europe, one may well pause here briefly to consider its position with regard to the relations it would establish between bishops and the abbots of the Benedictine system. St. Benedict recognized the right of the bishop to conduct or supervise and to confirm the election of the abbot, and to remove unworthy candidates from the abbatial office.[2] He acknowledged to the bishop a certain right of surveillance over monastic discipline whenever difficulties arose which the abbot could not effectively control, as when a monk-priest proved rebellious to the Rule and showed himself disinclined to amend his life.[3] Therefore St. Benedict acknowledged jurisdictional rights for the bishop in whose diocese the abbey was located.[4] But, on the other hand, in everything which pertained to the internal regime of the monastery, he carefully pointed out the magistral position of the abbot. To the abbot exclusively pertained the abbey's administration and organization, the choosing of the prior,[5] the punishment of errant monks, the making of important decisions, the setting of precedents. This was not to say that the Rule was in-elastic or rigid in its specifications of all relations with outside powers. The principle of autonomy was certainly an inherent quality of the Rule, and yet the precise connections with civil or church law were conditioned and regulated by the circumstances of the times, and the spiritual and temporal necessities of the monks. This status of inexactness was later to prove a sore point in the development of Benedictine history.

[2] *The Holy Rule of our Most Holy Father Benedict,* translated by Rev. Boniface Verheyen, O.S.B. (Atchison: Abbey Student Press, 1949), Chap. 64.

[3] *Holy Rule,* Chapter 62.

[4] *Holy Rule,* Chapter 64.

[5] *Holy Rule,* Chapter 65.

CHAPTER III

THE THIRD COUNCIL OF ARLES (455)

Less than five years after the Council of Chalcedon, in January, 455, a provincial council was called by Ravennius, metropolitan of Arles, with the object of settling a jurisdictional dispute between Faustus, abbot of Lérins, and Theodore, bishop of Fréjus, the diocese in which Lérins was located.[1] The dispute arose after Theodore's ascendancy to the episcopal office, since before that time the relations between the bishop and the monastery had been quite cordial in the diocese.[2]

Honoratus, founder and first abbot of Lérins, had entered into a pact with or received a privilege from Leontius, bishop of Fréjus, sometime between 419 and 426, which established a *modus vivendi* between the monastery and the diocese. Theodore in contesting the pact sought to exercise a greater influence over the monastery than did his predecessor. The argument assumed rather notable proportions when the bishops of the province sided with one or the other, causing a rift in the provincial unity, and a scandal for the Church.[3]

Theodore, unable to settle the matter, petitioned Ravennius to hold a provincial council to decide the matter. It was not the purpose of the council to pass judgment upon one or the other of the principals and to punish the guilty party; the council sought rather to establish a norm for the future relations between the two.[4]

[1] Hefele, *A History of the Councils*, IV, 5.

[2] Malnory, *Saint Césaire, Evêque d'Arles* (Paris, 1894), p. 272.

[3] Goux, *Lérins au Cinquième Siècle* (Paris, 1856), p. 178.

[4] Weigel, *Faustus of Riez, an Historical Introduction* (Philadelphia: Dolphin Press, 1938), p. 67: "From the account of the council (Arles), it is impossible to determine the guilty party. The bishops evidently did not wish to deal with that problem; they were interested only in the solution of the difficulties. They clearly were intent on mollifying Theodore, yet they do not censure Faustus. Theodore, as a bishop, was of course in the higher position and consequently the deferential manner in which he is treated does not indicate any guilt on the part of Faustus."

The Council wished to set up a practical machinery to prevent the recurrence of such jurisdictional disputes in the future.[5] The general wording of the canons of Chalcedon is not found here, but rather a quite exact delimitation of the jurisdictional powers of each. Thenceforward, in matters pertaining to the exercise of strictly episcopal functions such as the ordaining of clerics, the admittance of clerics into the community, the confirming of neophytes, the consecration of chrism, the granting of faculties to transient clerics, the bishop's exclusive rights were to be unquestioned. The abbot, on the other hand, was to have exclusive control in all matters pertaining to the internal government of the monastery, such as the jurisdiction over non-clerical members of the community and the naming of those who were to be ordained.

> Hoc tamen sibi tantummodo vindicaturus, quod decessor suus sanctae memoriae Leontius episcopus vindicaverat: id est, ut clerici, atque altaris ministri, a nullo nisi ab ipso, vel cui ipse injunxerit, ordinentur: chrisma non nisi ab ipso speretur: neophyti si fuerint, ab eodem confirmentur: peregrini clerici absque ipsius praecepto in communionem, vel ad ministerium, non admittantur. Monasterii vero omnis laica multitudo ad curam abbatis pertineat: neque ex ea sibi episcopus quidquam vindicet, aut aliquem ex illa clericum, nisi abbate petente, praesumat. Hoc enim et rationis et religionis plenum est, ut clerici ad ordinationem episcopi debita subjectione respiciant: laica vero omnis monasterii congregatio ad solam ac liberam abbatis proprii, quem sibi ipsa elegerit, ordinationem, dispositionemque pertineat; regula, quae a fundatore ipsius monasterii dudum constituta est, in omnibus custodita.[6]

[5] *Ibid.*, p. 68: "The line of action agreed upon by the council was practical...Matters that pertained to strictly episcopal jurisdiction...were reserved exclusively to the bishop...Matters pertaining to the internal government of the monastery...were given over exclusively to the abbot."

[6] Mansi, VII, col. 907-908.

It is important here to delineate the actual import of the canon, in what was expressly stated and tacitly assumed. The distinction made between monks and clerics was much more clearly expressed in the wording of this council's canon than in that of Chalcedon.[7] Thereafter, monks as monks were not to be considered as clerics, and accordingly the bishop could not exercise jurisdiction over them as he did over those whom he had raised to the clerical state. The non-clerical monks, therefore, were to look to their abbot rather than to the bishop in all monastic matters. When a monk became a cleric, the absolute jurisdictional rights of the abbot became limited to purely monastic matters, and the bishop had a canonical hold on the new cleric by virtue of the orders he had conferred upon him. Indirectly, therefore, the bishop could exert his influence over the community through the canonical ties with the clerics dwelling within it. The interference, by the very nature of the monastic life, would not be a welcome one.[8]

How the bishop proceeded to extend his influence over the community will be seen in the following pages. The community at the time, through a long-standing tradition,[9] enjoyed the right of choosing its abbot. Moreover, the bishop could exercise no authority over the temporal things of the monastery.[10] The decision of the council definitely favored the abbots, for it checked effectively the attempts of the bishops to exert undue power over them.[11]

Whether the decision of the council was meant to serve as a precedent for all monasteries of that or future times, or whether

[7] McLaughlin, *Le très ancien droit*, p. 114.

[8] *Loc. cit.*

[9] Lévy-Bruhl, *Elections Abbatiales en France*, p. 22.

[10] Viollet, *Histoire des Institutions Politiques et Administratives de la France* (2 tomes, Paris, 1890), I, 370.

[11] Cf. Delatte, *The Rule of St. Benedict* (New York, Cincinnati, Chicago, 1921), p. 429; Goux, *Lérins au Cinquième Siècle*, p. 180: "Le concile reconnaissait à la multitude laïque qui l'habitait une exemption complète de la juridiction épiscopale, et défendait même à l'évêque d'admettre aucun de ceux qui en faisaient partie à la clericature, sans une demande expresse de l'abbé."

it merely confirmed the privileged position of the single monastery of Lérins, is difficult at this late date accurately to determine. In so far as the council expressly confirmed the agreements made previously between Honoratus, abbot of Lerins, and Leontius, bishop of Fréjus, it seems that Lérins enjoyed a privileged position which other monasteries did not possess. Hence the decision was not meant to form a precedent for all of Gaul, nor to be of any consequence to any other monastic community than that of Lérins.[12]

A second possibility, convincing upon first inspection but actually quite unlikely, looked to the state of the Roman Law with respect to monasteries. This law system was thought by some to have limited the power of the bishop relative to the monasteries in his diocese, which were considered as "*piae causae,*" and the bishop therefore was to be regarded as encroaching upon rights which Lérins possessed simply in virtue of its being a monastery.[13] The abbot thus was protecting rights, and not assuming privileges. These rights derived from the very nature of his monastic community recognized as a legal and ecclesiastic entity by the Church and the State.

Some authors adverted to a third possibility. Theodore was merely applying in practice the measures recently enacted in Chalcedon. The correctness of this assumption likewise seems unlikely, for the influence of Chalcedon was not felt in the West before the following century. Then, too, if Chalcedon had been cited in his evidence by Theodore, the documents of the council would have made mention of it.

The canon of the council is mentioned only in two collections of this period.[14] Yet, in view of the importance of Lérins,

[12] McLaughlin, *Le très ancien droit,* p. 134; Lévy-Bruhl, *Elections Abbatiales en France,* p. 23: "Lérins était placé, en 455, dans une situation privilégiée, et la décision du concile d'Arles n'est qu'une sorte de confirmation de ce privilège. Nous ne saurions donc en tirer argument quant à la condition générale des monastères de Gaule."

[13] Bittermann, "The Council of Chalcedon and Episcopal Jurisdiction," *Speculum,* XIII (1938), *loc. cit.* Miss Bittermann, however, does not seem to distinguish clearly between the "*piae causae*" and *monasteria,* which distinction, it seems, should have been made before it could be assumed that both might fall equally under the precepts of the Roman Law.

[14] McLaughlin, *Le très ancien droit,* p. 134 (note.)

it is difficult to believe that Arles did not exert an influence of some note upon similar situations arising after it. This is not to say that the legislation of Arles exerted coercive power outside of the province, which would be a ridiculous assertion, nor even that Arles meant its canon to affect all other monasteries in the province, since this cannot be proved, but only that in so far as there were very few councils in this period which legislated *ex professo* upon the matter, and in so far as Lérins was well known throughout the West, and because the decision of the council confirmed rights of that community, in abstraction altogether from its privileged or non-privileged position, one is forced to conclude that the council played an important part in the determination of future relations between bishops and monasteries.[15]

[15] McLaughlin, *Le très ancien droit*, p. 133: "...Le synode convoqué par Ravennius, métropolitain d'Arles, régla le différend entre eux et établit en faveur du monastère une charte de liberté que les moines francs ne cesseront pas de revendiquer. Nous en retrouverons beaucoup de clauses dans les chartes d'émancipation." Cf. also Weigel, *Faustus of Riez*, p. 69: "After the council (Arles) no more is heard of the controversy. However, the council must have been of great importance for the whole of Gaul. It established a precedent whereby conflicts between monks and bishops could be decided." See also Arnold, *Caesarius von Arelate und die Gallische Kirche seiner Zeit* (Leipzig, 1894), p. 36 (note).

CHAPTER IV

THE REIGN OF POPE GREGORY THE GREAT

A part of the Church proper, and recognized as such since the Council of Chalcedon, monasticism received a yet closer association with it during the pontificate of Pope St. Gregory the Great (590-604).[1] This luminary himself wore the Benedictine habit at one time, knew well and popularized the Holy Rule, wrote the best-known life of St. Benedict, and even established several monasteries from his own patrimony. His familiarity with and concern for monasticism is therefore easily understandable.

During the Lombard invasions many of the monasteries had been sacked and pillaged and the monks dispersed. Imperial officials, eager to fill their own purses, impoverished the monasteries for personal gain.[2] Landowners gained frequently at the expense of the monasteries. Bishops,[3] profiting from the uncertain status of monks in the Church polity,[4] harassed the

[1] Actually, Gregory was not the first Pope to favor monasticism, since some years before (in 556) Pope Pelagius I (556-561) had established certain rights for the monasteries of Lucania and Samnium, recalling the decision of the III Council of Arles (455), in which the bishop was to have power over the abbey only in the sacramental ministrations. (Pelagius I, ad Joannem episcopum Larinatum—Jaffé, *Regesta Pontificum Romanorum ab condita Ecclesia ad annum post Christum natum MCXCVIII* (2. ed. correctam et auctam auspiciis Gulielmi Wattenbach curaverunt S. Loewenfeld, F. Kaltenbrunner, P. Ewald, 2 vols. in 1, Lipsiae, 1885-1888), n. 955 (hereafter cited as Jaffé).

[2] Snow, *St. Gregory the Great, his Work and his Spirit* (London, 1892), p. 213.

[3] "Les monastères ont déjà attiré des convoitises et ils sont parfois devenus assez riches pour tenter un évêque qui peut profiter se sa position pour augmenter les revenus de son église."—McLaughlin, *Le très ancien droit*, p. 182.

[4] Pöschl, *Bischofsgut und MENSA EPISCOPALIS*, Band I, pp. 83ff.; *Monumenta Germaniae Historica*, Epistolarum Tomus I et II, *Gregorii I Papae Registrum Epistolarum*, ediderunt Paulus Ewald et Ludovicus Hartmann (Berolini, 1891-1899), Tom I, pars II, p. 406; Jaffé, n. 1408 (1040); McLaughlin, *Le très ancien droit*, p. 182: "Jusqu'à son temps les limites de

monks and interfered unduly in their internal affairs. It was to protect the monks from external interference, lay and ecclesiastical, that Gregory strove to give them a definite and fixed status in the Church.

Although several councils reflected the policies of Gregory quite faithfully, one may well single out a few of his manifold letters, which indicate his personal feelings on the various relations between bishop and monastery. It was ever the belief of the pope-saint that monasticism was a complete separation from the world, and that one who accepted the vocation of a monk must devote himself to contemplation in a life of prayer and mortification.[5] A cleric, according to him, was not to be a monk and still carry on the active ministry of souls.[6] He forbade monks to occupy themselves with the secular affairs which could deprive them of the liberty necessary for devoting themselves to the service of God, the Divine Office, and prayer.[7] The monastic oratories, in Gregory's view, were to retain their proper character; they were not to be transformed into public oratories. He wished to preserve the tranquility of the monasteries, and forbade bishops to celebrate the public Masses which attracted the crowds.[8] For much the same reasons he criticised the too frequent visits of the bishops to the religious communities.[9]

In all of these cases, St. Gregory wished that a sharp distinction be made and preserved between the clerical and the monastic life.[10] If priests, deacons, and other clerics who were

la juridiction épiscopale n'ont pas été déterminées en termes précis. Le principe de sujétion des moines aux évêques a été posé mais les applications n'en ont pas été faites." Cf. also *ibid.*, p. 177.

[5] Paul the Deacon, *Vita*, *MPL*, 75, col. 43.

[6] *Gregorii I Papae Registrum Epistolarum* (hereafter Registrum), Lib. IX, n. 157—*MGH*, *Epistolae*, Tom. II, p. 159.

[7] *Registrum*, Lib. I, n. 67—*MGH*, *Epistolae*, Tom. I, p. 88.

[8] *Registrum*, Lib. V, n. 49—*MGH*, *Epistolae*, Tom. I, p. 349; *Ibid*, Lib. VI, n. 44—*MGH*, *Epistolae*, Tom. I, p. 419.

[9] *Registrum*, Lib. VIII, n. 17—*MGH*, *Epistolae*, Tom. II, p. 20.

[10] "Mais, de ce chef, on se trouvait en présence de deux dangers; le premier menaçait la vocation du moine enlevé à sa solitude et rejeté dans le monde; le deuxième ébranlait ou annulait l'autorité de l'abbé et compromettait les intérêts du monastère. La meilleure preuve que ces dangers n'étaient

engaged in the service of a church wished to enter into the monastic order, they were to renounce the service of the clericate.[11]

The monastery was an autonomous institution, placed naturally under the high surveillance of the diocesan bishop, but yet the organism was to function in complete freedom from outside control. The selection of the abbot belonged as a right to the community. When a monk's qualifications were duly known upon his selection by the community as abbot, the diocesan bishop could not rightfully refuse his blessing.[12] The administration of the monastic temporalities was removed from the power of the bishop. Since the abbot had full authority over his monks, the power of the diocesan bishop was limited; he could not, without the authorization of the abbot, elevate the monks to Orders, that is, bring them into his jurisdiction for diocesan work.[13] This was permissable only with the abbot's consent.[14] The pope was duly solicitous for the regular recitation of the Divine Office. If, however, there was a sufficiently large number of monks to take care of this, the abbot could, from the kindness of his heart, offer a monk to the bishop to help out in the diocese, but such a monk in the diocesan service lost his rights in the monastery.[15] On the other hand, some monks were to be ordained to serve the spiritual needs of the community life.[16]

To these examples one could feel tempted to add several letters which, however, in recent years have been accounted as

pas imaginaires, c'est que S. Grégoire le Grand fut obligé de légiférer, d'une part pour assurer la tranquillité des monastères et faire respecter l'autorité des abbés, et d'autre part pour sauvegarder les intérêts réels des diocèses."—Berlière, "L'Exercice du Ministère Paroissial," *Revue Bénédictine*, XXXIX (1927), 231-233.

[11] *Registrum*, Lib. IV, n. 11—*MGH*, *Epistolae*, Tom. II, p. 244.

[12] *Registrum*, Lib. V, n. 47—*MGH*, *Epistolae*, Tom. I, p. 346.

[13] *Registrum*, Lib. VIII, n. 17—*MGH*, *Epistolae*, Tom. II, p. 19. Lévy-Bruhl demonstrated that this point did not arise through Gregory's inventiveness; it existed even before Gregory's time. Cf. *Elections Abbatiales*, p. 177.

[14] *Registrum*, Lib. VI, n. 27—*MGH*, *Epistolae*, Tom. I, p. 405-406.

[15] *Registrum*, Lib. VII, n. 40—*MGH*, *Epistolae*, Tom. I, p. 489.

[16] *Registrum*, Lib. VI, n. 39—*MGH*, *Epistolae*, Tom. I, pp. 415-416.

spurious, in view of their broad concession of favors and privileges to monasteries. But the foregoing references seem sufficient to establish Gregory's position relative to monasticism.[17]

Gregory, by his own letters and the councils held during his pontificate, thus established the monastic system on a firm and definite basis. He gave the supreme sanction of the Holy See to the status of monks, secured the inviolability of their property, a freedom in the election of superiors, a certain amount of exemption from episcopal control, and practically the need of a submission to their own superiors only. It was clear that the rules set for his monks by St. Benedict were thenceforth officially recognized by the Church, and rightfully called for the personal respect of all members of the hierarchy and laity.

A theoretical contradiction seems to be present in Gregory's concept of clerical life as compared with the monastic life, since despite his sharp distinction between them he yet undertook to send monks on the mission which resulted in the conversion of the Angles. It is true that he believed that the two types of life could not be fulfilled in their entirety by one person, but he did not prohibit monks from undertaking clerical

[17] What Abbot Snow (*op. cit.*, p. 213) called the "*Magna Charta*" of monks (*Registrum*, Lib. V, n. 49—*MGH, Epistolae*, Tom. I, p. 348) is perhaps the best example of such spurious documents. It reads in part: "It is necessary ...that the bishops should observe the regulations which are below enumerated, so that by their means no occasion should afterwards be alleged for causing them annoyance. We interdict...any bishop or layman by any means in the future to diminish the revenues, property, or securities of monasteries, or cells, or farms which belong to them or attempt it by fraud or evasion. If any dispute shall arise...it shall be terminated without wilful delay...before Abbots and other God-fearing fathers...At the death of an abbot of any community, a stranger shall not be elected unless the united agreement of the brethren shall choose him...Nor let any person under any pretence be placed over constituted Abbot...etc." This pericope is variously cited as being either a letter written by Gregory in 595 or an excerpt from a council held in 601. Cf. Taché, "Notes sur l'Histoire des Exemptions Monastiques," Revue de l'Université d'Ottawa, XI (1941), p. 171* (Note); Mansi, X, col. 495; *MPL*, 77, col. 579-580; Hefele-Leclercq, *Histoire des Conciles*, III, 339. In the earlier edition of Jaffé (n. 998) the letter was accepted as genuine, but in the edition revised by Wattenbach it was rejected as spurious. (n. 1366). Although the letter is spurious, it may still have been circulated as a genuine document and have exerted accordingly not a little influence.

duties. He employed them himself and encouraged their employment by other bishops, but if they undertook such clerical duties they were not to live in the monastery, since the monastic discipline might thus be impaired.[18]

Gregory's employment of monks for the conversion of England prepared the way, even though involuntarily, for future exemptions. It was not the intention of Gregory to remove the monks from the jurisdiction of the bishops, but the circumstances of the conversion of England by a peculiarly monastic organization set the stage for many exemptions which were to follow.[19]

Although Gregory's letters were restricted to Italy, and did not receive wide circulation until over a century after his death, his decrees are traceable in the most notable collections of the Middle Ages. The actual diffusion of the letters began in the middle of the 8th century, after which their popularity and influence became immense.[20]

[18] Various solutions have been offered to bring about a state of concord between Gregory's ideals, as expressed in his letters and in his practice of employing monks in various clerical offices. A few of these may be traced in Berlière, *L'Ordre Monastique*, p. 41; McLaughlin, *Le très ancien droit*, p. 178; Porcel, *La DOCTRINA MONASTICA de San Gregorio Magno y la REGULA MONACHORUM*, The Catholic University of America Studies in Sacred Theology, n. 60 (Washington, D.C.: The Catholic University of America Press, 1952), pp. 158-159.

[19] Taché, "*art. cit.*," pp. 170 ff.

[20] "...ses décrets en faveur des moines trouveront place dans toutes les collections canoniques du moyen âge, notamment dans celle de Gratien qui en contient un grand nombre...Dans les collections canoniques de l'Espagne on trouve les lettres adressées par saint Grégoire aux personnages de ce pays. Il en est de même pour la France...Au temps de saint Boniface les lettres grégoriennes commencent à être connues en France et en Allemagne. Signalons les trois grandes collections du VIIIe siècle qui ont permis la reconstitution de registre de saint Grégoire; a) Une collection R, contenant 686 lettres, faite, il paraît certain, sur l'ordre du pape Hadrien I (772-795), et envoyée à Charlemagne; b) Une collection P, renfermant 53 lettres dont 21 ne sont pas dans le recueil précédent. Cette collection fut envoyée, peut-être par Paul Warnefrid, à Adalhard, abbé de Corbie; c) Une collection C, de 200 lettres dont 144 qui ne se trouvent pas dans les deux autres collections. Ce recueil date également du VIIIe siècle."—McLaughlin, *Le très ancien droit*, p. 180 (Text with note). Cf. also Berlière, "L'exercice du Ministère Paroissial," *Revue Benedictine*, *XXXIX* (1927), 232.

CHAPTER V

IRISH MONASTICISM

ARTICLE 1. RISE AND DEVELOPMENT OF IRISH MONASTICISM

The beginnings of Irish Christianity are somewhat of a mystery because of the paucity of historical records. It is known that Palladius made a "fleeting visit" to Ireland several years before St. Patrick arrived (432), the isle being subsequently won for the Church by its great patron.[1] A matter greatly disputed and only partially settled concerns St. Patrick's original ecclesiastical organization, i.e., whether he actually established episcopal dioceses or rather depended immediately upon monastic elements to spread the faith. Strongest proponents of the opinion that Patrick did establish an episcopal diocesan organization after the ordinary church methods are Fr. John Ryan (1894-1932) and Prof. J. B. Bury (1861-1927), who regarded it as apodictic,[2] whereas others

[1] Brennan, *Ecclesiastical History of Ireland* (Dublin, 1864), p. 3: "Palladius is the first Christian bishop whom the genuine annals of the Irish Church have upon record. He landed in the year 431." Gougaud, *Christianity in Celtic Lands* (London, 1932), p. 386: "...the neighboring island, called "barbarous" by Prosper of Aquitaine because it had never borne the Roman yoke, had already before the year 432 been visited by missionaries, notably by Palladius, who made but a fleeting stay; and in the course of the 5th c. it was won for the Gospel by St. Patrick." Bury, *The Life of St. Patrick* (London, 1905), p. 213: "He, Patrick, did three things. He organised the Christianity which already existed; he converted kingdoms which were still pagan, especially in the west; and he brought Ireland into connexion with the Church of the Empire, and made it formally part of universal Christendom."

[2] Ryan, *Irish Monasticism, Origins and Early Development* (Dublin and Cork, 1932), p. 167: "Bishops, as we have seen, were the ordinary (as far as evidence goes, the sole) rulers of the Church in Ireland from the days of St. Patrick to the third decade of the sixth century." Cf. *ibid*, p. 168, and also p. 96: "In a word, the place of monasticism in the Church founded by St. Patrick was important but secondary." Bury, *St. Patrick*, p. 379: "Patrick's organisation was from one point of view monastic, from another

seem disinclined to press the claim to that extent.[3]

The matter seems unsettled, at least for the first century after Patrick's arrival. If one assume Ryan's thesis, which is quite tenable to be sure, the territory within which the bishop exercised jurisdiction was assuredly not well defined, for the first definite and sure attempt to fix diocesan boundaries seemed to have been made in the beginning of the 12th century.[4] It seems, then, that the whole of Ireland was thus under the direct jurisdiction of Patrick, almost in the manner of a single diocese, with some secondary delegated jurisdiction being granted the bishops for small areas. It is small wonder, therefore, that after the death of St. Patrick this fragile organization gave way completely to the monastic.[5]

Alongside the diocesan organization Patrick established a monastic one. The training that Patrick had received in the abbeys of Gaul, principally at Lérins, led him to fashion a monasticism based upon the oriental Pachomian type of life,[6]

episcopal. It was monastic in so far as many of the churches in the various regions were connected with religious communities of a monastic character, and the clergy were largely monks. But this did not prevent it being episcopal in the sense that there were episcopal districts or dioceses. There was not a body of bishops without sees, who went around visiting churches promiscuously, but each bishop had his own diocese." *Cambridge Medieval History*, I, 531: "There is reason to think that territorial bishops were found in Ireland to begin with." Taché, *art. cit.*, p. 18*: "...de l'arrivée de saint Patrice en 432 à sa mort en 461, la part des moines dans le travail apostolique et le gouvernement des chrétientés naissantes fut secondaire."

[3] Lemarignier, *Les Privilèges Normandes depuis les Origines jusqu'en* 1140 (Paris: A. Picard, 1937), p. 2: "Les pays peuplés par les Celtes insulaires, c'est-à-dire, l'Irlande et les pays bretons, avaient alors un statut ecclésiastique très particulier. Ils n'étaient pas divisés en diocèses, et tout clergé séculier y était inconnu. Leur clergé était exclusivement régulier, et les seuls centres religieux étaient des monastères ayant juridiction sur des territoires plus ou moins précis." Gougaud, *Christianity*, p. 222: "The question whether there were episcopal dioceses in Ireland in the early centuries of the Middle Ages is still under discussion. The territory within which the bishop's jurisdiction was exercised was certainly not well defined."

[4] Gougaud, *Christianity*, p. 222.

[5] Bury, *St. Patrick*, p. 181.

[6] Ryan, *op. cit.*, p. 407: "The Irish system of monasticism is thus remotely Egyptian, but hails more proximately from Lérins, whence it came at first

but rather of a semi-cenobitical bent, with great emphasis on asceticism.[7]

Early in the sixth century a new element was introduced through Britain, which in being commingled with the localisms gave to Irish monasticism an eclectic character.[8] When the monastic element eventually dominated Ireland completely, jurisdiction fell principally into the hands of bishop-abbots and presbyter-abbots.[9] As the number of the abbeys mounted, jurisdiction became exercised over all persons within the territorial boundaries of each abbey.[10]

The presbyter-abbatial system eventually predominated over the other form,[11] with the bishops, as bishops, anomalously becoming subject to the jurisdiction of the priest-abbots, performing their episcopal functions of order at the behest of their abbot superior.[12] This did not, however, reflect any disdain for the episcopal office, since the bishops were chosen for the sanctity of their lives, and jurisdictional burdens were thought to be incongruous with their high office.[13] This strange

directly through St. Patrick...then early in the sixth century indirectly through Britain..." Cf. McLaughlin, *Le très ancien droit*, p. 29.

[7] Ryan, *op. cit.*, p. 407: "Severe bodily austerity is a marked feature of the Irish monastic system. This is found everywhere in Egypt..."

[8] Cabrol-Leclercq, *Dictionnaire d'Archéologie Chrétienne et de Liturgie*, Tom. II (Paris, 1925), col. 3211 (hereafter cited *DACL*).

[9] McLaughlin, *Le très ancien droit*, p. 29: "La hiérarchie du pays est monastique. La juridiction est exercée par des abbés-évêques ou par des abbés-prêtres, d'abord sur l'abbaye-mère, puis sur les autres monastères et paroisses de la circonscription. On trouve peu d'évêques qui ne soient pas moines à partir de cette transformation dans l'organisation ecclésiastique de pays au VIe siècle."

[10] Ryan, *Irish Monasticism*, p. 3.

[11] Taché, *art. cit.*, p. 19*; Gougaud, *op. cit.*, p. 223; Ryan, *op. cit.*, p. 175.

[12] Ryan, *op. cit.*, p. 170: "Some of the greatest monasteries of the country...had been ruled since their foundation by presbyter-abbots. As these had complete control within the monastic territory, which soon became very extensive, the monastery had perforce to secure the services of a bishop. For convenience sake, and, no doubt, also to safeguard monastic independence, one of the monks was chosen for promotion to the higher order." Cf. also *ibid*, pp. 3ff.

[13] Cabrol-Leclercq, *Dictionnaire*, Tom. II, col. 3213; Ryan, *op. cit.*, p. 409: "In a category by itself must be placed the prominence of the abbots as ecclesiastical rulers, a development which arose partly from the popu-

organization was vigorous enough to predominate until the 9th century with the invasion of the Danes.[14]

At the same time, Ireland, isolated as it was, developed a particularism which infiltrated the monastic system. Although this country remained within the framework of the Church,[15] as did the monastic order, they yet differed from the Church proper in several matters which rendered them suspect to the continental Church. Unlike traditional western monasticism, the Irish monastic system discountenanced the stability which characterized European monasticism, and combined the ideals of their anchoritic forebears with an apostolic leaning.[16] The Irish monks were ever on the move, regarding peregrination as practically the equivalent of the vows of present day religious congregations to spend part or all of their lives on foreign soil.[17]

Moreover, in contrast to Benedictine monachism, the monastic rule, if they had one, of the Irish system did not extend far beyond a mere penitential code, actual order within the cloister depending entirely upon the person of the abbot, his power being absolute, his authority in disciplinary matters unlimited.[18] In Ireland proper there was naturally no question of exemption, since of course the bishops as such had no actual jurisdiction attached to their office.[19] Their monastic tonsure

larity of the monastic institute and partly, perhaps, from an ascetical fear of the worldly advantages then commonly attached to the episcopal office in Christian lands."

[14] Taché, *art. cit.*, pp. 20*ff.

[15] Gougaud, *Christianity*, p. 213: "It is indeed abundantly clear that for long, in the bosom of the great Catholic unity, that Church stood a little aloof and in the shade and preserved a physiognomy all its own; but to assert hostility. . . distrust towards the Mother Church of Christianity is to flout our best sources of information."

[16] Ryan, *op. cit.*, pp. 407 ff.

[17] Fuhrmann, *Irish Medieval Monasteries on the Continent* (Washington, D.C., 1927), p. 2.

[18] McLaughlin, *Le très ancien droit*, p. 29.

[19] Taché, *art. cit.*, p. 19*; Ryan, *op. cit.*, p. 299: "To the question then, what were the relations between the monks and the ecclesiastical authorities in the sixth-century Ireland, the answer is that the monks themselves were the ecclesiastical authorities. Non-monastic bishops and bishoprics were of small, almost negligible importance. Did the Irish, we may ask, not know the general system of Church government, and did they

was *sui generis*, and they celebrated Easter at a time different from continental Christianity. Moreover, they did not conform to the canonical rule which required that at least three bishops should take part in the episcopal consecration.[20]

Article 2. Impact of Irish Monasticism on the Church Proper

Pushed by their apostolic ideals, the energetic Irish were unable to find full expression for their zeal for the faith at home. Some had already departed on missionary endeavors before 585, the year St. Columban (543-615) landed on the continent, but it was with this great missionary saint that "the most remarkable missionary effort known in Europe" was begun.[21] Settling in the kingdom of Burgundy, he soon established three monasteries, Anegray, Luxeuil, and Fontaine. Thrust out from his principal monastery, Luxeuil, by Brunhilde, he headed north to Champagne, preparing for the foundation at Rebais, and several women's monasteries at Faremoutiers and Jouarre. Turning east next, he passed by Lake Constance, where later arose the foundation of St. Gall. From there he penetrated the borders of Italy and founded Bobbio, where he died in November, 615.[22]

It was from these centers that a great number of other monasteries arose,[23] but it is somewhat difficult to accurately determine which monasteries of the period were "strictly

not feel their own system, so much at variance with it, to be an anomaly? They must have known the ordinary system of Church government, for St. Patrick had established it amongst them and they might likewise have seen it at work in Britain in the first half of the sixth century or even later."

[20] Gougaud, *Christianity*, p. 208.

[21] Fuhrmann, *op. cit.*, p. 5: "Most tenacious of Irish customs, fearless as St. Paul himself in expressing his convictions, Columbanus more than any one else transplanted the essentially monastic church discipline of Ireland to France, Germany and Switzerland."

[22] Cf. Gougaud, *Christianity*, p. 140; *Cambridge Medieval History*, II, 147 ff; Lemarignier, *op. cit.*, p. 3.

[23] Gougaud, *op. cit.*, p. 148: "The number of cloisters whose foundation was directly or indirectly due to their activity has been estimated at about fifty."

Irish" and which were merely influenced by them.[24] The present treatment will relate to all monasteries which looked to Columban directly or indirectly as their founder, and which housed Irish monks exclusively or had them in the majority.[25]

If one recalls the peculiarities of the Irish monks as mentioned above, one can readily understand that their advent into Gaul was not without some embroilment. There was an already established diocesan organization in Gaul, and its bishops were displeased with this unannounced "invasion" and unauthorized residence of Columban in their territory.[26] Frankish councils of the 6th and 7th centuries had placed monasticism largely under the jurisdiction of the bishop,[27] and these irregular entries were a direct violation of the conciliar canons and Gallican policy.[28] Columban either ignored the bishops'

[24] *Ibid*, p. 157: "There is, however, a tendency on the part of some writers to exaggerate the number of strictly Irish foundations. . . . The title, it seems, ought to be restricted solely to those cloisters which, in the years following their foundation or their restoration on the introduction of measures of reform, were governed by Irishmen and which, moreover, had a majority of Irish monks among their inmates. . ."

[25] *Ibid*, p. 151: "Scottic monks spread in considerable numbers from the sixth to the ninth century in all the territories subject to the rule of the Frankish monarchs. All grades of monks and abbots, bishops without a diocese (*episcopi vagantes*), abbot-bishops who either governed an abbey and a diocese simultaneously or exercised their episcopal functions only within their own monastery. Finally several of these *peregrini* were appointed to the rule of dioceses; one of them even occupied one of the most important metropolitan sees of continental Europe."

[26] Martin, *Saint Columban* (Paris, 1905), p. 76: "L'épiscopat pourtant n'était point très favorable à cet étranger qui, contrairement à la tradition des Eglises franques, avait installé ses colonies dans le diocèse de Besançon, sans avoir même songé à solliciter l'autorisation de l'ordinaire et qui avait appelé, pour consacrer l'autel de Luxeuil, non point l'évêque du diocèse, mais un prélat, semble-t-il, irlandais ou breton."

[27] Hauck, *Kirchengeschichte Deutschlands*, I, 245; Gougaud, *op. cit.*, p. 22; *Catholic Encyclopedia* (15 vols., Index and Supplements, New York, 1907-1922), IV, 138: "The councils of Gaul held in the first half of the sixth century had given to bishops absolute authority over religious communities, even going so far as to order the abbots to appear periodically before their respective bishops to receive reproof or advice as might be considered necessary." Taché, *art. cit.*, p. 20*.

[28] Martin, *op. cit.*, p. 76.

protestations altogether or used some ruse to bypass them.[29] It suffices to note here that Columban acted contrary to the continental policy, which had been active for some hundred years. Actual resistance to him did not appear at first, probably because the natives were overawed by his personality.[30]

The most striking encounter between the Irish monks and the bishops concerned the date of Easter. Being the pivot-festival of the church-year, on it depended the entire cycle of movable feasts, and a slight change could throw the entire liturgical year into confusion.[31] Briefly, the Roman Church celebrated Easter on the Sunday following the first full moon after the vernal equinox.[32] The Irish followed another computation, and even celebrated Easter on the day itself of the full moon if that day happened to fall on a Sunday. This was a scandal to the continental bishops, and the controversy reached such a pitch that in 603[33] the bishops assembled to judge Columban. They believed him a Quartodeciman. But instead of appearing, he blatantly[34] addressed a letter to them in which he advised them to hold synods more frequently, and pay more attention to matters of at least equal importance to that of the date of Easter.[35] He remained adamant[36] on the latter point, and even went so far as to address to Pope St. Gregory a letter in which he cited oriental views in defense of his own.[37]

[29] Lemarignier, *op. cit.*, p. 4: "Moine celte, il avait suivi les usages celtiques et ne s'était pas soucié de l'autorité diocesaine."

[30] Martin, *op. cit.*, p. 77.

[31] Gougaud, *op. cit.*, p. 185: "Consequently, from the second century on we find the Holy See busy seeking to suppress the different views which prevailed on this question in Christendom."

[32] Martin, *op. cit.*, p. 82: "Les divergences étaient inevitables: elles se produisaient presque chaque année."

[33] Gougaud, *op. cit.*, p. 191: ". . . Gaulish bishops assembled in council at Chalon-sur-Sâone in 603 to discuss his (Columban's) case. . . ."

[34] Cf. Taché, *art. cit.*, p. 21*: Martin, *op. cit.*, p. 82.

[35] *Catholic Encyclopedia*, IV, 138: "He did not appear lest, as he tells us, 'he might contend in words,' but instead addressed a letter to the prelates in which he speaks with a strange mixture of freedom, reverence, and charity."[36]

[36] Hauck, *Kirchengeschichte Deutschlands*, I, 257.

[37] Curtis, *History of Ireland* (London: Methuen and Co. Ltd., 1950), p.

The letter never reached its addressee, and hence no decision was effected. The matter was not settled in St. Columban's lifetime, and the latter held fast to his custom. This question of the Easter date, and the others of tonsure, etc., were matters of dispute for over a hundred years, but towards the beginning of the 8th century the Irish resistance was overcome, and contact became more frequent between the representatives of Celtic Christianity and those of the continental and English Churches.[38]

St. Columban, imbued with the practices common in Ireland,[39] personally did not countenance any interference in his abbey from bishops. This applied to things both of a spiritual and of a temporal nature. Perhaps he noted that the bishoprics of Gaul were too worldly in nature and were held by prelates of not altogether good character,[40] and accordingly determined to stay free of them. In the foundations reflecting his spirit, one finds that some received complete exemption by charter right. Most notable of these was the case of Bertulf (d. 640) second successor to Columban in Bobbio. He withstood the efforts of the Bishop of Tortona[41] to subject the abbey to his

151; Gougaud, *op. cit.*, p. 185: "In his letter he asserted that he took his stand on the authority of Anatolius of Laodicaea, whose work on Easter had, he said, been quoted by Eusebius of Caesarea and praised by St. Jerome, the oracle of the West. Anatolius, bishop of Laodicaea, in the third century, had, as a matter of fact, treated of the Paschal computus, but with conclusions as remote as possible from the views held by the Scots."

[38] Cf. Curtis, *History of Ireland*, pp. 151 ff.

[39] Bury, *St. Patrick*, pp. 180 ff., "When new monasteries (Irish) were founded, they determined to have bishops of their own, and to be quite independent of the bishops of the dioceses in which they were situated. This practice was not indeed confined to Ireland. There are several notable instances in Gaul. But whereas elsewhere it was the exception, in Ireland it seems to have become the rule;" Cf. Gougaud, *op. cit.*, p. 223.

[40] Ryan, *op. cit.*, p. 299 (footnote 4): "Bishoprics in Gaul, looked at from the worldly standpoint, were worth having, and were paid for by the ambitious. Where a bishop had acquired his see by simony there was little good to be hoped for from him. Here is the final reason for the desire that the bishop should be a monk, whose life would do credit to his high order. Hence, again, St. Columban's determination to keep free from the local bishops."

[41] Ryan, *op. cit.*, p. 299.

jurisdiction, and appealed to Pope Honorius in 628, "qui praebuit optatum munus; privilegia Sedis Apostolicae largitus est, quatenus nullu episcoporum in praefato coenobio quolibet jure dominare conaretur."[42] The privilege was important and was preserved as a model in the *Liber Diurnus* of the papal courts.

The Abbey of Rebais in Champagne received from King Dagobert I (629-634)[43] a large measure of exemption, and this was entered into the famous formulary of Marculf.[44] Not being a concession from Rome, it had to take second place to that of Bobbio.

In Columban's Rule there was no mention of exemption, since not only was the Rule lacking in legislative statutes, but it seemed simply to take this for granted. In the charter, however, of one foundation[45] from Luxeuil, that of Solignac, the principle was stated quite clearly: "The bishop or any other person shall have no right and no power whatsoever in the said cloister, neither with regard to its temporal goods, nor over the persons therein."[46] The exemption accepted by the local bishops was contained in all the foundations which used Luxeuil as a model. These all reflected the spirit of Columban. In Solignac's charter, moreover, St. Eligius (588-660), the founder, followed the practice of Luxeuil by removing the abbey from all external influence save from that of the king. He added that in case of laxity the Abbot of Luxeuil could undertake the reformation of the foundation. He also mitigated the strict Columban Rule by introducing the Benedictine Rule to become effective side by side with the other.[47]

It is thus evident that Columban's monasticism had given to the exemption movement a new impetus, which was only

[42] Jonas, *Jonae Vitae Sanctorum Columbani, Vedastis, Johannis*, ed. Bruno Krusch, *MGH, Scrip. Rer. Germ.* (62 vols., Hannoverae et Lipsiae, 1905), Vol. 35, p. 283; Jaffé, n. 2017 (1563).

[43] Taché, *art. cit.*, p. 149*.

[44] *Formulae Merovingici et Karolingici Aevi*, ed. K. Zeumer—*MGH, Leges*, V, 39-41.

[45] Gougaud, *op. cit.*, p. 224.

[46] Hauck, *Kirchengeschichte Deutschlands*, I, 285.

[47] Gougaud, *op. cit.*, p. 225.

germinally present before.[48] Even when the Rule of Columban began to give way to the Benedictine Rule[49] less than fifty years after Columban's death, the remnants of the Irish principles remained in privileges already granted and preserved both in Rome and in the private charters[50] by way of local grants. The movement inaugurated by the Irish monks was not, however, halted when the Benedictine Rule at first became commingled with and later replaced completely that of Columban.[51]

[48] Bittermann in an article ("The Influence of Irish Monks on Merovingian Diocesan Organisation," *American Historical Review*, XL (1934-1935). 232-245) attempts to debunk the traditional opinion on the contribution of Irish Monasticism to the origin of monastic liberties. According to Lemarignier (*Les Privilèges*, p. 2), Ryan (*op. cit.*, p. 108) has weakened Miss Bittermann's thesis by pointing out the influence of the Celts over Lérins. The point seems well taken. Cf. Levillain's review of Bittermann's article in *Le Moyen Age*, XLV (1935), 236-237.

[49] Hauck, *op. cit.*, I, 282: "Der Einfluss, welchen Columba auf die Geschichte des Mönchtums in Frankreich übte, war mächtig, aber er war nicht dauernd. Die Regel Columbas wurde verhältnismässig rasch verdrängt durch die Benedikts von Nursia." Cf. also *ibid*, p. 283 (note).

[50] Taché, *art. cit.*, p. 150*: "...en moins de cinquante ans en effet, la règle celtique fut supplantée par celle de saint Benoît. Si l'exemption s'est maintenue il faut l'attribuer au fait qu'elle a trouvé un cadre juridique dans l'immunité franque; d'où l'on peut concevoir une idée encore plus haute de l'importance de celle-ci dans la domaine ecclésiastique."

[51] Hauck, *op. cit.*, I, 285.

CHAPTER VI

PRIVILEGES AND FACTORS CONTRIBUTING TO THE EXEMPTION MOVEMENT

Whereas the Irish undoubtedly gave to the monastic exemption movement a great spur, there were other stirrings from various directions which also advanced the forward movement of monasticism towards independence from the diocesan bishop.[1] A more important step in that direction was that of the privilege, an act which regulated the relations of the monastery with the diocesan authority.[2] The monks themselves, frequently oppressed or greatly vexed by episcopal intrusions in the monastic life, appealed to the pope, the metropolitan, the kings or the dukes to free them. Their petitions, as the evidence of preserved privilege formularies demonstrates, were heard. In a later chapter it will be seen that these appeals must have been frequent enough to cause the bishops some concern, for they thought it necessary to legislate against them.[3]

At times the monasteries were founded by royalty, whether for pious motives or some other reason, and endowed by a founding charter with full or partial exemption from the bishop by way of privilege. If lesser personages founded the monasteries, and were unable to exempt them without the bishop's

[1] Lemarignier, *Les Privilèges Normandes*, p. 4: "Son [St. Columban's] influence n'est d'ailleurs pas la seule qui se soit fait sentir."

[2] Levillain, "Etudes sur l'Abbaye de Saint-Denis à l'époque mérovingienne," *Bibliothèque de l'Ecole des Chartes* (Tom. 87 (1926)), p. 21. Although a certain freedom is exercised by authors, the proper meanings of exemption, immunity and privilege should be distinguished. Exemption is a privilege through which a person, withdrawn from his immediate superior, is placed under the power of an intermediary superior or of the supreme authority. Immunity is reserved for the most part to cases of exemption from the secular powers. Privilege has taken on the meaning of a particular favor having only an indirect relationship with exemption.—Taché, "Notes sur l'histoire des exemptions monastiques," *Revue de l' Université d'Ottawa*, XI (1941), 9* - 14*.

[3] Vide, e.g., *infra*, ch. VII.

approval, this was often obtained as a condition without which the project would not be commenced. The signature of the bishop sufficed for granting it perpetual independence, or at least for endowing it with other privileges of whatever sort. Exemption arising from the beneficent initiative of the bishop was also occasionally found, but less frequently, since the monasteries were rich prizes, and not to be lost without a struggle.[4] The bishop's motive, if he in fact exempted the monastery, could also be its protection from the potential abuse of his own successors.

The classic formula for preserved privileges is that of Marculf, the chart of privileges granted to Rebais by Dagobert I, which one might accept as a pattern for the others of that time.[5] Two distinct sections open the formula, the first, "*De privilegio,*" and the second, "*Cessio regis de hoc privilegium.*" (sic) The first is an episcopal privilege, and the second is a confirmation of this privilege.[6]

The formulas take up both the matter of monastic temporalities and its more spiritual affairs. Emancipation from the bishop with regard to temporalities was quite complete in the document, so much so that the Abbot was able to manage all matters without interference from the bishop—even without having to render account to him, a requirement in the Frankish legislation.[7] With regard to the bishop's more spiritual rights, the abbot was no longer nominated by the diocesan bishop but by the community, although the bishop still held fast to his right to bless the abbot. In addition, ordinations depended upon the bishop, as did the consecration of altars. These remained in the hands of the bishop, some slight defense against the total independence of the abbey. Leclercq men-

[4] Lafontaine, *L'Evêque d'Ordination*, p. 97: "C'est au VIIe et au VIIIe siècle que les monastères connurent la plus grande prospérité en richesse foncière. Sous les Carolingiens, Saint-Germain-des-Prés possédait un domaine d'environ trente-trois mille hectares (128 milles carrés), avec une population de douze à quinze mille âmes. Même en 816, après les déprédations de Charles Martel, certaines abbayes possédaient un domaine foncier de trente à cent mille hectares (115 à 386 milles carrés)."

[5] *MGH, Leges*, V, 39-41.

[6] Cf. Leclercq, "Exemption Monastique," *DACL*, V, col. 952 ff.

[7] Vide *infra*, p. 68.

tions that the abbatial power in some cases became so great within the diocese, that the abbot delighted in "inviting" the bishop to perform the same ceremonies which the diocesan prelates previously did independently of the abbot's consent.[8]

Marculf was imitated in many of the formularies, although the latter appear in a variety of forms, and contain diversiform privileges. There is no certainty regarding how many such charts of emancipation were extant in the Merovingian and Carolingian period, but according to Lafontaine, who has written a fine treatise regarding them,[9] only fourteen have come down to us. He excluded from his consideration the documents relative to the foundations of the monasteries of women, the charters of lay founders or of abbots, the apocryphal charters, lost charters whose one-time existence is beyond question but which are not to be found, the incomplete charters, and the episcopal charters which contained no specific privilege of exemption. Leclercq lists twenty,[10] but he seems to have been less selective. Taché lists only four charts which explicitly remove the monks from submission to the episcopal power.[11] A few outstanding examples of these privileges are worthy of mention.

St. Gregory the Great granted to monasteries in Gaul several privileges benefiting the monastery of St. Trophimus of Arles and the monasteries founded at Autun by Brunhilde and Thierry II.[12] These privileges were limited to two points: the temporalities and the free election of the abbot, leaving to the bishop the disciplinary surveillance and the various exercises of his order. These two currents, the Irish and Gregorian, opposed in the beginning, tended both to fuse and to clash in the course of the 7th and 8th centuries until the Irish was finally

[8] Leclercq, "Exemption Monastique," col. 957.

[9] Lafontaine, *L'Evêque d'Ordination*, 117-157.

[10] "Exemption Monastique," col. 957.

[11] "Notes sur l'histoire des exemptions monastiques," p. 158*.

[12] Lemarignier, *Les Privileges Normandes*, p. 4: "Ce dernier cas, surtout, est digne d'intérêt. C'est à la demande de Brunehaut que le pape expédia les bulles, et il n'est pas impossible que la reine ait voulu opposer à la formule irlandaise de liberté la formule romainé." Cf. *supra*, Brunhilde's attitude toward Columban.

eliminated by the other.[13]

Moreover, St. Gregory, in utilizing the monks for the conversion of England, prepared indirectly for innumerable subsequent privileges.[14] In the diocese of Strassburg, Germany, Bishop Widegern, the ordinary, completely exempted the abbey of Murbach,[15] permitting the community to have its own bishop. This confirmed and extended King Theodoric V's (727) charter, which permitted the monks to call in the local ordinary for episcopal functions, but if he was detained, if he refused, or if he demanded remunerative considerations, any other bishop could be summoned in place of him. Freedom in abbatial elections was likewise among the concessions.[16] Bishop Widegern granted by it all privileges possessed by the monasteries of Lérins, Agaune, and Luxeuil in regard to episcopal functions and exemptions. The charter was remarkable also for having mentioned for the first time the existence of a Benedictine Congregation of monasteries, permitting Murbach to elect a member of another house of the congregation of St. Pirmin if they so chose. This seems to be the first known attempt to form a Benedictine congregation.[17]

In Germany, under Willibrord (d. 739), monasticism had made a somewhat hesitant debut, and understandably succumbed in the face of the revolt of the Frisian, Radbod, in 716.[18] To St. Boniface (680-755) goes the credit of not only winning

[13] Cf. *infra*, pp. 58 ff.

[14] Taché, *art. cit.*, p. 170*.

[15] Fuhrmann, *Irish Medieval Monasteries*, p. 48. Taché believes that the document granting privileges to Murbach is not to be trusted. "On pourrait ajouter celle de Thierry IV au monastère de Murbach (727), *MGH*, n. 95, mais elle est fort suspecte, précisement à cause des termes qu'elle emploie pour l'exclusion des évêques: il semble qu'il y ait eu dans cette partie interpolation d'un extrait d'une bulle pontificale.—*art. cit.*, p. 159* (note).

[16] Fuhrmann, *op. cit.*, p. 49.

[17] Fuhrmann, *op. cit.*, p. 50: "Apparently, then, St. Pirmin was the first to establish a closer union between Benedictine communities. His work in this line preceded by nearly a hundred years the more radical innovation of Benedict of Aniane."

[18] Hauck, *Kirchengeschichte Deutschlands*, I, 404; Berlière, *L'Ordre Monastique*, p. 57.

the Frisians and the surrounding areas for the Church, but also of reconstituting Christianity on a monasticism which was strongly and successfully rebuilt on the feeble foundation of his forerunner.[19] With the reception of the archiepiscopal dignity, his influence extended to the entire trans-Rhenish area submitted to the Franks: Alemannia, Hessia, and Thuringia.[20]

Boniface, trained in the English Benedictine traditions carried there from Rome by St. Austin (d. 604), was aided in his work of converting the Germans by other Anglo-Saxon monks. The work of conversion consequently followed the pattern outlined by St. Gregory for Austin.[21] He created a network of monasteries, and made the Benedictine Rule compulsory throughout his jurisdiction,[22] thus also setting the norm for the bishop-monastery relations as outlined by St. Benedict, and sanctioned by Pope Gregory the Great. Boniface's hierarchical organization was, then, merely the "juxta-position of the episcopal dignity to the abbatial authority already existing."[23]

There are few recorded conflicts between Boniface and the Benedictine monasteries in his archdiocese, but one instance may be mentioned, since it casts light upon the attitude of the German saint toward the Irish peculiarities. Virgilius, successor to Bishop John, whom St. Boniface had placed over the see of Salzburg, was ruling the diocese as a presbyter-abbot. Virgilius was Irish-born, and for episcopal functions called upon Dubdachrich, also Irish, and quite likely one of the "*episcopi vagantes*" who were consecrated in Ireland and roamed about as the non-possessors of any see. Boniface held these clerics in reproach, and complained to the pope about them.[24]

[19] Hauck, *op. cit.*, I, 408.

[20] Kurth, *Saint Boniface* (Milwaukee, 1935), pp. 52 ff.; Berlière, *op. cit.*, p. 61.

[21] Berlière, *loc. cit.*

[22] *MGH*, *Epistolae Selectae*, LVI, p. 99; Kurth, *op. cit.*, p. 90.

[23] Berlière, *L'Ordre Monastique*, p. 64.

[24] Fuhrmann, *op. cit.*, p. 45; Gougaud, *Christianity in Celtic Lands*, p. 24: "St. Boniface, in the course of his missions, met more than one adventurer of this type whom he did not hesitate to have condemned by the councils and the Holy See. In order to put a stop to these disturbers, the first Germanic general council (Conc. Germanicum, ch. 4; Mansi, XII, 367)

Few details of the encounter have been preserved. It is known only that Boniface and Virgilius differed on points of doctrine and discipline. The source of the difficulty probably can be attributed to the unrenounced Irish customs of Virgilius, although it is certain that the Easter date did not enter into the dispute.[25] Virgilius was consecrated a bishop after the death of Boniface, and nothing further indicated the presence of any difficulty, so that it may be presumed that his singular position as presbyter-abbot with jurisdictional power over the diocese was the core of the dispute.[26]

It was to Fulda that Boniface directed his principal attention. Although the other abbeys were subject to the church under the Benedictine Rule that followed the course of England, Boniface asked papal immunity from Pope Zachary for Fulda, which he had not petitioned for any of the other monastic foundations.[27] The request was granted. By the privilege the monastery of Fulda was to be subject to no other jurisdiction than that of the pope himself. No religious function was thenceforth to be performed, not even Mass itself, without the express authorization of the abbot. This seems to be the first occasion that so close a bond was established between the Holy See and a monastery in Frankish territory, and hence also the first occasion when the canonical relations between bishops and abbots were canonically so widely divorced in this area.

In contradistinction to this trend toward exemption were

held in April 742 at St. Boniface's instigation, but in what place is not known, began by decreeing that unknown bishops and priests should not be allowed to exercise the sacred ministry until they had been examined in council. The Council of Soissons (Conc. Suessionense, ch. 5) further enacted that the said strolling bishops and priests should obtain the approval of the bishop of the diocese. The councils of Ver (Conc. Vernense, ch. 13; Mansi, XII, 583) (755), of Mainz (Conc. Moguntiacum, ch. 22; Mansi, XIV, 85) (813), and of Tours (Conc. Turonense III, ch. 13; Mansi, XIV, 85) (813) issued still further edicts against them. The twenty-second canon of Mainz describes these nomads as "*acephali*. . .*hippocentauris similes, nec equi nec homines*," and threatens them with excommunication and prison."

[25] Kurth, *op. cit.*, p. 81.

[26] Gougaud, *op. cit.*, p. 148.

[27] Kurth, *op. cit.*, p. 106.

other efforts, not inimical to monasticism, but quite firmly set against monastic independence. St. Owen, bishop of Rouen from 641-684, himself deeply influenced by St. Columban, was yet unwilling to constitute monasticism after the latter's passion for independence.[28] Friendly to monasticism, he founded the abbeys of Fontanelle, Jumièges, Fécamp, Pavilly and Monte-villiers.[29] To none of these did Owen grant the slightest privilege;[30] but he held them strictly under his authority, at times choosing their abbot for them.

From the foregoing it is apparent that conciliar and private law would strive for hegemony until the question would finally have to be decided for or against monastic independence.

[28] Hauck, *op. cit.*, I, 286.
[29] Lemarignier, *op. cit.*, p. 22.
[30] *Ibid.*, p. 21.

CHAPTER VII

OCCIDENTAL LEGISLATION UNTIL BENEDICT OF ANIANE (Ca. 750-821)

ARTICLE 1. LEGISLATION IN MEROVINGIAN GAUL

Before considering the legislation in Gaul during this period, one must of necessity recall the impact of the Council of Chalcedon (451) and the III Council of Arles (455) upon the West. Neither one, however, was definitive in deciding the full extent or the limits of the bishop's power, Chalcedon using a vague wording and Arles making its direct effects applicable to one monastery alone.[1] And yet, after the year 455, although there were held many councils which treated of bishop-monastery relations, very few of them rejected Chalcedon, and most of them either cited Chalcedon directly or embraced its tenets and adopted a similar phraseology. Arles, although influential, was not a general council, and probably was not thought worthy of citation in these later codifications (although the charters mention it.)

Many councils thought it necessary to restate the general submission of the monastery to the bishop which Chalcedon had first instituted.[2] Chalcedon's fourth canon had made the founding of a monastery depend upon the consent of the bishop, which decree was renewed in the councils of Agde and Epaone.[3] It is interesting to note that as a means of assuring

[1] McLaughlin, *Le très ancien droit*, p. 136.

[2] The V Council of Arles (554), can. 2—*MGH*, Legum Sectio III, *Concilia*, Tom. I, *Concilia Aevi Merovingici* (ed. F. Maassen, Hannoverae, 1893), p. 118; Mansi, IX, col. 702; Bruns, II, 218; Hefele, *History of the Councils*, IV, 376: "Ut monasteria ei subsint episcopo in cujus territorio sita sunt." See also the II Council of Orleans (533), can. 2—*MGH*, *ibid.*, p. 61; Mansi, VIII, col. 838; Bruns, II, 187; Hefele, *History of the Councils*, IV, 187; also the I Council of Orleans (511), can. 19—*MGH*, *ibid.*, p. 1; Mansi, VIII, col. 354; Bruns, II, 164; Hefele, *History*, IV, 89.

[3] The Council of Agde (506), can. 27, 58;—Bruns, II, 151; Hefele, *History*, IV, 81: "Monasterium novum nisi episcopo aut permittente aut probante nullus incipere aut fundare praesumat." (27) "Cellulas novas aut

this power of surveillance over the monasteries the bishops demanded that the monasteries be located near cities to make them more accessible to inspection.[4] McLaughlin mentions that this was necessary for the purpose of combating the tendency of monks to make new establishments almost at personal whim.[5]

In whichever way the Fathers at the Council of Chalcedon determined monastic goods to be subjected to episcopal jurisdiction, the bishops of this era seemed to interpret it generally in their own favor. Alienation of any monastic goods, for example, was forbidden to the abbot on his own initiative, but became permissible with the bishop's approval and signature.[6] The punishment for the infraction of this decree was severe—excommunication for the abbot, and the return of the object that had been alienated.[7] Administrators appointed by the bishop and stationed in the abbeys came as the result of one council's legislative activity.[8] A bishop, however, was forbidden to enrich himself with the goods of a defunct priest or abbot.[9]

congregationculus monachorum absque notitia episcopi prohibemus instituti" (58). The Council of Epaône (517), can. 10—MGH, *ibid.*, p. 15; Mansi, VIII, col. 560; Bruns, II, 168; Hefele, *History*, IV, 110.

[4] Lesne, *Histoire de la propriété ecclésiastique en France* (5 vols., Tom. 1 (Paris, 1910), I, 88.

[5] *Le très ancien droit*, p. 136.

[6] The IV Council of Orleans (541), can. 11—MGH, *ibid.*, p. 86; Mansi, IX, col. 115; Bruns, II, 203; Hefele, *History*, p. 212: "Monasteriis aut parochiis collata sibi abbates et presbyteri non vindicent nec alienent sine episcopi consensu. Si quid abbatibus aut sacris monasteriis aut parochiis pro Dei fuerit contemplatione collatum, in sua proprietate hoc abbates vel presbyteri minime revocabunt, nec alienare quod cunctis fratribus debetur quacumque occasione praesumant; quibus si fuerit necessarium ut statuta convellant, non aliter valeat, nisi fuerit episcopi sui subscriptione firmatum." See also the III Council of Orleans (538), can. 23—*MGH*, *ibid.*, p. 72; Mansi, IX, col. 17; Bruns, II, 199.

[7] The III Council of Orleans (538), can. 26—*MGH*, *ibid.*, p. 81; Bruns, II, 199.

[8] The III Council of Orleans (538), can. 21 (18)—*MGH*, *ibid.*, p. 79; Bruns, II, 198.

[9] The Council of Chalon-sur-Saône (644), can. 7—*MGH*, *ibid.*, p. 210; Mansi, X, col. 1191; Bruns, II, 266; Hefele, *History*, IV, 464: "Res defuncti presbyteri vel abbatis intactae permaneant. Ut defuncto presbytero vel abbate nihil ab episcopo auferatur vel archidiacono, vel a quocumque de

The practice of making visitations in the monasteries gave the bishops the opportunity to demand large gifts or taxes for their troubles. Since the parishes served as models in this practice, the monasteries were relegated to the position of parish churches with regard to temporal or fiscal matters.[10] To increase his own diocesan clergy, the bishop frequently ordained monks without consulting the abbot, which practice serves to explain the prohibition of such action by at least one council.[11]

The bishop generally exercised a right over the selection of the abbot in the monasteries of his territory. The sole restraining force was his own conscience, for the councils required him to act honorably and with a just reason in choosing abbots.[12] Such a power could betray the bishop to withhold his choice of an abbot and in the meanwhile to collect revenues from the abbey. It was probably in an attempt to check such an abuse that the Council of Chalon (644) permitted the abbot to choose a successor.[13] Abbots could be summoned to the regular annual diocesan synods, at which they had to render an account of all their abbatial activities and to report on the discipline of the abbey.[14]

The monks desired to shake off the oppressive and restraining influence of the bishop, for they made overtures to secular

rebus parochiae vel xenodochii vel monasterii aliquid debeat minuere: quod qui fecerit, juxta statuta canonum debeat coerceri."

[10] Lesne, *Histoire de la propriété*, I, 67.

[11] The Council of Agde (506), can. 27 "...Monachi etiam vagantes ad officium clericatus ne ordinentur nisi iis testimonium abbas suus dederit, nec in civitatibus nec in parochiis ordinentur..."—Bruns, II, 161; Hefele, *History*, IV, 81.

[12] Council of Epaone (517), can. 19: "Abbas si in culpa reperiatur aut fraude, et innocentem se asserens ab episcopo suo accipere noluerit successorem, ad metropolitani judicium deducatur."—*MGH*, *ibid.*, p. 24; Mansi, VIII, col. 561; Bruns, II, 169; Hefele, *History*, IV, 111. Cf. also McLaughlin, *Le très ancien droit*, p. 89.

[13] Can. 12—*MGH*, *ibid.*, p. 210; Mansi, X, col. 1191; Bruns, II, 266; Hefele, *History* ,IV, 462. The same canon forbade any abbey to have two abbots.

[14] I Council of Orleans (511), can. 19—*MGH*, *ibid.*, p. 7; Mansi, VIII, col. 354; Bruns, II, 164; Hefele, *History*, IV, 91: "...Abbates...qui semel in anno in loco ubi episcopus elegerit accepta vocatione conveniant."

princes to aid them. The bishops, however, prohibited such undertakings.[15] They assumed the right and the power to excommunicate a malefactor as a penal sanction for this rule. The rule seemed more specifically directed against the Irish monasteries of St. Columban, who probably ignored the bishops as a regular practice.[16] Over the abbot the bishop exercised other powers. The bishop's permission was needed if the abbot absented himself from the abbey for a time.[17] Excommunication, a severe penalty, attended the abbots' solicitation of secular aid, their disdain for episcopal ordinances, alienation of abbey goods, admittance of women into their monasteries.[18] Removal of the abbot to another monastery was the penalty for his neglecting to report a crime of one of his subjects to the

[15] I Council of Orleans (511), can. 7—*MGH, ibid.*, p. 4; Mansi, VIII, col. 353; Bruns, II, 162; Hefele, *History*, IV, 89: "Ut clerici sine commendatitiis episcopi sui ad regem non accedant. Abbatibus, presbyteris omnique clero vel in religionis professione viventibus sine discussione vel commendatione episcoporum pro petendis beneficiis ad domnos venire non liceat: quod si quisquam praesumpserit, tam diu loci sui honore et communione privetur, donec per poenitentiam plenam ejus satisfactionem sacerdos accipiat." The Council of Chalon-sur-Saône (644), can. 15: "Ut abbates et monachi saeculari patrocinio non utantur et principem sine episcopi sui permissu non adeant. . . quod si fecerint, a suis episcopis excommunicentur" —*MGH, ibid.*, p. 210; Mansi, X, col. 1191; Bruns, II, 266; Hefele, *History*, IV, 462.

[16] McLaughlin, *op. cit.*, p. 138.

[17] The V Council of Arles (554), can. 3—*MGH, ibid.*, p. 119; Mansi, IX, col. 702; Bruns, II, 218; Hefele, *History*, IV, 376: "Ut abbatibus longius a monasterio vagari sine episcopi sui permissione non liceat; quod si fecerint, juxta antiquos canones ab episcopo suo regulariter corrigantur." The Council of Agde (506), can. 38—Bruns, II, 153; Hefele, *History*, IV, 82: ". . . Servandum quoque de monachis, nec iis ad solitarias cellulas liceat a congregatione discedere, nisi forte probatis post emeritos labores aut propter infirmitatis necessitatem asperior ab abbatibus regula remittatur. . ."

[18] The I Council of Orleans (511), can. 7—*MGH, ibid.*, p. 4; Mansi, VIII, col. 353; Bruns, II, 162; Hefele, *History*, IV, 89; also can. 15—*loc. cit.*; the II Council of Orleans (533), can. 21—*MGH, ibid.*, p. 64; Mansi, VIII, col. 838; Bruns, II, 187; Hefele, *History*, IV, 188; the III Council of Orleans (538), can. 26 (23)—*MGH, ibid.*, p. 81; Mansi, IX, col. 18; Bruns, II, 199; the II Council of Tours (567), can. 17 (16)—*MGH, ibid.*, p. 126; Mansi, IX, col. 796; Bruns, II, 229; Hefele, *History*, IV, 391; the Synod of Auxerre (580), can. 26—*MGH, ibid.*, p. 182; Mansi, IX, col. 914; Hefele, *History*, IV, 414.

bishop.[19] On the other hand, the bishops were no longer able to depose an abbot uncanonically,[20] or without consulting the other abbots to effect such a deposition in the annual synods.[21] And yet privileges of one sort or another frequently freed the abbeys from the interference of the bishop in regard to the abbey's material goods.[22]But the rest of the abbeys, if they were not so fortunate as to be privileged, continued subject to the bishop's authority over monastic goods.[23] This authority evinced a twofold element, reflecting indeed a vexing irritation to the monks, but likewise, at least occasionally, a necessary protection.[24] The maintenance of monastic discipline was assumed by the bishop as a personal chore, regardless of the abbot's residence or non-residence in the monastery.[25] The bishop took it upon himself to establish a rule for the monasteries, especially where many rules were extant before the advent of the Benedictine Rule.[26]

[19] The Synod of Auxerre (580), can. 23—*MGH, ibid.*, p. 181; Mansi, IX, col. 914; Hefele, *History*, IV, 413: "Si monachus in monasterio adulterium commiserit, aut peculiare habere praesumpserit aut furtum fecerit, et hoc abbas per se non emendaverit aut episcopo aut archidiacono non innotuerit, ad poenitentiam agendam in alio monasterio retrudatur."

[20] Council of Paris (614), can. 4—*MGH, ibid.*, p. 187; Mansi, X, col. 540; Hefele, *History*, IV, 438: "We have unanimously decreed that if a bishop deposes an abbot uncanonically (*quia fratres nostri sunt*), which will probably never happen, the latter shall appeal to the Synod..."

[21] The II Council of Tours (567), can. 7—*MGH, ibid.*, p. 124; Mansi, IX, col. 796; Bruns, II, 226; Hefele, *History*, IV, 390: "Ut episcopus nec abbatem nec archipresbyterum sine omnium suorum compresbyterorum et abbatum concilio de loco suo praesumat ejicere, neque per praemia alium ordinare, nisi facto concilio tam abbatum quam prebyterorum suorum, quem culpa aut negligentia ejicit, cum omnium presbyterorum consilio refutetur."

[22] Lesne, *Histoire de la Propriété*, I, 130: "L'administration du temporel monastique échappe à l'évêque; tout doit être remis à l'abbé ou à l'abbesse. Un grand nombre de monastères s'émancipèrent ainsi, au temporel, de l'autorité épiscopale. Les abbés purent gérer en toute indépendance les biens de la communauté. Ces monastères furent des propriétaires libres."

[23] Lesne, *loc. cit.*

[24] Lesne, *Histoire de la propriété*, I, 414.

[25] The V Council of Arles (554), can. 2, 5—*MGH, ibid.*, p. 119; Bruns, II, 218; Mansi, IX, 702; Hefele, *History*, IV, 376.

[26] DeClercq, *La Législation Religieuse Franque de Clovis à Charlemagne*

Although most of these canons seemed to favor the bishop in defining his rights over the monastery and the abbot, they also served to limit his rights in view of the principle of law, "*generi per speciem derogatur*," inasmuch as the general statute of Chalcedon became modified and restricted by statutes enacted in the local councils.[27] A summary view indicates the current tendency on the part of the bishops to become ever more possessive with reference to the monasteries in their dioceses, and the resulting resistance to this on the part of the monks in their striving to obtain greater freedom from the power wielded by the bishops.

ARTICLE 2. SPANISH LEGISLATION TO THE INVASION OF ISLAM

Spain, closer to Gaul than Africa, was able to associate itself more intimately with Gaul's legislation than was Africa. Therefore as early as 524 in the Council of Lerida[28] approval was given in its 3rd canon to the ordinances of the Council of Agde (506) and the I Council of Orleans[29] (511), in their legislation regarding monks. Moreover the Council of Lerida added in its third canon that "the bishop has the right, with the consent of the abbot, to ordain for the service of the Church those monks whom he knows to be qualified."[30] Then, with reference to the material goods of the abbey: "Anything which has been given to the monasteries as a present is not at the disposal of the bishop. A layman who wishes to obtain the consecration of a church built by him must not withdraw it from the authority of the bishop under the pretext that it is a monastic church, if no monks reside thereat and no rule for it has been drawn up by the bishop."[31] Thus the Spanish council went a

(Louvain, Paris: Bureaux du Recueil Bibliothèque de l'Université, 1936), p. 301.

[27] Reiffenstuel, *Jus Canonicum Universum* (5 vols. in 7, Parisiis, 1864-1882), VII, 82, Rule 34.

[28] Mansi, VIII, col. 612; Bruns, II, 21; *MGH*, Legum Sectio III, *Concilia*, Tom. I, *Concilia Aevi Merovingici*, pp. 35-39; Hefele, *History*, IV, 524.

[29] Can. 3—Mansi, VIII, col. 625; *MGH*, *ibid.*, pp. 35-39; Bruns, II, 21; Hefele, IV, 133.

[30] Hefele, *loc. cit.*

[31] *Loc. cit.*

step farther than the Council of Agde and the I Council of Orleans, which it had endorsed, by making a clear distinction between the monastic and diocesan church with regard to the bishop's jurisdiction.

The tenor of this first council was confirmed and extended by others in later years. Chalcedon's general statement of bishop-monastery relations was reiterated.[32]

Bishops freely permitted clerics to enter the monastic life, recognizing its higher spiritual status.[33] Several measures of these councils confirmed the material holdings of monasteries against possible encroachments from outside powers.[34] The monasteries were favored by a decree which permitted the bishops to give a fiftieth of their fortune to build monasteries, while they were limited to a 100th of their fortune in the construction of a church.[35]

A provincial council in 619 anathematized the plundering of monasteries by bishops.[36] "The newly-erected monasteries in the province of Baetica were confirmed and every kind of plundering or the removal of a monastery was forbidden to

[32] Council of Barcelona (540), can. 10—Hefele-Leclercq, *Histoire des Conciles*, II, 1163; Mansi, IX, col. 110; Bruns, II, 28: "De monachis vero id observari praecipimus quod synodus Chalcedonensis constituit."

[33] The IV Council of Toledo (633), can. 50: "Clerici, qui monachorum propositum appetunt, quia meliorem vitam sequi cupiunt, liberos eis ab episcopo in monasteriis largiri oportet ingressus, nec interdici propositum eorum, qui ad contemplationis desiderium transire nituntur."—Mansi, X, col. 631; Bruns, I, 235.

[34] The III Council of Toledo (589), can. 3: "Haec sancta synodus nulli episcoporum licentiam tribuit res alienare ecclesiae, quoniam et antiquioribus canonibus prohibentur; si quid vero quod utilitatem non gravet ecclesiae pro suffragio monachorum ad suam parochiam pertinentium dederint, firmum maneat"—Mansi, V, col. 1010; Bruns, I, 213; *ibid*, can. 4: "Si episcopus unam de parochitanis ecclesiis suis monasterium dicare voluerit, ut in ea monachorum regulariter congregatio vivat, hoc de consensu concilii sui habeat licentiam faciendi; qui etiam si de rebus ecclesiae pro eorum substantia aliquid quod detrimentum ecclesiae non exhibeat eidem loco donaverit, sit stabile."

[35] *Ibidem*, can. 5.

[36] II Council of Seville (619), can. 10: "Decima actione poscentibus monasteriorum patribus pari sententia statuimus, ut coenobia super condita in provincia Baetica sicut et illa quae sunt antiqua, immobili et inconcussa stabilitate permaneant solidata."—Mansi, X, col. 560; Bruns, II, 72.

bishops on pain of missing salvation."[37] McLaughlin believes that the majority of the bishops favored monasticism the while but a small minority were bent on subduing it.[38] The strong wording of the conciliar decrees seems to confirm this.[39] The bishops were not to overtax the monasteries;[40] "No bishop could in the future demand more than two *solidi* yearly . . . the convent churches were quite free from this tax."[41] Because of the failure of the bishops to watch over the abbeys, many had fallen into ruins.[42]

The Spanish abbots enjoyed a higher status than the abbots of Gaul, since they could attend all councils as abbot-prelates.[43] This was not to say that the abbots were the peers of the bishops, since conciliar action quite definitely decided against such a view. The abbots owed the same obedience to the bishops as the secular clerics, and could expect regular visitations from the bishop, who was to be well and honorably received.[44]

In the liturgy the abbeys were not independent, for the bishop could permit only the particular practice of the private recitation of the Divine Office; in the public recitation there

[37] Hefele, *History*, IV, 443.

[38] *Le très ancien droit*, p. 144.

[39] I.e., the IV Council of Toledo (633), can. 51: "Nuntiatum est praesenti concilio, quod monachi episcopali imperio servili opere mancipentur et jura monasteriorum contra instituta canonum illicita praesumptione usurpentur . . ."—Mansi, X, col. 631; Bruns, I, 235.

[40] The VII Council of Toledo (646), can. 4: ". . . non amplius quam duos solidos unusquisque episcoporum . . . monasteriorum tamen basilicis ab hac solutionis pensione sejunctis."—Mansi, X, col. 768; Bruns, I, 263.

[41] Hefele, *op. cit.*, IV, 467.

[42] The IX Council of Toledo (655), can. 2: "Quia ergo fieri plerumque cognoscitur, ut ecclesiae parochiales vel sacra monasteria ita quorumdam episcoporum vel insolentia vel incuria horrendam decidant in ruinam, ut gravior ex hoc oriatur aedificantibus moeror, quam in construendo gaudii extiterat labor."—Mansi, XI, col. 472; Bruns, I, 292.

[43] McLaughlin, *Le très ancien droit*, p. 145.

[44] Council of Merida (666), can. 11: ". . . Placuit huic sancto concilio, ut tam a presbyteris quam ab abbatibus sive etiam a diaconibus episcopo honor debitus impendatur, ut a nullo contumelium pati videatur, et quandoque contigerit eum juxta canonicam sententiam visitare suam parochiam, et digne eum suscipiant et prout habuerint aut ratio permiserit illi praeparent quae fuerint necessaria. . . ."—Mansi, XI, col. 75; Bruns, II, 89.

was to be conformity with the practice in use at the metropolitan church.[45] "Worship was everywhere to be conducted as in the metropolis. Only the convents were enabled to have some special *officia* with the permission of the bishop."[46] As in Gaul, the abbots were required to attend the annual diocesan synods, and to give an account of their office for the past year.[47] The abbot had to receive the penitents sent to the abbey by the bishop or else be suspended by him.[48] In the choice of an abbot, the diocesan bishop could institute him along with the other monastic officers, watch over the discipline of the house, and punish any violations which occurred.[49] Levy-Bruhl believed that the word "*instituere*" pointed inclusively to the naming of the abbot.[50]

It is obvious that Gaul and Spain followed more or less the same pattern with regard to bishop-monastery relations. However, a few points of difference may be mentioned. Whereas the councils of Gaul negatively outlined the prohibitions with regard to both bishops and monasteries, the Spanish councils positively defined quite precisely the rights of both. McLaugh-

[45] The XI Council of Toledo (675), can. 3: "...unam eumdemque in psallendo teneant modum, quem in metropolitana sede cognoverint institutum...abbatibus sane indultis officiis, quae juxta voluntatem sui episcopi regulariter illis implenda sunt..."—Mansi, XI, col. 138; Bruns, I, 309.

[46] Hefele, *History*, V, 488.

[47] The Council of Huesca (598), can. 1: "...ut annuis vicibus unusquisque nostrum omnes abbates monasteriorum vel presbyteros et diaconos suae diocesis ad locum ubi episcopus elegerit congregari praecipiat, et omnibus regulam demonstret ducendi vitas, cunctosque sub ecclesiasticis regulis adesse praemoneat..."—Mansi, X, col. 482; Bruns, II, 65.

[48] The Council of Narbonne (589), can. 6: "...ut quicumque fuerit culpabilis inventus clericus, aut honoratus de civitate et ad monasterium fuerit deputatus, sic abbas qui est praedictus cum illo qui dirigitur agat, sicut ab episcopo manifesta correctione fuerit ordinatus..."—Mansi, IX, col. 1014; Bruns, II, 60.

[49] The IV Council of Toledo (633), can. 51: "Quapropter monemus eos qui ecclesiis praesunt, ut ultra talia non praesumant, sed hoc tantum sibi in monasteriis vindicent sacerdotes, quod praecipiunt canones, id est monachos ad conversationem sanctam praemonere, abbates aliaque officia instituere."—Mansi, X, col. 631; Bruns, I, 235.

[50] *Elections Abbatiales*, p. 26.

lin notes[51] that at least from the VIII Council of Toledo (653) abbots were adding their signatures to the decrees, which indicated a certain status far above that of the abbots of the Frankish kingdoms, who were required to attend, but only in the capacity of subjects of the bishops, or possibly as delegates of the bishops, in which case the abbots were probably the heads, not of a monastery, but of the clerics attached to a basilica.[52]

ARTICLE 3. AFRICAN LEGISLATION TO THE INVASION OF ISLAM

African monasticism, it seems, enjoyed a freedom from the jurisdiction of the diocesan bishop which was unknown in Europe until much later. The monasteries were numerous and rich, and in consequence of the influence of St. Augustine, particularly, they had procured in Africa a *modus vivendi* quite independent of the episcopacy.[53] As early as 525, the complete independence of monasteries from clerical jurisdiction was already recognized by the Council of Carthage.[54] And even in those dioceses wherein the bishops strictly enforced the fourth canon of Chalcedon, the monasteries found a means of putting themselves beyond the reach of the local episcopal power, by

[51] *Le très ancien droit*, p. 146.

[52] McLaughlin, *op. cit.*, p. 146 (note).

[53] Lévy-Bruhl, *Elections Abbatiales*, p. 24.

[54] Mansi, VIII, col. 656: "Erunt igitur omnia omnino monasteria, sicut semper fuerunt, a conditione clericorum modis omnibus libera, sibi tantum et Deo placentia." There is some question about the use of the term "*conditio clericorum*" here, but both the Council itself and the commentators understood it to mean full independence, even though the latter avoided translating the passage as such. Two authors, Ceillier (Remi Ceillier (1688-1761), *Histoire Generale des auteurs ecclésiastiques* (2. ed., Paris, 1865), XV, 831) and Richard (Ch. L. Richard (1711-1794), *Analyse des conciles generaux et particuliers* (5 vols. in 4, Paris, 1772-1777), I, 507), translated and used "*conditio*" in the precise sense of "jurisdiction." Blaise (Albert Blaixe, *Dictionnaire Latin-Français des auteurs Chrètiens* (Revu spécialement pour le vocabulaire théologique par Henri Chirat, Paris: Librairie des Meridiens, 1954)) applied the meaning of "that to which one is submitted" to "*conditio*" as found in the Council of Carthage of 535, which was contemporary to this one. Hence the expression as used there seemed to carry this sense of "subjection" or "jurisdiction."

attaching themselves to a bishop other than the local diocesan.[55]

In 534 another council was held in Carthage. It was attended by 217 bishops,[56] and may thus be considered as echoing the official voice of the African hierarchy on the bishop-monastery relations during that period. The Council decided quite definitively that monasteries were to be independent of the bishops.[57]

Except for a few monasteries, the rest of the convents in Africa,

> should enjoy the fullest liberty as far as the Councils allow. If they wish that clergy should be ordained or oratories consecrated, this shall be done by the bishop of the place or of the neighborhood. In other respects, however, the monasteries are independent of the bishop, and have no duties to render to him. Moreover, the bishop must not erect a chair (*cathedra*) for himself in any monastery, nor must he ordain anyone without consent of the abbot. When the abbot dies, the whole society (of the monastery) shall elect a new one; and the bishop shall in no way usurp the right of election. If a dispute arises respecting the election (among the monks), other abbots shall decide; if the dispute continues, the matter shall be brought before the primate of the province. At divine service the bishop should read aloud (from the diptychs), among the others whom he has ordained, also the monks of his district whom he has ordained.[58]

It is not known for certain whether this was merely a private opinion regarding the decree of the Council, since the decree itself seems to have been lost, and this statement by one who seemed to be the reporter of the assembly alone is preserved. However, since the Council favored the one who presented the complaint to which these words served as a reply, it may safely be thought that the sentiments of the Fathers present was duly expressed in this passage. Taché believes that, since the

[55] Lafontaine, *L'Evêque d'Ordination*, p. 63.

[56] McLaughlin, *Le très ancien droit*, p. 141.

[57] Mansi, VIII, col. 841.

[58] Hefele, *History*, IV, 189; Mansi, VIII, col. 841.

decisions of the two councils of Carthage were used more frequently later, they may be regarded as being more important than the III Council of Arles (455).[59] It is interesting to note that reference in support of the pericope is made both to a sermon of St. Augustine (*De Moribus Clericorum*, I, II) and to the decision of the Council of Arles in 455.

The Council of Carthage was regional, and yet its influence upon Europe must have been great, particularly since the ideas of St. Augustine had received such a wide diffusion in the 7th century, and this decision restates his views on monasticism.[60] This independence of the monasteries in Africa from the jurisdiction of the bishop was accomplished by means of a general law in that part of the Christian world. In Gaul, private law carried similar views in contrast to the conciliar position.

ARTICLE 4. ANGLO-SAXON LEGISLATION DURING THE MIDDLE AGES

The problem of bishop-monastery relations can hardly be posed with regard to Britain, since the episcopal offices were by and large held by monks from their advent in 597 with St. Austin of Canterbury until the invasion of the Danes around the year 835. There was some kind of separation between the two orders beginning about the 7th century, and there is a hint of some difficulties existing between them in the granting of privileges of exemption from the diocesan bishop. Encroachment by the local bishop undoubtedly existed in view of the several privileges which protected the monastic temporalities from the hands of those who could be tempted to seize them.[61]

In the Penitential of Theodore (830/847) is enumerated a

[59] "Notes sur l'Histoire des Exemptions Monastiques," *Revue de l' Université d'Ottawa*, XI (1941), 27*.

[60] McLaughlin, *Le très ancien droit*, p. 142.

[61] E.g., the privilege of Pope Adeodatus to the monastery of St. Peter and Paul (St. Austin's), Canterbury. Cf. Haddon and Stubbs, *Councils and Ecclesiastical Documents Relating to Great Britain and Ireland* (3 vols. in 4, Oxford, 1869-1878), Vol. III (1871), 123-124, and the privilege of Pope Constantine to the Monasteries of Bermondsey and Woking.—*ibid.*, III, 276; Jaffé, n. 2148.

list of privileges which set limits to the local bishop's powers, and defined the positive rights of the abbots.[62] The document allowed the monks to elect their own abbot; the abbot could not be forced to remain within the monastery by the bishop; the monastery could not be confiscated by the bishop in case the abbot had committed a serious offense; etc.

Inasmuch as most of the bishops were chosen from monastic communities, the bishops were charged with the duty of surveillance of the communities within the diocese.[63]

In the Legatine Synod of 766, a distinction was made between the canons and the monks, and the bishops were cautioned to see to it that both classes remained faithful to their customs and peculiar norms.[64] The bishop was empowered, however, to send to another abbey any abbot who had committed a serious fault,[65] to examine and bless the abbatial candidate,[66] to examine candidates for the priesthood chosen from the monasteries,[67] and to authorize the foundation of new religious houses.[68]

Thus England also reflected the granting of innumerable privileges, even though, perhaps, because of the close link

[62] Theodores *Pentitential, op. cit.*, III, 195-196 (Taken from C.C.C.C. Ms. 320).

[63] Council of Clovesho (747), can. 4: "...Ut episcopi in suis parochiis abbates atque abbatissas moneant, quatenus seipsos primo ponant exemplum bene vivendi, deinde subjectos sibi ut regulariter conversantur, diligenti cura exerceant...;"—*op. cit.*, III, 364. Cf. also Hauck, *Kirchengeschichte Deutschlands*, I, 554. See also can. 20: "Episcopi in suis parochiis, ut sint monasteria juxta vocabulum nominis sui, id est, honesta silentium, quietorum, atque pro Deo laborantium habitacula, et non sint ludicrarum artium receptacula...ne aliquid intra claustra monasterii aliter quam decet videant vel audiant."—Haddan and Stubbs, III, 20.

[64] "Ut episcopi diligenti cura provideant, quo omnes canonici sui canonice vivant, et monachi seu monachae regulariter conversentur, tam in cibis quam in vestibus, ut discretio sit inter canonicum et monachum vel secularem..."—*op. cit.*, III, 450.

[65] Theodore's *Penitential*, Cap. VI, can. 5—*op. cit.*, *loc. cit.*

[66] Council of Clovesho (716)—*op. cit.*, III, 300; Council of Clovesho (742)—*op. cit.*, III, 360.

[67] Legatine Synods (766-791), can. 5—*op. cit.*, III, 450.

[68] Council of Celchyth (816), can. 8—*op. cit.*, III, 582.

between monasticism and the active ministry, there was less conflict between the two elements.

Article 5. Legislation in Carolingian Gaul

During the Carolingian period, one naturally meets a formulary repetition of the conciliar legislation regarding monks which appeared in the preceding centuries, even reaching back to Chalcedon. The monasteries were still, with all special privileges barred, under the jurisdiction of the bishop, although the language was frequently not as absolute as before.[69] In this period there was no mention of the bishop's competence to exert his authority with relation to the material goods of the abbey, so that the abbeys seem to have assumed some control themselves.[70] This control, however, was very limited, since the abbeys become the property of the king and his sycophants.[71] Charlemagne (768-814) had instituted his highly organized "*missi dominici*," and these, combined with bishops, inspected and corrected abuses in the abbeys.[72] The monks were forbidden to hold parishes, a sore point for the simple reason that Germany had been constituted upon monastic

[69] Capitulare Aquisgranense (801-813), cap. 1: "Ut episcopi circumeant parrochias sibi commissas, ...Et ut monachi per verbum episcopi et per regimen abbatis et per bona illorum exempla regulariter vivant, prout loca locata sunt...;"—*MGH*, Legum Sectio II, *Capitularia*, Tom. I, *Capitularia Regum Francorum* (ed. Boretius, Hannoverae, 1893), p. 170; Concilium Vernense (755), cap. 3: "Ut unusquisque episcoporum potestatem habeat in sua parrochia, tam de clero quam de regularibus vel secularibus, ad corrigendum et emendandum secundum ordinem canonicam spiritale, ut sic vivant qualiter Deo placere possint."—*MGH*, *ibid.*, p. 135; Capitula vel Missorum vel Synodalia (813), can. 4—*MGH*, *ibid.*, p. 182; Admonitio ad omnes Regni Ordines (823-825), cap. 10—*MGH*, *ibid.*, p. 305; etc.

[70] McLaughlin, *Le très ancien droit*, pp. 170 and 161.

[71] Lesne, *Histoire de la Propriété Ecclésiastique en France*, T. II, *La propriété ecclésiastique et les droits régaliens à l'époque carolingienne*, fasc. II, *Le droit du roi sur les églises et les biens d'Eglise* (1926), pp. 502-503.

[72] Concilium Moguntinense (813), cap. XX: "Deinde dignum ac necessarium est, ut missi per quaeque loca directi simul cum episcopis uniuscuiusque diocesis perspiciant loca monasteriorum canonicorum pariter et monachorum..."—*MGH*, Legum Sectio III, *Concilia*, Tom. I, *Concilia Aevi Karolini* (ed. A. Werminghoff, Hannoverae et Lipsiae, 1908), p. 265; Pipini Capitulare Italicum (801-810), cap. X—*MGH*, *ibid.*, p. 209.

foundations, and the application of this precept was to cause some vexation there.[73] In case of any conflicts between ecclesiastics, which included abbots and monks, it was through the bishops' courts that judgment was rendered. An appeal could then be made to the metropolitan.[74] The abbot and the bishop were able to choose the candidates for the priesthood, which undoubtedly gave the bishop certain rights over the clerical monk.[75] It was the abbot who granted permission to his monks to temporarily leave the monastery, but in order to prevent abuse, if too great a number wished to absent themselves, only the bishop could give such permission.[76]

Abbatial elections took place only with the permission of the king and the bishop.[77] Abbots still had to attend the synods, although their presence was more an act of obedience than a designation of status.[78] Clerics and monks were still prohibited from appealing over the head of the bishop to the king.[79] Monks unhappy with the discipline of a monastery could, with the permission of the bishop, change their house

[73] Concilia Rispacense, Frisingense, Salisburgense (800), cap. 25: "Ut qui monachico voto est constitutus nullo modo parroechiam teneat nec ad judicia secularia accedere praesummat."—*MGH*, *ibid.*, 206. The actual limits of the "*parroechia*" during these centuries are difficult to determine from a simple reading of the conciliar texts. It is possible that at times the word referred to a diocese rather than a mere parish. Cf. Imbart de la Tour, *Les Paroisses rurales du V au XI siècle* (Paris, 1900), pp. 50-73; 88-105; Amann-Dumas, *L'Eglise au pouvoir des Laïques* (888-1057) (Paris: Bloud and Gay, 1940), pp. 177-179.

[74] Concilium Francofurtense (794), cap. VI: "Statutum est..."—*MGH*, *ibid.*, p. 167; Capitulare de Justitiis Faciendis (811-813), cap. II—*MGH*, *ibid.*, p. 176.

[75] Capitulare Missorum Generale (802), cap. XVI—*MGH*, *ibid.*, p. 94.

[76] *Ibidem*, cap. XVII.

[77] Concilium Francofurtense (794), cap. XVII: "Ut abbas in congregatione non elegatur, ubi jussio regis fuerit, nisi per consensum episcopi loci illius."—*MGH*, *ibid.*, p. 167; Episcoporum ad Imperatorem de rebus ecclesiasticis Relatio (821), cap. IX—*MGH*, *ibid.*, p. 369.

[78] Concilium Vernense (755), cap. IV: "Ut bis in anno sinodus fiat...et illi episcopi ibidem conveniant, quos modo vicem metropolitanorum constituimus, et alii episcopi vel abbates seu presbiteri, quos ipsi metropolitani aput [*sic*] se venire jusserint, ibidem in ipsa secunda sinodo convenire faciant."—*MGH*, *ibid.*, p. 32.

[79] *Ibidem*, cap. VIII.

and enter another monastery where the observance was better.[80] Permission of the bishop was required for one who aspired to live his life as a recluse.[81] Participation in civil court suits was permissible only on approval from the bishop.[82] The abbot could be punished by the bishop.[83]

It is quite evident that the monasteries were slowly withdrawing from the episcopal power as such. Legislation treating directly with the monks became rarer, and revealed itself in an exhortative rather than a preceptive tone. Privileges of one sort or another made this period a crazy-quilt of legislation and private law.[84] The rights of the bishop over the temporal goods of the abbeys received small mention during this period, but when special rights could not be urged and vindicated, the bishop retained a right of surveillance of the monastic communities in his territory.

[80] *Ibidem,* cap. X: "...Et si talis causa evenerit, quod absit, quod ille abbas sic remissus vel neglegens inveniatur aut in manus laicorum ipsum monasterium veniat, et hoc episcopus emendare non potuerit, et aliqui tales monachi ibidem fuerint qui propter Deum de ipso monasterio in alterum migrare vellent propter eorum animas salvandas, hoc per consensum episcopi sui licentiam habeant, qualiter eorum animas possint salvare."

[81] Concilium Francofurtense (794), cap. XII: "Ut reclusi non fiant nisi quos ante episcopus provinciae atque abbas comprobaverint, et secundum eorum dispositionem in reclusionis loco ingrediantur."—*MG H*, *ibid.*, p. 167.

[82] Concilium Moguntinense (813), cap. XII:—"Hoc tamen omnino volumus, ut monachi ad saecularia placita nullatenus veniant, neque ipse abbas sine concilio episcopi sui et, cum necessitas exigit, tunc per jussionem et consilium episcopi illuc vadat, nequaquam tamen contentiones aut lites aliquas ibi movere praesumat, sed... per advocatos suos hoc faciat."—*MG H*, *ibid.*, p. 209.

[83] Capitula vel Missorum vel Synodalia (813), cap. IX: "Ut clerici vel ...:"—*MG H*, *loc. cit.*: Episcoporum ad Imperatorem de Rebus Ecclesiasticis Relatio (821), cap. XI: "A quo et quomodo corrigi abbas neglegenter agens debeat, canon Calcidonensis titul. VIII, videnter exponit cum ab episcopo loci dissilienter communione privare non ambigat."—*MG H*, *ibid.*, p. 369.

[84] McLaughlin, *Le très ancien droit*, p. 168.

CHAPTER VIII

THE REFORM OF BENEDICT OF ANIANE (Ca. 750-821)

Charlemagne (742-814) had during his reign (768-814) promoted the wide adoption of the Benedictine Rule, even though he did not especially favor this form of religious life over the others. His interests, by this course of action, were not to deepen the spiritual life of the monastic houses so much as to use them to strengthen his own hold over his vast empire and to further his personal interests.[1] It was during this period of his rule that the monasteries began to be accepted not primarily as centers of spiritual formation but rather as the depots of intellectual culture, fortresses manned by monk-soldiers, even as "political plums" to be doled out to those who were most obsequious to him.[2] From his tenure until the tenth century, except for a brief period during the reign of his son, Louis the Pious, secularization was to infect monasticism.[3] Abbeys became the prize possessions of Emperor, bishop, and noble. Charlemagne was reluctant to give up any hold whatsoever over such foundations. As an exception to his general policy

[1] E. Amann, *L'Epoque Carolingienne* (Paris: Bloud & Gay, 1937), p. 259: "Charlemagne aimait l'Ordre et même l'uniformité. . . De même qu'il avait prescrit l'adoption de la liturgie romaine dans toutes les églises de l'Empire franc, de même demanda-t-il à l'abbé du Mont-Cassin une copie type de la règle de saint Benoît et il décida que, dorénavant, on se conformerait dans tous les monastères à ses dispositions;" Narberhaus, *Benedikt von Aniane, Werk und Persönlichkeit,* (Münster in Westf., 1930), p. 2: "Wenn seine Bemühungen um die zerrüttete Klosterordnung auch nicht gering sind, so war es doch weniger die Wiederherstellung echt monastischen Lebens im Sinne Benedikts von Nursia, die ihm im Sinne lag, also vielmehr die Einstellung des Mönchtums in dieselbe Richtung, in der er die Kirche überhaupt benutzte, in den Dienst des Staates und seiner Kulturaufgaben." Cf. also Hauck, *Kirchengeschichte Deutschlands,* II, 520; Knowles, *The Monastic Order in England* (Cambridge: University Press, 1949), p. 28; Schmitz, *Histoire de l'Ordre,* I, 92.

[2] Amann, *L'Epoque Carolingienne, loc. cit.*; Lavisse-Rambaud, *Histoire Générale du IVe Siècle à nos Jours* (Paris, 1922), I, 351.

[3] Schmitz, *Histoire de l'Ordre,* I, 106.

of the centralization of power, Benedict of Aniane (Ca. 750-821) received a grant of immunity in the original charter of his monastery at Aniane, completed about 782 with the help of the dukes and counts.[4] Rarer, perhaps, than a grant of immunity of this type was the right of communities to choose their own abbot as the Benedictine Rule (Ch. 64) ordained.[5] Charlemagne's own personal hold was enhanced by choosing these himself, or by having the bishops or nobles do so with his approval.[6] He was not rigorous in his demands that the Benedictine Rule alone hold sway, for it was during his reign that the Rule for Canons, less severe than the Benedictine, was permitted to ease its way into many monasteries.[7] And even in the Benedictine Rule a very special application was accorded this venerable document by Charlemagne, since he authorized only those portions which were favorable to his interests, evidently excluding from them Chapter 64 of the Benedictine Rule.[8]

Canon law regarding monasteries and their relations with bishops in this period, as well as in the preceding one, was determined for the most part by conciliar decisions and by

[4] "Vita Benedicti:"—*MGH*, *Scriptores*, XV, 207: "...ut nullus comes neque episcopus aut ulla judiciaria potestas...ingredi audiat vel exactare presumat..."

[5] Schmitz, "Benoît d'Aniane," *Dictionnaire d'Histoire et Géographie*, Tom. VIII, col. 181: "Parmi ces privilèges monastiques, l'un des plus importants consiste dans la libre élection de l'abbé choisi au sein même de la communauté. En ce temps-là [time of Charlemagne], cette liberté n'existait guère pour les monastères..." Amann, *L'Epoque Carolingienne*, p. 259: "Il [Charlemagne] se montra donc extrèmement parcimonieux dans l'octroi à certains monastères privilégiés de la faculté d'élire leur abbé."

[6] Amann, *loc. cit.*: "Il tenait beaucoup à en réserver la nomination direct au pouvoir royal."

[7] Amann, *loc. cit.*: "Un autre indice que le pouvoir central ne se mettait pas trop en peine de l'observation exacte de la règle bénédictine, c'est que, sous le règne de Charlemagne, se poursuivit le mouvement qui amenait, dans bien des couvents, la substitution à la règle monastique de la règle canoniale beaucoup plus douce; les moines se muaient en chanoines, même à Saint-Martin de Tours, même à Saint-Denis, les deux grandes abbayes royales de l'ancienne France."

[8] Amann, *op. cit.*, p. 259: "A vrai dire, il ne tint pas très énergiquement la main à la mise en pratique du texte qu'il fit expédier à tous les abbés."

capitularies sent out from the imperial palace, both of which were in many ways repetitious and vague on this point.

Louis the Pious (778-840) assumed the reins of government of the empire in 814. Deploring the decadent state of monastic life[9] Louis was advised by St. Benedict of Aniane concerning means to correct this appalling state.[10]

Benedict believed that the principal weakness in monasticism was its lack of uniformity, both in rule and in practice. Although Louis' father had firmly implanted the Benedictine Rule in monasteries and suppressed the others (except, as seen, the Rule for Canons), there were extant many interpretations of this Rule which occasioned diversity of practice and minimal standards of monastic life. It was the purpose of Benedict, therefore, to unify the monastic Rule and to establish for it a single practice.[11]

[9] Amann, *L'Epoque Carolingienne*, p. 259: "Un point surtout le frappe, les moines de son temps font trop fi de cet esprit de pauvreté et de pénitence que le patriarche de Mont-Cassin voulait faire prévaloir. Ils vivent bourgeoisement, confortablement, préférant au travail des mains, aux rudes labeurs de l'agriculture les délassements que donnent les besognes intellectuelles. Au travail de l'esprit l'on sacrifie volontiers la prière elle-même, l'office divin, qui doit être selon le sens étymologique, le vrai devoir du religieux."

[10] Ardo, Benedict's biographer, reported that the saint was the reformer first "*omnium monasteriorum tam in Provincia, quam in Gotia seu Novempalitana provincia,*" ("Ardonis Vita Benedicti Abbatis Anianensis et Indensis," *MGH, Scriptores*, XV, 208), but upon invitation from others (see text) his influence was extended more broadly. At Louis' request, while the latter was still king of Aquitaine alone, Benedict extended his reform to all of that kingdom (*Ibid.*, p. 211). Becoming the successor to Charlemagne upon the latter's demise, Louis sent him throughout Francia: "Franciae eum partibus ire jussit."—(*Ibid.*, p. 215).

[11] Louis set out to implement the initial reform with an assembly in which monks of many monasteries agreed upon a number of reforming measures and techniques which were presented to and approved by the king. Reference to this is made in Ardo's life of Benedict. (*MGH, Scriptores*, XV, 215). One version of the Capitulary of this assembly with a commentary can be found in the *Statuta Murbacensis*, Mansi, XIV, 349 ff. Cf. also Berlière, "Les coutumiers monastiques des VIIIe et IXe siècles," *Revue Bénédictine*, 25 (1908), p. 105: "Un synode de 816 a discuté les observances bénédictines, dont on retrouve le formulaire dans les statuts dits de Murbach, qui seraient antérieurs au synode de 817, "dans les *Capitula novitiorum* envoyés à l'abbé

To accomplish his first purpose, Benedict set about writing the *Codex Regularum* and *Concordantia Regularum*,[12] which were collections of the monastic Rules of former periods up until his day, and all were intended as a commentary and explanation of the Benedictine Rule. In July, 817,[13] the abbots of the empire were convoked in Aix-la-Chapelle, where Benedict instructed them on the interpretation of the Rule. At the meeting the abbots concurred[14] in the publishing of the *Capitulare Monachorum*, a set of 75 norms for the regulation of monastic life.[15]

The *Capitulare* was more than a norm to be posed as an ideal for the abbeys to refer to from time to time. The emperor reinforced Benedict's policies by delegating *Missi* to see to their implementation,[16] although since the session was at-

de Saint-Gall, dans les capitula envoyés à Reichenau par les moines Tatto et Grimald (816-817)."

[12] *MPL*, CIII, 703.

[13] The monastic assembly of 817 was preceded in the previous year by one designed to reform the "*canonici*" and the "*sanctimoniales sub canonica vita degentes*." Since Ardo does not mention Benedict's presence, the saint was probably hostile to the canonical order, somewhat less severe than the monastic. Cf. Lesne, "Les Ordonnances Monastiques de Louis le Pieux et la Notitia de Servitio Monasteriorum," *Revue d' Histoire de l'Eglise de France*, VI (1920), 161; 321; 449. In this assembly 27 statutes were passed and redacted for the monasteries of the strict observance. In July of 817 the 27 statutes were revised in the monastic session and enlarged to form the *Capitulare monasticum*.

[14] Not without some opposition. Cf. Graham, *English Ecclesiastical Studies, Being Some essays in Research in Medieval History* (London, 1929), p. 153.

[15] According to Schmitz, *Histoire de l'Ordre*, I, 95-96, there exist two recessions of the Capitulary, the shorter one being the original. For example, Schmitz himself in the work here cited gives 75 as the number of chapters, and also in his article "Benoît d'Aniane," col. 180, as does Graham (*op. cit.*, p. 153), but *MGH* (*Cap. Reg. Fr.*, I, 343), de Valous (*Le Monachisme Clunisien des Origines au XV Siècle* [Ligugé, 1935], p. 10) and Amann-Dumas (*L'Eglise au Pouvoir des Laïques*, 888-1057, [Paris: Bloud & Gay, 1940], p. 317) name 83 as the number of the chapters. Cf. Berlière, "Les Coutumiers monastiques des VIII et IX siècles," p. 105.

[16] To check on the progress of his general reform, Louis convoked a synod in Aix-la-Chapelle in 818-819, which undoubtedly included the monks and the regular *missi*. Cf. Lesne, "Les Ordonnances Monastiques de Louis le Pieux et la Notitia de Servitio Monasteriorum," p. 624.

tended by the monks alone, the resolutions could not go under the head of purely canonical legislation in the sense that those of the assembly held the previous year could.[17] It could be compared to the constitutions of modern congregations of monks,[18] since it possessed the same force as the Rule itself, but in this case had the added sanction of imperial authority behind it. The actual *Capitulare* recounted the monastic obligations, but did not state its rights and privileges. With regard to these latter, there was mentioned another "*scedula*,"[19] which recounted favors accorded to the monasteries by Louis the Pious. Unfortunately, this latter is not preserved for us, and the most one can find are veiled allusions to it. Ardo indicated that it was the purpose of the *scedula* to protect the

[17] The *Capitulare Monasticum* cannot be called an imperial capitulary, since neither was the emperor present nor did he officially approve the decree, although his actions indicated that he thoroughly supported the assembly's acts. When "*Missi*" is used here, it refers to the *Missi* commissioned to reform the monasteries, and not to the regular corps of the same. They were not the bishops, dukes, laymen, but only the most select monks chosen by the emperor himself. Cf. Ermoldi Nigelli, "Carmina in honorem Hludowici," *MGH*, *Poetae Latini*, t. II (Berolini, 1884), p. 489. Cf. also Lesne, *art. cit.*, p. 173. The *missi* did not just visit a monastery once and then depart, but in order to assure a complete reform they made repeated visitations. Cf. "Vita Hludowici," Ch. XXVIII, *MGH*, *Scriptores*, II, 622.

[18] Butler, *Benedictine Monachism*, p. 221.

[19] Ardo reported that the monastic rights were written in an imperial document, and that among the rights was one that permitted the monks to choose their own abbot from among their numbers. (*ex his*). Add to this the fact that in his *Concordia Regularum* Benedict had consecrated an entire chapter to the election of the abbot and had joined the portions of other Rules which substantiated the free election of the abbot, and then one may assume that the free election was promoted not a little before Louis by the saint (*MPL*, CIII, 755 ff.) The *Statuta Murbacensia* likewise made mention of this (Mansi, XIV, 350). The bishop-abbot who reported on the latter *Statuta* was vague in his explanation of the synodal acts, which indicated to Lesne (*art. cit.*, p. 325, footnote) that there was some difficulty for him to live the common life and maintain his episcopal position. The rights and the privileges of the monks were discussed less publicly at another time when the emperor could grant whatever rights appeared to him to be just. For mention of the "*scedula*" cf. *MGH*, *Cap. Reg. Fr.*, I, 276. Cf. also Lesne, *art. cit.*, p. 322; Schmitz, "Benoit d'Aniane," p. 181.

regular observance.[20] Later he showed that free election, being one of these rights, was not to be granted to all, but some abbeys still fell under the power of the state, acting through secular abbots.[21]

The importance of the right of free election cannot be overemphasized, since upon it depended to a large extent the possibility of monastic quietude, free from the disturbances of outsiders. Lévy-Bruhl believed that even with such a grant of free elections the individual communities would still seek charters that gave their own monasteries such liberty. The reason may be that the general privilege had to be confirmed by a special one, before the reception of which the other would be ineffectual. Then, also, the possession of a charter of this kind offered a permanent assurance in the event that the emperor pass away, the law be repealed, or even totally ignored.[22]

Benedict's relations with the bishops were in general very friendly.[23] Whether this was due to the emperor's support and the consequent discouragement of opposition cannot be ac-

[20] "Ardonis Vita Benedicti," p. 217: "Cernens quoque nonnullos totis nisibus anhelare in adquirenda monachorum coenobia, eaque non tantum precibus, ut obtineant, verum etiam decertare muneribus, suisque usibus stipendia monachorum expendi, ac per diruta nonnulla, alia vero, fugatis monachis, a secularibus obtineri clericis, adiit hac de causa piissimum imperatorem precibusque pulsat, ut ab hujuscemodi contentionibus clericos, monachos vero ab hoc redderet periculo extorres. Adsensum prebet gloriosissimus imperator, monasteria in regno suo cuncto prenotata, in quibus ex his regulares abbates esse queant, decernit ac per scripturam, ut inconcussa omni meaneant tempore, firmare precepit suoque anulo signavit; sicque multorum cupiditatem, monachorum nihilominus pavorem extersit." That this conforms with the *Capitulare Ecclesiasticum* is maintained by Lesne, *art. cit.*, p. 325 ff., and by Lévy-Bruhl, *Les Elections Abbatiales*, p. 36.

[21] "Ardonis Vita Benedicti," p. 218: "His vero monasteriis quae sub canonicorum relicta sunt potestate."

[22] Lévy-Bruhl, *Les Elections Abbatiales*, p. 37; cf. also Lesne, *art. cit.*, p. 329.

[23] Narberhaus, *Benedikt von Aniane*, p. 44: "Benedikt bewegt sich auf derselben Linie. Wenn auch das Papsttum und die Kirche als solche kein einziges Mal in der *Vita* erwähnt werden, so sprechen für Benedikts kirchliches Denken Artikel 6 des Konzils von Arles i. J. 813, seine freundschaftliche Stellung zum Episkopat...;" Canon 6 of Arles as mentioned here asserted the duty of the bishops to watch over the conduct of the canons

curately determined, but they seemed to follow the general lines of relations extant in this period, in which the monasteries were still under the observation of the bishops, who stepped in when they saw the necessity.[24] Benedict wrote to Bishop Nibridio (of the See of Narbonne, 797-827) a letter which has a friendly, even an intimate, tone, and indicates mutual trust and cordiality.[25] There is no instance, to the writer's knowledge, of the bishops' opposition to Benedict through canonical or other means in his reorganization of monastic life, although some opposition arose in the Council of Aix-la-Chapelle in 817 on the part of the abbots and monks present.[26] There were, however, several instances wherein the bishops invited Benedict into their dioceses to either reform the houses or to establish new foundations there. On the petition from the Archbishop of Lyons, Leidrade, he reformed the monastery of Ile-Barbe.[27] To Theodulph (761-821), Bishop of Orleans (797-818), he sent four of his personally trained monks to restore the abbey of St. Maxime to its one-time wide renown.[28] Others,

and monks. Cf. Hefele-Leclercq, *Histoire des Conciles*, III, 1135; *MGH*, Legum Sectio III, *Concilia*, I, *Concilia Aevi Karolini*, pp. 245-247.

[24] Smith, *Monastery of Cluny* (London, 1920), p. 8: "That he [Benedict] succeeded as far as he did was largely due to the imperial support without which the movement would have collapsed after his death (821)."

[25] "Ardonis Vita Benedicti," p. 220: "Venerabili in Christo patri Nibridio archiepiscopo Benedictus ultimus omnium abbatum abbas sempiternae felicitatis salutem opto in Domino. Eia, vir Dei, pareat modo karitas ac dilectio seu benivolentia, qua semper modo, in quantum potes...ut orationibus tam in psalmis quam in missis pro me ad Dominum fundere non cessent...etc."

[26] Graham, *English Ecclesiastical Studies*, p. 153.

[27] Mabillon, *Annales Ordinis S. Benedicti Occidentalium Monachorum Patriarchae* (6 vols., Lucae, 1739-1745), V, 208: "Leidradus Archiepiscopus Lugdunensis in epistola ad Carolum Magnum, Monasterium regale Insulae Barbarae, inquit, situm in medio Araris fluvii, quod antiquitus est dedicatum in honore S. Andreae Apostoli...ibidem praefecit domnum Benedictum Abbatem." Cf. Mourret-Thompson, *History of the Catholic Church* (7 vols., St. Louis, 1930-1955), III (1933), 382; Amann, *L'Epoque Carolingienne*, p. 261.

[28] "Ardonis Vita Benedicti," p. 209: "Theodulphus quoque Aurelianensium presul, cum monasterium Sancti Maximi construere vellet, a iam prefato viro postulat regularis disciplinae peritos cui mox adsensum prebuit et bis denos illi monachos, prefecto magistro, misit."

it is true, were not constructed or reformed at the insistance of the bishops, but there is no indication that, once the petitions coming from non-episcopal personages had been answered by Benedict, any unfavorable actions were taken by the local bishops. For example, Cormery in Touraine, and Gellone, or St. William of the Desert, were Aniane's accomplishments, not in answer to bishops' requests, indeed, but to those of the famous Alcuin (d. 804) and William of Aquitaine (d. 812). Nobility thus played its role in bringing Benedict into new territories, and it is difficult to know whether their purpose in bringing him there was in any way different from the bishops' purpose.[29] Besides doing this work himself, Benedict sent abbots whom he had trained to head the new or reformed abbeys, and there is no record of any differences between them and the bishops of the dioceses of their locale. Thus, from negative proof, it seems that the bishops offered no notable canonical resistance to Benedict's work. If it did not endure, it was due not to the presence of episcopal resistance but rather to other reasons which will be pointed out later.

In the *Concordantia Regularum* are a few references to bishops and their authority over the abbots and monasteries. The actual tenor of Benedict's work favored the traditional attitude, except, as we have seen, in the election of abbots, which he believed to be the rights of the monks, as vindicated in the Benedictine Rule itself. Fr. Menard (1585-1644), the Maurist scholar, indicated Benedict's views in his commentary on Chapter 62 of the Rule of St. Benedict as quoted in the *Concordantia*:

> Itaque olim ejusmodi presbyteri monasteriorum non solum erant sub abbate, sed etiam sub episcopo, ut patet ex epistola Friderici archiepiscopi Coloniensis ad Adelberonem episcopum Leodiensem ex hoc S. Benedicti loco (Apud Ruperium, lib. IV, in Reg. S.

[29] Lavisse-Rambaud, *Histoire Générale*, I, p. 324: "C'est que les évêques étaient parties intégrantes de l'Etat. Ils sont, pour Charlemagne, les collaborateurs des comtes. Il s'inquiète de leurs rapports avec ceux-ci. Une des questions addressées aux missi est: Comment les comtes s'entendent-ils avec les évêques?" For monasteries founded by counts for Benedict, cf. Mabillon, *Annales*, V, 210 ff.

> Benedicti, cap. 2): "Neque a solo abbate, inquit, super monachum presbyterum judicium est diffiniendum, nisi episcopus adhibeatur in testimonium juxta ipsius S. Benedicti institutum sanum et legitimum." Qui supra in eadem epistola omnes sacris ordinibus initiatos ait sub cura esse tum episcopi, tum abbatis. Concilium Arelatense tertium omnes clericos monasterii Lirinensis subjicit episcopo, laicos vero abbati (tom. I, conc. Galliae), "Hoc enim et rationis et religionis plenum est, ut clerici ad ordinationem episcopi debita subjectione respiciant; laica vero omnis monasterii congregatio ad solam ac liberam abbatis proprii, quam sibi ipse elegerit, ordinationem dispositionemque pertineat." Sed modo propter exemptiones alio jure vivitur. Et sane olim hoc tolerabile erat, cum pauci essent in monasteriis sacerdotes seu clerici."[30]

The commentator, therefore, divided the authority over the priest-monks between the bishop and the abbot. The subjection to the abbot came probably through the profession, although this was not asserted, and to the bishop through ordination. He justified the exemptions which removed the monasteries from the control of the bishops by the paucity of monks in the monasteries who were priests or clerics.

The bishops were also cooperative in spreading the reform by choosing some of the inspectors who were to carry out the reform in the monasteries.[31] Ardo, the biographer of Benedict of Aniane, added that it was largely due to the bishops that

[30] *MPL*, CIII, col. 1325. Dom Cuthbert Butler (1858-1934) said of Dom Ménard in his *Benedictine Monachism*, p. 181: "Dom Hugues Menard, one of the earliest of the Maurist scholars, edited it in 1638, adding most excellent notes to all the Rules. Those on St. Benedict's Rule must secure for this work a place among the best of the commentaries."

[31] Schmitz, *Histoire de l'Ordre*, I, 95 ff.: "Ces inspecteurs devaient dénoncer les abbés récalcitrants à l'évêque du lieu d'abord, puis si besoin était, aux synodes ecclésiastiques. Ces zélateurs étaient choisis parmi les disciples éprouvés de Benoît; celui-ci d'ailleurs remplit plusieurs fois cette délicate mission. En général, ils étaient nommés par les évêques. Grace à eux, ajoute Ardo, la réforme gagna du terrain;" Schmitz, "Benoît d'Aniane," col. 181, "Benoît lui-même remplit souvent cette fonction. En général, ils etaient nommés par les évêques."

the reform gained any headway at all.[32] The inspectors were to denounce the recalcitrants to the local bishop, and if this brought no results they could go to the councils or to the emperor for a higher sanction. The net result of the reformation, where it was thus enforced, i.e., in most of what is now France, and in parts of present-day Germany.[33] was to make all of the monasteries blue-prints of Benedict's, not only in the Rule but also in the most minute details of the diurnal horarium.[34] The conclusion is not difficult to draw: Since Benedict was on the best of terms with the bishops, and made it a policy to continue the traditions of his predecessors except in the presence of privilege (which, as was seen above, he always attempted to acquire through his patron Louis), the

[32] "Ardonis Vita Benedicti," p. 220; cf. also Amann, *L'Epoque Carolingienne*, p. 266: "Benoît d'Aniane est mort le 11 février 831. Son oeuvre se continua dans les années suivantes et le triomphe que remporte à Saint-Denis la cause de la réforme montre que le souverain et les évêques, tantqu'ils eurent les mains libres, ne se laissèrent pas détourner de cette grande tâche."

[33] Mourret-Thompson, *History of the Catholic Church*, III, 382: "Louis the Pious called St. Benedict of Aniane to the Council of Aachen and commissioned him to visit all the monasteries of his empire. Thus his work extended to most of the abbeys of the West." Mabillon, *Annales*, V, 208: "Quam Anianae disciplinam instituit Benedictus, eamdem in varia Franciae ac Germaniae monasteria propagavit." Berlière, "Les Coutumiers monastiques," p. 105: "Ce qu'Aniane est pour le sud de la France, Cornelimunster le sera pour la Germanie..." (Cornelimünster was Benedict's abbey of Inde near the imperial palace—the fountainhead of the reform after Louis was made emperor).

[34] Cf. "Ardonis Vita Benedicti," p. 215; Mansi, XIV, 352; Benedict's abbey, Inde, near to Louis' palace, became the school or model for all other abbeys in the reform. Cf. Nigelli, "Carmina in honorem Hludowici," p. 41: "Quo, Benedicte, tua regula, sancte, viget. Namque idem Benedictus erat pater illius aedis, / Et Hludowicus adest Caesar et abba simul. / Haec loca saepe colit, properatque revisere caulas, / Ordinat et sumptus, munera larga parat." It is apprent from these stanzas that much of the success of Benedict's reform can be attributed to the close harmony between him and the throne. Without Louis' backing (...*Caesar et abbas simul*...) Benedict might have achieved far less than history has ascribed to him. Cf. also Butler, *Benedictine Monachism*, p. 221: "Every monastery and every monk in all his master's realms was to be like to himself and his. He aimed at a cast-iron system of uniformity, and herein lies the essential antagonism of spirit between Benedict of Aniane and the great Benedict."

other monasteries acted in like manner. The bishops, through the reform, were certainly not passed by, since they still appointed the inspectors. They were effectively moderated, since the same inspectors appointed by them had to be approved by Benedict or by Louis. The legislation still gave the bishop the right of surveillance, and the refractory monks were referred in the first instance to the bishops for correction, then to a council where many bishops would be the judges. It is difficult to envision the bishops effectually extending these prerogatives of surveillance beyond the pale of Benedict's supervision, since the latter was thorough to the point of being picayunish. Then, also, the presence of exemptions, now beginning to flower in Louis' regime, made the encroachments of bishops in the monks' inner discipline a smaller and smaller threat to monastic autonomy. Like a giant web, the system of Benedict of Aniane extended over the West. The slightest deviation from his policy could be instantly corrected and Benedict's will could prevail. This removal of the all-pervading will of the bishop from monastic inspection, and the entrusting of the same into the hands of the monks themselves is one of the first attempts for the instituting of congregations, as we know them today.[35]

Much depended upon the personality of the figure in charge of the reformation, Benedict himself. Probably all too aware of this, the saint appointed a successor for himself, undoubtedly an *alter ego*, to continue his work in the same vein as it had been inaugurated.[36]

"Benedict of Aniane," as Dom Thomas Symons concludes, "had left his mark on the whole of western monasteries, and his ideas underlay, in a general way, all the continental re-

[35] Butler, *Benedictine Monachism*, p. 221: "...up to 817 no organic union existed between monasteries." But, as was noted in a preceding chapter, according to Fuhrmann, *Irish Medieval Monasteries*, pp. 50-51, St. Pirmin preceded Benedict by one hundred years in the congregational plan, which in the latter case was only more intensive than the one of Pirmin.

[36] *MPL*, CIII, col. 1429: "Notum sit omnibus fidelibus nostris, quia vir venerabilis Benedictus abba una cum consensu Georgii abbatis Anianensis monasterii, quem ipse ibidem successorem elegerat..."

forms of more than a century later."[37] Although Benedict's policy was not in strict accord with the true Benedictine spirit,[38] still, in the matter of bishop-abbot relations, nothing was essentially changed from the legislation which preceded this era. An additional check upon episcopal encroachment was had in Benedict's personal overall authority of the monastic life, while on the other hand bishops could still appoint the special *missi*, and correct the errant monks. Monasticism was now, in a very real sense, given over more completely to the monks themselves than under the rule of Charlemagne. Moreover, Louis the Pious was more liberal than his father had been to grant privileges to the monastic houses, and this represents another step in the trend toward the exemption movement exemplified in its most developed stage in the Cluniac reform of the following century, itself, according to most recent scholarship, only the logical development of the movement initiated by the Saint of Aniane.[39]

[37] *Regularis Concordia*; *The Monastic Agreement of the Monks and Nuns of the English Nation*; translated with notes by Dom Thomas Symons (New York: Oxford Univ. Press, 1953), p. XLVII.

[38] Knowles, *The Monastic Order in England*, p. 28: "Thus, by a natural, but in a sense paradoxical development, the monastic life of the West, while becoming more explicitly "Benedictine" than before, became also identified with a way of life which was a Carolingian modification of the scheme of the original legislator;" Butler, *Benedictine Monachism*, p. 221: "His scheme of a rigid uniformity among the monasteries of the Empire, secured by the appointment of himself as General, aided by an agent or inspector in each house—an idea wholly alien to the most elementary conception of Benedictine life..."

[39] Cf., e.g., Guy de Valous, *Le Domaine de l'Abbaye de Cluny aux Xe et XIe siècle*, p. III.

CHAPTER IX

LEGISLATION DURING THE RULE OF LOUIS THE PIOUS (816-840)

Since the most important features of Louis' reign regarding the relations between the bishops and abbots have been already delineated in the last chapter, it remains only to indicate the nature of the conciliar and capitulary legislation substantiating his general policy.

It has been explained that the traditional pattern regarding the bishop-abbot relations was continued without any essential change during Louis' reign. The statutory foundation for this pattern was the one established in Chalcedon—that the monks were to be subject to the local bishops, which was interpreted as the duty of the bishop to see that the monastic observance be always such as to edify the Church. In the era under consideration, therefore, this also appeared as the prevalent policy. Bishops were themselves to furnish edification, but they were further to see to it that those who had made profession in some religious order were to live up to their vows, whether the vows bound them to a canonical or a monastic community.[1]

According to one capitulary, the authority of the bishop regarding the religious house was further defined through his office of teaching and counseling them concerning the full import of their way of life.[2] The "lay abbots" mentioned in this

[1] Admonitio ad omnes Regni Ordines (825), cap. 4: "Sed quoniam scimus, quod specialiter pertineat ad episcopos, ut primum ad sacrum ministerium suscipiendum juste accedant et in eodem ministerio religiose vivant et tam bene vivendo quam recte praedicando populis sibi commissis iter vitae praebeant et ut in monasteriis in suis parroechiis constitutis sancta religio observata fiat et ut unusquisque juxta suam professionem veraciter vivat. . ."—*MGH, Capitularia Regum Francorum,* I, 303.

[2] Ansegisi abbatis capitularium collectio (789-827) (These dates indicate not the time of the composing of the capitularies but rather the time of their collation. There were other collections, but this is perhaps the most important and best known. About it F. L. Ganshof [*Wat Waren de Capitularia* (Brussel: Paleis der Academien, 1955), p. 99 of the French summary]

text represent an abuse of this period. It began as far back as the time of Charles Martel (689-741). Founders or proprietors of the abbeys considered the latter as personal property, to be dealt with as any other item of estate. The abbey or "*abbatia*" included the ensemble of goods and effects on the abbatial property as well as the monastery proper and the church. They came to be considered as a means of deriving rich income rather than primarily as a religious retreat, and hence it was not thought a profanity to call a lay person the "abbot" of this material possession.[3] Besides earning a comfortable revenue from the abbeys, those laymen who owned the abbey but were interested only in the temporal, and accordingly bore the name "lay abbots," also were instrumental in determining many matters which today would be considered strictly monastic, i.e., pertaining to the inner life of the community.[4]

It was during this period, and perhaps more truly so somewhat earlier, that the abbeys came to fall under the power of the king or the bishop, and accordingly were known as royal or episcopal abbeys. It was frequently to escape the episcopal domination that they became royal.[5] However, many fell by donation into the hands of dukes and counts, and came to be considered as nothing more than benefices or honors, the

writes: "La plus considérable (of these collections) et la plus célèbre est celle que constitua l'abbé de Saint-Wandrille, Ansegise; elle comprend les capitulaires de Charlemagne et de Louis le Pieux, groupés en quatre livres. Terminée en 827, elle fut à partir de 829, la collection à laquelle le Palais se référa quand il fallait citer un capitulaire antérieur."), lib. 1, cap. 8: "Abbatibus quoque et laicis specialiter jubemus, ut in monasteriis quae ex nostra largitate habent episcoporum consilio et documento ea quae ad religionem canonicorum, monachorum, sanctimonialium pertinent peragant et eorum salubrem admonitionem in hoc libenter audiant et oboediant."—*MGH*, *Cap. Reg. Fr.*, I, 416. The term "*documento*" as used here seems to indicate a lesson or an example to be given by the bishop (cf., e.g., Lewis and Short, *A Latin Dictionary*, [Oxford: Clarendon Press, 1951]," Documentum").

[3] Cf. Amann-Dumas, "*L'Eglise au Pouvoir des Laïques*, p. 296.

[4] Schmitz, *Histoire de l'Ordre*, I, 257: "Le séculier ou le laïque qui avait été pourvu de *l'abbatiat* d'un monastère possédait toutes les prérogatives de l'abbé régulier dans le gouvernement de sa maison. Sa qualité d'abbé l'autorisait à intervenir dans la conduite de sa communauté."

[5] Cf. Amann-Dumas, *op. cit.*, pp. 298 ff.

revenues falling into the hands of him to whom the abbey was given. New abbeys strove to place themselves under royal protection or "*tuitio*" rather than under that of the bishops or nobles, since the king was usually quite generous in granting broad privileges to the abbeys under his control.[6] At times the bishops and nobles placed the abbeys under royal patronage to keep them from becoming the property of their enemies.

There were two types of monasteries for men indicated in this passage—those of monks and those of canons. The monks were guided by the Benedictine Rule almost exclusively, while the regular canons followed the Rule which took shape in 817, modeled after that of St. Chrodegang (d. 766). There were many similarities and some differences between the two, but since a complete comparison of the two types of life is not possible here, it may suffice to indicate that the canons regular had a rule which somewhat mitigated the stricter regime of the monks.

The abbots were reminded that they were to fulfil their office not altogether autonomously, but always under the bishop's surveillance, lest they act against their charters or the spirit of the Church.[7] For those abbots who were not observant of their duties, a punishment by the bishop was prescribed in correction of them, the principle stemming from Chalcedon, title VIII, which punished the malefactors by means of a canonical censure (deposition) if they were clerics, or of excommunication if they were monks or laymen.[8] Canonical

[6] Lévy-Bruhl (*Elections Abbatiales*, p. 114) likens royal protection with its advantages to an "*abbatia nullius*;" "Celui-ci faisait si peu peser sur les monastères son droit de propriété, qu'un peu plus tard on donnera comme synonymes les deux expressions, "*abbatiae regales*" et "*abbatiae nullius juris*." Cf. Sickel, *Beiträge zur Diplomatik* (Wien, 1863), ch. IV: "Die Mundbriefe, Immunitaeten und Privilegien der ersten Karolingern," p. 29.

[7] Concilium Aquisgranense (836), cap. 25: ". . . et inquantum ipsi abbates abbatumque subiecti episcopis propriis pro se suisque omnibus rationem reddituros noverint, tanto eorum consilio atque auctoritate modis omnibus mancipentur."—*MGH*, Legum Sectio III, *Concilia*, Tom. II, *Concilia Aevi Karolini*, Pars II (ed. Societas Aperiendis Fontibus, Hannoverae et Lipsiae, 1908), p. 711.

[8] Episcoporum ad Imperatorem de Rebus Ecclesiasticis Relatio (821), cap. 11: "A quo et quomodo corrigi abbas neglegenter agens debeat, canon

abbots[9] received special consideration in one council. They were advised to act according to their Rule, and under correction to be obedient, or else to be sent on to the episcopal court or to the emperor.[10] At the same time the abbots were permitted, if they thought themselves wronged, to look beyond the bishops by appealing to the "higher" authority of the king in vindication of their rights.

For reasons of good order within a diocese, the monks along with the priests and clerics were advised not to become involved in secular activities.[12] Permission to have such dealings in a case of necessity had to be procured from the bishop.[13]

Calcidonensis titul. VIII evidenter exponit, cum ab episcopo loci dissilienter communione privare non ambigat."—*MG H, Cap. Reg. Fr.*, I, 368; Concilium in Francia Habitum (816-829), cap. 12—*MG H*, Legum Sectio III, *Concilia*, Tom. II, Pars II, 591.

[9] Amann-Dumas, *L'Eglise au Pouvoir des Laïques*, p. 294: "Entre la règle bénédictine et la règle canoniale il y avait de grandes ressemblances. Les moines et les chanoines menaient la vie commune à l'intérieur d'un cloître... Tous, ils étaient astreints à célébrer l'office divin à des heures marquées suivant un rituel à peu près identique. Tous, ils étaient soumis à une exacte discipline sous la direction d'un abbé."

[10] Concilium Parisiense (829), cap. 37: "Decet, immo necesse est, ut abbates canonicorum adtendant, ut quid abbates vocentur. ...Unde etiam summopere episcopis, ad quorum curam pertinent, providendum est, ut huiuscemodi abbates ab inlicitis se abstineant et dictis et exemplis sibi subditis ad vitam aeternam ducatum praebere contendant. Quodsi episcopo suo oboedire superbiendo rennuerint, synodali judicio aut corrigantur aut certe principali auctoritate interveniente honore praelationis priventur."

[11] Concilium Moguntinense (829), Relatio: "Licebat tamen abbatibus ab episcopo ad principem et concilium provocare, ut apparet ex Rabani epistola ad Otgarium de causa Saxonis fugitivi monachi."—*MG H*, Legum Sectio III, *Concilia*, Tom. II, Pars II, 605.

[12] Ansegisi Capitularium Collectio (789-827), cap. 22: "Ut nec monachi nec clerici nec presbyteri in secularia negotia transeant."—*MG H, Cap. Reg. Fr.*, I, 399.

[13] Concilium Aquisgranense (836), cap. 26: "...Ipsos etiam monachos passim et quasi absque canonicae auctoritatis jugo effrenatos per secularia negotia minime oportet discurrere et villicis atque saecularibus curis inservire, sed secundum institutionem canonicam in quibus renuntiaverunt contentos esse et neque saecularibus neque ecclesiasticis negotiis nisi in causa necessitatis, accepta tamen propriae civitatis episcopi licentia interesse."—*MG H*, Legum Sectio III, *Concilia*, Tom. II, Pars II, 711.

The wording of this decree seemed to single out the canonical abbots, and this was quite in keeping with the reform proceedings under Benedict of Aniane, for although Louis' intention was to reform *in globo* the state of the religious in his empire, the reforming personality of Benedict of Aniane was especially energetic with respect to the Benedictine houses, since he seemed to disparage the canonical state for its laxity, and only incidentally became involved in the reform of these ranks, namely through the overall effect of his reform. If his efforts were productive and effective, then the later legislation seemed directed against the canonical order rather than his own when the legislation was corrective in its nature. Perhaps the bishops depended too much upon the efforts of Benedict, for a decree from the proceedings of one council called the bishops to task for not being vigilant in caring for the monastic houses in their dioceses.[14]

The proximity of bishop to abbot in a diocese always set the stage for possible provocation, and accordingly the two were advised to live in a spirit of peace and harmony that could prove conducive to forwarding the ends of the Church.[15] In those cases wherein there arose a conflict which could not be resolved between themselves, the emperor was to be approached for a settlement of the matter.[16]

[14] Concilium Aquisgranense (836), cap. 1: "Didicimus sane nonnullos episcopos in gubernandis congregationibus sibi subiectis, canonicis videlicet et monachis et sanctimonialibus, hactenus valde neglegentes exstitisse et ob id multos in sui detractionem et contemptum provocasse, ita ut nonnulli alii praelati in eorum parochiis constituti, eorum prava exempla secuti, suas similiter congregationes neglexerint. Quos et fraterno et synodali conventu admonendos esse necessario duximus, ut ab hac neglegentia deinceps se cohibeant et ceteris se imitabiles praebeant. . ."—*MGH*, Legum Sectio III, *Concilia*, Tom. II, Pars II, 704.

[15] Ansegisi Abbatis capitularium Collectio (789-827), lib. 1, cap. 59: "Ut pax sit et concordia et unanimitas cum omni populo christiano inter episcopos, abbates, comites, judices et omnes ubique seu maiores seu minores personas, quia nihil Deo sine pace placet nec munus sanctae oblationis ad altare, sicut in evangelio ipso Domino praecipiente legimus. . ."—*MGH*, *Cap. Reg. Fr.*, I, 399 ff.

[16] *Ibid*, cap. 77: ". . . Ut episcopi, abbates, comites et potentiores quique, si causam inter se habuerint ac se pacificare noluerint, ad nostram jubeantur

A constant source of controversy was undoubtedly the presence of secular and religious clerics active in the ministry of the same diocese. The Council of Aix-la-Chapelle (836) had forbidden the monks to occupy themselves with secular and ecclesiastical affairs,[17] and one does not have to stretch his imagination to include parish work under the expression "ecclesiastical affairs."[18] Perhaps it was for this reason that controversies arose over real or supposed conspiracies instigated against the bishop (pastor) in the diocese.[19] Although the right of the monks to serve in the capacity of parochial minister was challenged by the secular clergy, the Council of Toul (838) did not mince words in declaring the rights of the religious to do so. In the decision, a church located outside the monastery portal (*ante fores ipsius monasterii*), called the church of St. Maximus, was given perpetual parochial status and was to be administered by the monks.[20]

venire praesentiam neque illorum contentio aliubi diiudicetur, ne propter hoc pauperum et minus potentium justitiae remaneant."—*MGH*, *loc. cit.*

[17] Concilium Aquisgranense (836), cap. 26—*MGH*, Legum Sectio III, *Concilia*, Tom. II, Pars II, 707.

[18] Cf. Berlière, "L'Exercice du Ministère Paroissial par les Moines dans le Haut Moyen-Age," *Revue Bénédictine*, XXXIX (1927), p. 237: "Le concile d'Aix-la-Chapelle de 836 interdit aux moines de s'occuper des affaires séculaires et ecclésiastiques, et, en cas de necessité, le consentement de l'évêques doit être requis; parmi ces affaires ecclésiastiques il y a lieu de supposer que l'on comprend aussi le ministère paroissial."

[19] Ansegisi Capitularium Collectio (789-827), lib. I, cap. 29: "...ut nec clerici nec monachi conspirationem vel insidias contra pastorem suum faciant;"—*MGH*, *Cap. Reg. Fr.*, I, 399 ff.; Capitulare Olonnense Ecclesiasticum Alterum (825), cap. 7a; "De monasteriis et senedochiis inordinatis et destructis ad palatium vel ad quorumcumque jura pertinentibus qui admonitionem episcoporum contemnunt, placuit nostrae imperialis providentiae judicio reservari."—*MGH*, *Cap. Reg. Fr.*, I, 328; Concilium Aquisgranense (836), cap. 27: "Monachi interea non debent parvipendere pastores suos in cuiuscumque parrochia consistentes, sicut aliqui faciunt."—*MGH*, Legum Sectio III, *Concilia*, Tom. II, Pars II, 707.

[20] Concilium Tullense (838), (decisio): "Hoc ergo testimonio, ancipiti submota sententia, decernimus et consulto totius synodi statuimus, ut secundum praefixum terminum praedicta ecclesia ius parrochiale in perpetuo possideat. Obsecramus autem ac sub invocatione nominis divini obtestamur unumquemque antistitum successorum nostrorum, ne in aliquo praedictam determinationem violari patiatur, ut, dum particeps fit nostrae

This was a period of secularization, as noted in the last chapter, and many abbeys forfeited their Benedictine character to adopt the life of the canons, at times the simple canonical, at times the canonical-regular life. In the *vota* of the bishops there is evidence of their attempt to settle the doubts concerning the monastic status of communities by giving many of them the choice of becoming the one or remaining the other.[21] At the same time the emperor certainly, but the bishops also, must have been frequently vexed by monasteries changing their Rules, for the assembled bishops protested against such whimsical conversions of life.[22] Likewise, for peace in the diocese, the desire of the bishops undoubtedly supported the *placitum* of the abbots that the monks who had been raised to the dignity of clerics should not thereupon give up their vows, but rather should remain in their monastic profession and not leave their community.[23]

With Europe in the grips of the feudal system, serfdom was an accepted social caste. However, when the documents referred to serfs with relation to monasteries, it was to be quite generally assumed that these serfs became part of the "*familia*" of the monastery voluntarily in order to gain spiritual and even temporal security by such voluntary bondage to the abbey, or more properly to the "saint" in whose honor the mon-

bonae voluntatis, sit et remunerationis."—*MGH*, Legum Sectio III, *Concilia*, Tom. II, Pars II, 783. Cf. also Berlière, "L'Exercice du Ministère Paroissial par les Moines dans le Haut Moyen-Age," p. 237.

[21] Capitula ab Episcopis Imperatori proposita (825), cap. 2: "Ubi vero fuerunt et non sunt, vivant (canonice) excepto si XII vel amplius fuerint; si XII inventi fuerint et locus ac res permittant, sint monachi. Ubi autem dubietas est, utrum canonice an monachice [sic] sint, et oportunitas loci aut quantitas substantiae hoc fieri permittit, detur eis optio, utrum monastice an canonice vivere velint."—*MGH*, *Cap. Reg. Fr.*, I, 358.

[22] *Ibid.*, cap. 1: "Videtur nobis, si domino nostro placet, ut providentia missorum nostrorum commitetur, ut, ubicumque monachi aut monachae modo sunt, et oportunitas loci seu quantitas permittat, maneant in ipso proposito."—*MGH*, *loc. cit.*

[23] Ansegisi abbatis Capitularium collectio (789-827), cap. 27: "Item in decretis Innocentii papae de eadem re, ut monachus, si ad clericatum provehatur, propositum monachicae professionis non amittat."—*MGH*, *Cap. Reg. Fr.*, I, 399 ff.

astery was dedicated.[24] These serfs, for the sake of order and with a view to their certified vocation to the clerical life, were not to be permitted promotion to the clerical state until they had attained full freedom from their lords, i.e., from the abbots in the monasteries to which they were bound by their monastic profession. Legislation dealing with these serfs forbade their ordination until they had attained full freedom, lest the very office of the priesthood itself become the object of servile subjection.[25] Neither bishop nor abbot could seek to attract such servants from the other in order to swell their numbers.[26]

The controversy surrounding the temporalities of monasteries occupied the attention of several capitularies, which reflected the tendency to balk the efforts of some, undoubtedly bishops among them, from usurping the monastic goods for personal gain.[27] One of the greatest protections to the abbey

[24] Schmitz, *Histoire de l'Ordre,* I, 287: "La *familia* monastique ne comprenait pas seulement tous les serviteurs de condition libre qui remplissaient un office auprès de l'abbaye, elle englobait encore les serfs qui étaient à son service. Ceux-ci occupaient dans le servage une situation privilégiée. Cette supériorité provenait du fait que le serf monastique était considéré comme le serf du saint, patron de l'abbaye, et partant comme le serf de Dieu."

[25] Capitulare Ecclesiasticum (818-819), cap. 5: "De servorum vero ordinatione, qui passim ad gradus ecclesiasticos indiscrete promovebantur, placuit omnibus cum sacris canonibus concordari debere; et statutum est, ut nullus episcoporum deinceps eos ad sacros ordines promovere praesumat nisi prius a dominis propriis libertatem consecuti fuerint. . . . Similiter quoque de his agendum est, quos laici de familia ecclesiarum ad sacros ordines promovere voluerint; sed et de his quos praepositi canonicorum aut monachorum ordinandos expetiverint eadem forma servanda est."—*MGH, Cap. Reg. Fr.*, I, 277. Ansegisi abbatis Capitularium Collectio (789-827), cap. 82—*MGH, Cap. Reg. Fr.*, I, 399 ff.

[26] *Ibid.*, cap. 22: "Praecipitur ut servum alterius nullus sollicitet ad clericalem vel monachicum ordinem sine voluntate et licentia domini sui."—*MGH, loc. cit.*

[27] Capitulare de Monasterio S. Crucis Pictaviensi (822-824), cap. 3: "Similiter ut res monasterii, quas modo habent, non prius ab ullo auferantur quam aut ante domnum Pippinum aut ante comitem palatii illius praefata ratio reddatur"—*MGH, Cap. Reg. Fr.*, I, 302: Ansegisi Abbatis Capitularium Collectio (789-827), cap. 31: "Item in eodem, ut loca quae semel Deo dedicata sunt, ut monasteria sint, maneant perpetuo monasteria, nec possint ultra fieri secularia habitacula."—*MGH, Cap. Reg. Fr.*, I, 399 ff.

by way of privilege was that of immunity, which was the root of a great many other privileges.[28] It was, in effect, a prohibition to outsiders to exercise any claims with regard to the monastic temporalities. During Louis' period such a grant was extended to a large number of monasteries, a condition urged by Benedict of Aniane. To protect this grant of immunity, one capitulary threatened all, inclusive of the bishops, with a severe penalty of 600 *solidi* for violating it.[29] The bishop was also to be penalized for attempting to form a contract with another when it involved a monastery of his diocese for purposes of personal gain.[30]

To undertake the reform of the monasteries as noted in the last chapter, the abbots and holy monks were the ones chosen ordinarily by the emperor—but also by the bishops with the emperor's consent—to make the visitations and to correct the abuses in the individual monasteries. Although abbots were occasionally included in the framework of the original "*missatici*" system, which reached back to a time prior to the reign of Louis the Pious, at a later period abbots were almost exclusively selected to see to the implementing of the reform. It was the bishop's duty to instruct these *missi* on points which needed particular attention and correction in the religious communities. The bishops in an imperial capitulary were advised on the manner of directing the special *missi* whom they had chosen, informing them regarding the methods to be adopt-

[28] Cf. Schmitz, *Histoire de l'Ordre*, I, 342.

[29] Ansegisi Capitularium Collectio (789-827), cap. 26: "De immunitate, si aliquod damnum ibi factum fuerit. Si quis in immunitate, damnum aliquod fecerit, sexcentos solidos componat. Si autem homo furtum aut homicidium vel quodlibet crimen foris committens infra immunitatem fugerit, mandet comes vel episcopo vel abbati vel vicedomino vel illi quicumque locum episcopi vel abbatis tenuerit, ut reddat ei reum... etc."—*MGH, Cap. Reg. Fr.*, I, 415 ff.

[30] Capitulare Olonnense (825), cap. 1: "Si quis episcopus aut propinquitatis affectu aut muneris ambitione aut causa amicitiae senodochia aut monasteria vel baptismales ecclesias suae ecclesiae pertinentes cuilibet per enfitheuseos contractus dederit se suosque successores poena multandos conscripserit, potestatem talia mutandi (immutandi) rectoribus ecclesiarum absque poenae conscriptae solutione concedimus."—*MGH, Cap. Reg. Fr.*, I, 316.

ed in the making of these visitations.

> Abbates, qui ab episcopis electi sunt ad conspiciendum regulae observationem in monasteriis, istum debent tenere modum in his quae eis iniuncta sunt. 1) Primo, quia subito et in brevi spatio pleniter cognoscere non valent conversationem fratrum in illo monasterio ad quod tunc veniunt, nisi aliquibus diebus ac noctibus cum eis conversentur, cum tali ad eos veniant paucitate, ut monasterium non gravent. 2) Deinde si intellexerint abbatem neglegentem suum ministerium agere aut de semetipso aut de fratribus suis, secundum regulae auctoritatem eos commoneant illum. Similiter etiam faciant, si ex fratribus fuerint neglegentes inventi: cum abbate suo secundum regulae auctoritatem eos commoneant. Si ignorantia est, per eandem regulam docendo corrigant eos; si autem voluntate delinquunt et emendaverint per eorum admonitionem, bene; quod si noluerint, nuntient synodali conventui. 3) Si vero questio aliqua fuerit de regulae capitulo, et non potuerint inter se definire, nuntient synodo, et ibi auctoritate episcoporum sacrior decernatur sensus; et per vim nihil agere qui missus est presummat. 4) Consuetudines autem ubi invente [sic] fuerint noxia, et hoc, ut supra dictum est, nuntient.[31]

The order highlighted four recommendations: 1) If the *missi* needed several days to inspect a community, they were to spend their time residing in the house of visitation; 2) Practices of the community as a whole, or those of individuals, were to be corrected if they did not conform to the Rule adopted in the place of visitation. Malefactors were to be announced to the local bishops, and, if the matter was not settled there, to the synodal inquest; 3) In doubt as to the meaning of some chapter of the Rule, the synod was to decide its sense; 4) Customs contrary to the spirit of the Rule were to be called to the attention of the bishop.

Who constituted the diocesan synods for judging the matters in question? Very likely such synods were composed of

[31] Capitula de inspiciendis monasteriis (817)—*MGH, Cap. Reg. Fr.*, I, 321.

the bishops and abbots, along with the proprietors of the monasteries, for one capitulary indicated the emperor's desire that the bishops and abbots aid the counts in the rendering of justice to the wrongdoers.[32]

Ecclesiastical amenities on some occasions must have been such as to bring the bishop and the monastic community together for meals from time to time. Since the bishop was not obligated to follow the rigors of a monastic rule, he probably expected that those who dined with him could relax their ascetical practices in order to partake of a meat dish ordinarily prohibited by their Rule. He could indeed have commanded some monks, therefore, to break their Rule on such an occasion. Any such episcopal practice was condemned by one non-imperial or episcopal capitulary, in which the bishop was advised not to force the monks to eat even fowl.[33]

Most frequently mentioned, perhaps, during the reign of Louis were the avid aspirations of the monks to seek a greater measure of freedom from the bishop(not to mention the other impinging influences) by being permitted to elect their own abbot. In this period it was the all-consuming endeavor of the reform to return to the full practice of the Rule of St. Benedict (Ch. 64), which assumed all lack of interference and prescribed a full measure of freedom in the abbatial elections.

This and other sections of the Rule were set aside, however, during the time of Charlemagne, with a view to the greater unification of the empire, and the religious spirit suffered as a result. Benedict of Aniane urged greater freedom and carried his influence to the imperial throne, believing that this greater freedom could favor the restoration of the religious life to a fuller vigor. Hence, undoubtedly in consequence of this pressure, this concern was made manifest from time to time in Louis' reign. The purpose was usually stated in the decrees—to insure internal peace for the monks in their monastic life untrammelled by the disturbances arising from sources out-

[32] Ansegisi Capitularium (789-827), cap. 9: "Episcopis iterum, abbatibus et vassis nostris et omnibus fidelibus laicis dicimus, ut comitibus ad iustitias faciendas adiutores sitis."—*MGH, Cap. Reg. Fr.*, I, 415 ff.

[33] Capitulare Monasticum (817), cap. 9: "Ut nullus episcoporum monachis volatilia comedere praecipiat."—*MGH, Cap. Reg. Fr.*, I, 343.

side the monastery.[34] These texts were quite vague, however, and hardly indicated any radical break from the past. Custom, more than canonical legislation, seemed to provide the final determinant of whether an abbey did or did not choose its own abbot.[35]

The privilege of free election usually included the necessity of having the local bishop approve the candidate elected. Although this could seem to restrict the communities in their choice, nonetheless the bishop was prevented from an outright choosing of someone in order to impose him upon the monastery.[36]

If the election of the abbot was withheld from the bishop's exclusive powers, the monastic communities were admonished to choose their abbots with care.[37] The abbot, moreover, had to be an ordained priest in order to accommodate the necessities of a more autonomous community.[38] Even a single ruling

[34] Ansegisi Abbatis capitularium collectio (789-827), cap. 1: "Monachorum siquidem causam, qualiter Deo opitulante ex parte disposuerimus, et quomodo ex se ipsis sibi eligendi abbates licentiam dederimus et qualiter Deo opitulante quiete vivere propositumque indefessi custodire valerent ordinaverimus, in alia scedula diligenter adnotari fecimus; et ut apud successores nostros ratum foret et inviolabiliter conservarentur, confirmavimus."—*MGH, Cap. Reg. Fr.*, I, 399 ff. Cf. also Capitularium Monasticum (818-819), cap. 5—*MGH, Cap. Reg. Fr.*, I, 343.

[35] Lévy-Bruhl, *Elections Abbatiales*, p. 39: "Tout ce que nous avons pu noter, c'est le *désir* des évêques, manifesté dans les textes conciliaires assez vagues, de devenir les maîtres de la dévolution de l'abbatiat, et c'est le *désir* de la législation séculière de sauvegarder le principe de l'élection abbatiale. Nulle part de règles de droit communément acceptées. Il est impossible de dire; ici finit le droit, ici commence l'abus...En l'absence d'une règle supérieure, s'imposant théoriquement à tous, l'élection abbatiale est une matière purement coutumière."

[36] Concilium in Francia Habitum (816-829), cap. 10: "Quoniam liquido constat monachorum congregationem absque abbate eiusdem ordinis esse non posse, eligendus est inter eos vir modestus et prudens una cum consensu episcopi civitatis..."—*MGH*, Legum Sectio III, *Concilia*, Tom. II, Pars II, 591 ff. Cf. also Episcoporum ad Imperatorem de Rebus Ecclesiasticis Relatio (821), cap. 8—*MGH, Cap. Reg. Fr.*, I, 368.

[37] *Ibidem*, cap. 8: "...vir modestus et prudens;"—also Concilium in Francia Habitum (816-829), cap. 10—*MGH*, Legum Sectio III, *Concilia*, Tom. II, Pars II, 591 ff.

[38] Eugenii II Concilium Romanum (826), cap. 27: "Abbates etenim per

of this sort, as emanating from the Holy See, indicated the trend of the papal influence in its enhancement of the abbatial dignity and its vindication of monastic independence.

Principal, then, among the measures raised in Louis' regime concerning the relations between the bishops and abbots through legislative action was the increase in grants of privileges of immunity and exemption, of which the most regular and important one was freedom in the abbatial elections. As it was noted, the repercussions of this movement were felt in the Eternal City itself, where an added impetus was given to the transalpine stirrings. The bishops were urged to regard the monasteries principally as centers of spiritual life rather than as sources of income, although the monasteries continued to serve this end where the traditionally established order of things could not prudently be altered. Monks, mostly canons regular it seems, were active in parishes, and bishops still retained the primacy of discipline over these as it was most conducive to the well-ordering of the diocese that such should be the case.

Many smaller matters, it has been seen, were raised and considered regarding the bishop-abbot relations, many of which pointed toward the gradual withdrawal of the monasteries from the former complete episcopal domination. The fourth canon of Chalcedon, however, retained its force, but the interpretation of the monks' subjection to the bishop underwent some mitigation as the result of Benedict of Aniane's desire to give the Benedictine Rule full play. After Louis the Pious' reign, there followed the attempt to reinstate the former order, and to set aside the overtures that had been made by the emperor. Thus a new era of monastic freedom was tc dawn.

coenobia, velut instanti tempore nuncupantur monasteria, tales constituantur qui sui vocabuli ministerium Deo possint indubitanter supplere, ita docti, ut, quandoque fratrum neglegentia acciderit, omnino cognoscere possint et emendare; sacerdotalem quoque sint honorem adepti, ut peccantium sibi subiectorum fratrum valeant omnimodis neglecta refrenare et amputare commissa, et ita observent, ut statuta regularum per omnia non inveniantur delinqui."—*MGH, Cap. Reg. Fr.*, I, 375.

CHAPTER X

LEGISLATION FROM 840 TO 900

The death of Louis the Pious shattered the final vestiges of organization in the empire. In the battle of Fontenoy, Lothaire I (840-855) was defeated, France's last unifying potentiality. The monastic reform had leaned heavily upon royal support, and without it the grand projects courageously initiated in the first half of the ninth century were all but neutralized by its withdrawal. Secularization now had the opportunity of free sway, and added to this and even promoting it was the increasing threat of the invaders, who had already devastated England and Belgium and the coasts of Italy, Sicily and southern France.[1] From the middle of the ninth century until 892, when they were finally expelled from northern France and Belgium in the battle of Löwen[2] the raiders from the north wreaked havoc on the religious centers. Few monasteries escaped. The monks scattered in the majority of cases; those who remained paid such heavy tributes that they became impoverished and had to seek means of sustenance from extra-claustral sources. Legislation still emanated from a weakened royalty and from the councils, and indeed seemed to be abundant enough, for in the thirty-four years of Charles the Bald's rule alone fifty-six councils and synods met in France. Church legislation could almost be said to have replaced the civil law.

[1] De Charmasse, "L'Ordre de Cluny du Xe au XIIe Siècle," *Revue des Questions Historiques*, VI (1869), pp. 265 ff.: "...à peine la réforme d'Aniane commençait-elle à faire sentir partout ses bons effets, que la présence de nouveaux barbares, remettent en question l'existence même de la civilisation, précipita la société monastique dans un état pire encore que le premier."

[2] Actually the repulsion was not complete, but there was diminished the ferocity of the attacks. Cf. de Moreau, *Les Abbayes de Belgique (VII-XII siècles)*, (Bruxelles: La Renaissance du Livre, 1952), p. 39: "La victoire remportée par Arnoul de Carinthie sur les Vikings, en 892, ne mit pas absolument fin à leurs incursions. Mais les plus durs moments étaient passés."

[3] Rocher, *Histoire de l'Abbaye Royale de Saint-Benoît-sur-Loire*, (Orleans,

Soon after the death of Louis, a council met in Mayence (Mainz). In it the ecclesiastical disciplinary personnel were separated into two "*turmae*," one made up of the bishops and their legates, and the other composed of the abbots and their legates, each of which was to see to it that the observance was intact in their separate spheres.[4] Abbots were urged to take a leading role in the maintenance of good observance in the monastic domain.[5] The kingdom was falling apart and the Church was using every means to retain the modicum of organization necessary for its functioning. Now a special accent was placed on the need of cooperation between bishops and abbots.[6]

Although the abbots had special responsibility over the monks, the bishops' duty of surveillance was not dispensed

1865), p. 110: "Au IXe siècle, en effet, la royauté tombait, la féodalité montait. L'une avait perdu sa force; l'autre n'avait pas encore acquis celle qu'elle eut bientôt; l'Eglise seule avait toute la sienne. Rien ne lui manquait: supériorité de lumière et de moralité, foi ardente des populations, riches domains. Enfin, alors que tout se divisait, et que la société civile et la société politique s'en allaient en miettes, le corps ecclésiastique montrait son unité...Les évêques n'étaient pas seulement les ministres de la religion; ils participaient dans ce siècle à l'administration publiques..."

[4] Concilium Moguntinum (847)—*MGH*, Legum Sectio II, *Capitularia Regum Francorum*, Tom. II, Pars I, pp. 173 ff.: "Convenit inter nos de nostro communi collegio clericorum atque monachorum duas facere turmas, sicut et fecimus, ita ut in una turma considerent episcopicum quibusdam notariis legentes atque perscrutantes cunctum evangelium necnon epistolas et actus apostolorum, canones quoque ac diversa...opuscula...In alia vero turma sederunt abbates ac probati monachi regulam sancti Benedicti legentes atque tractantes diligenter, qualiter monachorum vita in meliorem statum atque augmentum cum Dei gratia perducere potuissent..."

[5] Capitulare Missorum (865), cap. 5: "Directi abbates monasteria monachorum et puellarum ac senodochia circumeant; si, unde administrantur, debita obsequia habeant et concorditer degant, inquirant; quicquid inordinatum reppererint, regulariter corrigant..."—*MGH*, *ibid.*, p. 94.

[6] Capitula Pistensia (869), cap. 12: "Ut episcopi atque abbates et comites ac vassi nostri et omnes fideles laici concordi dilectione et unanimi voluntate ad Dei et sanctae ecclesiae ac nostrum et regni nostri honorem et statum atque communem nostram salvationem sine invidia et malevolentia atque indebita contentione communiter decertare procurent, ut pax et justitia et vera cum Dei voluntate concordia inter nos omnes et in regno nostro maneat..."—*MGH*, *ibid.*, p. 336. Synodus Pontegonensis (876), cap. 2—*MGH*, p. 351; Capitulare Missorum Suessionense (853), cap. 5—*MGH*, *ibid.*, p. 267.

with, but episcopal investigation of the monastic observance still continued.[7] It should be noted that the consent of the proprietor or the holder of the *Jus Abbatiae*[8] seemed to be necessary also for the making of these investigations, indicating a resurgence of the secularization suspended temporarily during the reign of Louis the Pious. Though the bishops themselves were one of the culpable elements in the secularization[9] of the monasteries, they showed their opposition to it in conciliar action.[10] They framed their words sharply and demonstrated their bitterness to the practice which was gaining momentum with each succeeding year.[11] Much of the responsibility for this

[7] Capitula Episcoporum Papiae Edita (845-850), cap. 9: "Et ea quidem monasteria, quae adhuc statum suum retinent unumquemque episcoporum, in cuius parroechia constituta sunt, providere oportet, utrum ordinem suum teneant; qui si aliter invenerit, una cum rectore monasterii corrigere debebit."—*MG H*, *ibid.*, p. 82; Capitulare Missorum Suessionense (853), cap. 2: "Ut missi nostri diligenter investigent per singulas parrochias simul cum episcopo de monasteriis quae Deum timentes in suis proprietatibus aedificaverunt."—*MG H*, *ibid.*, p. 267; *ibid.*, can. 1: "Ut missi nostri per civitates et singula monasteria, tam canonicorum quam monachorum sive sanctimonialium, una cum episcopo parrochiae uniuscuiusque, in qua consistunt, cum consilio etiam et consensu ipsius, qui monasterium retinet, vitam ibi degentium et conversationem inquirant, et ubi necesse est, corrigant;"—*MG H*, *loc. cit.*; Concilium Tullense I (859), cap. 9: "Ut congregationes canonicorum et monachorum...a propriis episcopis strenue visitentur...." —Mansi, XV, 539; Concilium Ticinense (Cisalpinorum Episcoporum) (855) —Mansi, XV, 18; etc.

[8] Capitulare Missorum Suessionense, cap. 1: "...qui monasterium retinet,"—*MG H*, *ibid.*, p. 267.

[9] Lesne, *Histoire de la Propriété*, II, I, 255: "Benoît III faisait tomber le blâme partiellement sur les évêques (for the secularisation) qui, comme le leur reprochait le concile de Meaux (Concilium Meldense (845)—*MG H*, *ibid.*, pp. 400 ff.) favorisent par leur silence ceux qui jettent la désordre dans les monastères."

[10] Cf. Lesne, *op. cit.*, II, I, 179: "...C'est à ces sécularisations toutes récentes et qui se continuent sous leurs yeux, que les évêques font allusion, quand à l'assemblée de Ver, ils se plaignent qu'à l'heure présente les biens d'église sont détenus par des séculiers." Cf. "Gesta episcoporum Autisidorensium," *MG H*, *Scriptores*, XIII, 385: "...ecclesiae facultates..., nunc in usu saecularium detinentur."

[11] Halphen, "The Church from Charlemagne to Sylvester II," *Cambridge Medieval History*, III, 446: "...the prelates of France, a few months later (June, 845) ventured to put forward, at the Synod of Meaux, a whole series

secularization, as the bishops pointed out in the Council of Meaux, could be laid to the imperial charge.[12]

A new note of equality appeared in the legislation regarding the status of the abbot as compared with that of the bishop, for both took on equal measures of responsibility toward their separate interests of guarding the subjects under their jurisdiction. That the basis of this equality was not a canonical one, however, is shown by the fact that the bishop and the abbot were held equal with the count, who represented a non-canonical, non-ecclesiastical hierarchical rank.

The genesis of this equalization, as was previously indicated, was traceable to the organizational plan of the Carolingians, whereby the abbey was just another "outpost" of the royalty. When the king wished to reward his subject, he could bestow upon him an abbey.[13] The abbey was his by right of founda-

of claims directed not less against their king than against the whole lay aristocracy, reproaching both alike with hindering the free exercise of religion. Their reproaches were carried to such a height that the king, with the support of the magnates, resisted." Concilium Meldense-Parisiense (845), cap. 10: "Perventum est siquidem ad nos, quod auditu lugubre et dictu nefas actuque horribile ac nimis triste dinoscitur, quia contra omnem auctoritatem, contra patrum decreta et totius christianae religionis, consuetudinem in monasteriis regularibus laici in medio sacerdotum et levitarum ac ceterorum religiosarum virorum ut domini et magistri resideant et velut abbates de illorum vita..."—*MGH, Cap. Reg. Fr.*, II, II, 1, p. 400.

[12] Lesne, *op. cit.*, II, II, 502: "...ces bénéfices, évêchés, abbayes, le monarque les donne, les retire, les garde à son gré en sa main...cette sécularisation d'ordre théorique a été le fondement juridique de toutes les pratiques spoliatrices dont ont souffert les églises." Tellenbach, *Church, State, and Christian Society at the Time of the Investiture Contest* (tr. by R. F. Bennett; Oxford: Basil Blackwell, 1948), p. 89: "Since the ninth century, however, the sacred power of the king had been revered by all. It was accepted as natural that the ruler should lead the people in Church affairs as much as in matters of politics. He summoned synods and councils, fixed their agenda, and presided over them either in person or by deputy...it was a firmly established custom that a bishopric might be obtained at the hands of the king. The monastic reformers of the tenth and early eleventh centuries had...little thought of raising objections to it, and were on the contrary full of praise for devout princes, entered into close relations with them, and gave enthusiastic approval to their intervention in the most intimate ecclesiastical affairs."

[13] Amman-Dumas, *L'Eglise au Pouvoir des Laïques*, p. 300: "Tantôt le

tion or endowment.[14] Other abbeys were placed under his protection against the usurpation of those who hoped to enrich themselves by their appropriation.[15] The abbeys came to be regarded as a useful part of the kingdom, even as the abbots came to be considered as functionaries of the crown. Unlike the holders of bishoprics who were required by canon law to receive the episcopal rank, the abbatial blessing was not so indispensable in the conferring of an abbey. A lay person could be an abbot as well as a cleric could.[16] Since abbeys were conferred on or fell into the hands of nobles and bishops principally, the three ranks of abbot, bishop, and count became, by popular estimation, confused. Legislation followed popular preference, and the three terms appear side by side.[17] Capitulary notices were addressed to bishops and abbots without the former sharp distinctions of rank.[18] In the councils, the abbots sat together with the bishops to manage affairs of the Church.[19]

roi entendait récompenser personnellement un de ses fidèles, en lui donnant une abbaye en bénéfice."

[14] Schmitz, *Histoire de l'Ordre*, I, 346: "En vertu du droit d'appropriation ecclésiastique (Eigenkirchenrecht) le roi carolingien est entré en possession des monastères qu'il a fondés ou dotés."

[15] *Loc. cit.*, "...il devient propriétaire encore des maisons qui lui ont été expressément cédées par le fondateur ou le propriétaire. Remettre une institution entre les mains du souverain, c'était, semblait-il, en garantir le plus surement l'avenir, en assurer le mieux les intérêts matériels et spirituels. Même au Xe siècle, à une époque où l'usurpation fait passer au pouvoir des grands un nombre de plus en plus considérable de monastères royaux, on estime encore qu'il est nécessaire, pour sauvegarder la pleine indépendence d'un établissement, de le mettre aux mains du roi."

[16] Amman-Dumas, *op. cit.*, p. 306.

[17] Capitulare Carisiacense (877), cap. 3: "De tertio vos, sicut melius Deo inspirante vidistis, regni vestri defensionem atque tuitionem et filii vestri custodiam per fideles vestros, tam per episcopos, quam abbates et comites dispositum habetis, et necessarium esse cognoscimus;"—*MGH*, *ibid.*, p. 355.

[18] Karlomanni Capitulare Vernense (884): "In nomine sanctae et individuae trinitatis. Karlomannus gratia Dei rex omnibus venerabilibus episcopis, abbatibus, comitibus, judicibus omnibusque sanctae Dei ecclesiae et nostris fidelibus;"—*MGH*, *ibid.*, p. 371.

[19] Synodus Pontegonensis (876), cap. 2: "Congregata igitur in Romana Urbe sancta synodo ante adventum praedicti domni imperatoris misit cum consensu omnium epistolas Hludowico regi, filiis quoque ipsius, archiepiscopis, episcopis, abbatibus, ac reliquis primoribus regni;"—*MGH*, *ibid.*, p.

The actual voting status of the abbots was indeterminate, although it seems that they were influential in episcopal elections.[20] Likewise the voting status of the monks serving in parishes was obscure. If they had a vote, it represented that of their abbot and community.[21] The fact that the bishops and abbots acted together in official meetings indicated a progression in the former extremely inferior status of the abbots with respect to the bishops. These latter at the same time underwent a loss in prestige, against which the councils vehemently inveighed.[22]

The reason for the ascendancy of the abbatial office was undoubtedly due to the convulsion of the times, although Benedict of Aniane had contributed to it by evoking the emperor's support. In face of the invasions, more than before, the abbots had to assume the position of protectors of the kingdom,[23]

351. Pistensis Synodus (862): "...itaque Carolus, episcopi, abbates quoque et comites convenere, nempe in locum, qui pistis dicitur..."—Mabillon, *Annales Ordinis S. Benedicti Occidentalium Monachorum Patriarchae* (6 vols., Lucae, 1739-1745), III, 86; Wormaciensis Synodus (868): "...septemdecim episcoporum et unius chorepiscopi signa et nomina subscripta habentur, et sex abbatum;"—Mabillon, *Annales*, III, 141; Concilium Cabilonense (873) —Mabillon, *Annales*, III, 169; etc.

[20] Imbart de la Tour, *Les Elections Episcopales dans l'Eglise de France du IX au XII siècles* (Paris, 1890), p. 14: "...il est certain que les chefs des monastères prenaient part à l'élection, (of the bishops) mais nous ignorons s'ils avaient un droit de vote personnel ou s'ils exprimaient le vote de la communauté;" *ibidem*, p. 214, "N'oublions pas que l'influence, dans le corps électoral, appartient en partie aux chefs des églises et aux abbés. Les intérêts religieux, que ces derniers surtout représentent, leurs richesses, leur crédit, pèsent d'un grand poids sur les élections..."

[21] *Ibid.*, p. 14: "Il est probable que ceux d'entre eux qui n'étaient point sous la juridiction de l'évêque ou n'avaient pas charge d'ames n'étaient pas convoqués à l'élection, sans qu'on puisse cependant rien affirmer à ce sujet. Nous ignorons également quelle était la situation des moines chargés d'une paroisse."

[22] Concilium Triburiense (895), Prologus: "Anno incarnationis Domini DCCCXCV sedente ad Triburian oppidum glorioso rege Arnulfo congregati sunt episcopi numero XXVI cum abbatibus monasteriorum ... contra plerosque etiam seculares, qui episcopalem auctoritatem imminuere temptabant, episcopis et sancte synodo vigore regio favebat;"—*MGH*, *ibid.*, p. 213.

[23] Lévy-Bruhl, *Elections Abbatiales*, p. 192: "...on peut dire que l'abbé mérovingien est un ascète tandis que l'abbé carolingien est un fonctionnaire."

and upon attack they were to unite with the bishop and the neighboring abbots and abbesses to repel the siege.[24] The abbeys now more than ever before became property of the proprietors, to be used primarily for lucrative purposes.[25] They apparently, rather than the bishoprics, became the centers of wealth and power. It was for this reason, probably, that the Northmen looked principally to the abbeys for the tribute they demanded.[26] In addition to the monks subjected by vow to them, the abbots also had vassals under their charge. The feudal concept of the abbatial title was evident in an edict which removed the title from an abbot who failed to watch the conduct of his vassals.[27] The once exclusive power of the

[24] Capitulare Tusiacense in Burgundiam Directum (865), cap. 13: "Ut, si infideles nostri se adunaverint ad devastationem regni nostri, fideles nostri, tam episcopi, quam abbates et comites et abbatissarum homines, sed et ipsi comites ac vassi nostri seu ceteri quique fideles Dei ac nostri de uno missatico se in unum adunare procurent. . ."—*MGH*, *ibid.*, p. 331.

[25] Amann-Dumas, *L'Eglise au Pouvoir des Laïques*, p. 296: "Au VIIIe et surtout au IXe siècle, l'idée de la propriété s'était détournée sur la personne de l'abbé. Placé à la tête de l'établissement, il gouvernait l'église monastique et les biens qui en dépendaient; il en avait la possession. A une époque ou la propriété ne se manifestait que par la possession, il était naturel de le considérer comme un propriétaire au moins temporaire. La basilique, le monastère et l'ensemble des biens y affectés furent envisagés comme faisant partie de *l'abbatia*. Par ce mot on entendait primitivement la charge de l'abbé avec toutes les attributions qu'elle comportait: soins spirituels, direction des moines, administration et jouissance des biens. Comme l'abbé tenait en sa main toutes les propriétés monastiques, *l'abbatia* se confondit avec le temporel du monastère."

[26] Edictum Compendiense de Tributo Nordmannico (877): "Unusquisque episcopus, qui habet abbatiam, aut abbas, qui similiter habet abbatiam, aut comes qui habet abbatiam, de suo manso indominicato similiterque et de vassallorum accipiat de manso indominicato denarios duodecim. . ."—*MGH*, *ibid.*, p. 354.

[27] Constitutio de expeditione Beneventana (866), cap. 4: "Quodsi comes aut bassi nostri alique infirmitate (non) detenti remanserint, aut abbates vel abbatissae si plenissime homines suos non direxerint, ipsi suos honores perdant, et eorum bassali [sic] et proprium et beneficium amittant;"—*MGH*, *ibid.*, p. 96; Lesne, *Histoire de la Propriété*, II, II, 76: "L'évêché, l'abbaye, l'usage d'une église épiscopale d'un monastère royal, quels que soient le mode juridique et le bénéficiaire de cette prise de possession constitue un *honor* tenu du souverain comme des autres *honores regni*. Les évêques du synode de Ver de 755 paraissent déjà considérer le gouvernement d'un

bishop, namely to choose those for the clerical status whom he deemed suited, was checked by the necessities which gave rise to the demands of lesser prelates and of the faithful themselves.[28]

The influence of the bishop decreased steadily over the monasteries not held by him as proprietor. Where their office had been used *per fas vel nefas* to divert the wealth into the "*episcopatum*" upon the departure of one of the monks from a monastery of the diocese, it was now to go to the abbots and the monastery.[29] If for some reason one of the opulent faithful could not be buried near the episcopal church, where this burial would have brought a rich stipend for the bishop, leave was granted for the burial to be made in monastic ground.[30]

More wandering monks than formerly roamed ahead of the invaders and at times broke away from their monastic observances. They had to be held in check.[31] In the distress of

monastère comme un *honor* que perdra celui qui n'aura pas su y rétablir l'observance. Quand Charlemagne, au synode de Francfort, restitue à l'évêque Pierre ses anciens honneurs, l'évêché est sans doute l'un de ces *honores*. Cf. also by the same author, "Les diverses acceptions du terme Beneficium du VIIIe au XIe siècles," *Revue Historique du Droit*, XLVII (1924).

[28] Capitula Pistensia (869), cap. 9: "Ut, si abbates vel abbatissae aut comites seu vassi nostri aut ceteri laici clericos probabilis vitae et doctrinae episcopis canonice consecrandos suisque in ecclesiis constituendos obtulerint, nulla qualibet occasione eos episcopi vel ministri eorum reiciant; et episcopi praevideant quem honorem presbyteri pro ecclesiis suis senioribus suis tribuere debent."—*MGH*, *ibid.*, p. 335.

[29] Additio tertia (Capitulis), cap. 66 (late ninth century): "Si monachus laicus fuerit, honore et cingulo expolietur, et res ejus monasterio adiiciantur." —Mansi, XVI, 583; *Ibid.*, cap. 67: "Si monachus monasterium suum dimiserit, omnia bona ipsius, et quae in monasterio introduxit, et quae non introduxit, dominio monasterii sint, et ipse officio Praesidis servire cogatur." —Mansi, *loc. cit.*

[30] Concilium Triburiense (895), cap. 15: "...sepulturam morientium apud ecclesiam, ubi sedes est episcopi, celebrari. Si autem hoc propter itineris longinquitatem, aut adiacentem alicuius inoportunitatis difficultatem inpossibile videatur, expectet eum terra sepulturae suae, quo canonicorum aut monachorum sive sanctaemonialium congregatio sancta communiter degat..."—*MGH*, *ibid.*, p. 213.

[31] Concilium Tullense II (860), cap. 5: "Quia peccatis nostris agentibus plurima loca Deo sacrata incensa et vastata sunt a perfidis Christianis, et a crudeli etiam gente Northmannorum, sub hac occasione multi lascivi

the times there may have been many who posed as monks, but were actually only playing the part for personal advantage, being better able in this role to partake of monastic temporalities. Bishops and abbots both were to be vigilant in respect of these.[32] Episcopal authority thus reinforced that of the abbots in eradicating abuses of this kind. Scrutinies were frequently held under episcopal direction for determining the standing of these vagabonds. One council demanded that, since some of these monks were spreading false doctrines, they should all be subjected to episcopal examination.[33] Perhaps with a view to suppressing such practices, and to distinguishing the monks of good faith from the others, one council decreed that commendatory letters be issued to such itinerant monks.[34] If these monks or other clerics wished to preach, permission was not to be given easily, but only after examination by the bish-

clerici et monachi relicto religionis habitu retro abierunt, et absque ulla canonica licentia et reverentia vagabundi feruntur, ab ovili gregis Dei errantes. Ideoque patrum auctoritate volumus, ut talibus omnibus necessitas imponatur, quatenus ad ordinationem et dispositionem episcoporum et abbatum suorum revertantur, et sub disciplina eorum maneant."—Mansi, XV, 560.

[32] Concilium Vernense (844), cap. 3: "In locis sanctis, hoc est monasteriis, alios studio, nonnullos desidia, multos necessitate victus et vestimenti a sua professione deviare comperimus. Quod petimus, ut in omnibus parroechiis directi a vestra mansuetudine religiosi atque idonei viri cum notitia episcoporum scrutentur et corrigant ac singulorum locorum statum vestrae celsitudini et nostrae mediocritati tempore a vobis constituendo renuntient."—*MGH*, *ibid.*, p. 384; *ibid.*, cap. 4: "Monachos, qui cupiditatis causa vagantur et sanctae religionis propositum impudenter infamant ad sua loca jubemus reverti et regulariter abbatum sollertia recipi. . ." *Loc. cit.*; Capitularia Italica (Hlotharii), Hlotharii Capitulare de expeditione contra Sarracenos facienda (846), cap. 4: "Et imprimis monachi, qui ordinem suum per desidiam aut cupiditatem seu secularem ambitum deseruerunt, admoniti ab episcopis et abbatibus emendentur. . ." *MGH*, *ibid.*, p. 65.

[33] Synodus Papiensis (850), cap. 21: "Quidam clericorum vel monachorum peregrinantes per diversas vagando provincias et civitates multiplices spargunt errores et inutiles questiones disseminant decipiente corda simplicium; de his decrevit sancta sinodus, ut ab episcopo loci detineantur et ad metropolitanum deducti discussione ecclesiastica examinentur. . ."—*MGH*, *ibid.*, p. 122; Synodus Regaticina (850), cap. 14—Mansi, XIV, 937.

[34] Additio quarta (capitulis) (Late ninth cent.), cap. 157—Mansi, XVI, 627.

op.[35] Since stability in a monastery became, perhaps, less attainable, some relaxations occurred in the legislation regarding those monks who chose to leave an abbey for one reason or another. The bishop had to be informed of such a departure and had to give his consent to it.[36] Likewise the bishop had to be consulted when an entire community wished to change its status from that of canons to that of monks, or vice-versa.[37]

The bishop's act of surveillance covered a broad and unprecise range, and was probably not uniform over the expanse of the empire. Capitularies and edicts of councils indicated the exercise of this duty in manifold fashion. One council forbade the rejection of any monk who had been duly accepted by a monastery without the knowledge of the local bishop.[38] Another forbade ordinations of monks to the priesthood unless they had a proper means of habitation, and prohibited the practice of their living with non-clerical persons.[39]

[35] *Ibidem*, cap. 33: "Illud quod nobis propter improbitatem quorundam monachorum verbo mandasti, speciali et praedictorum patrum statuta firmantes statuimus ut praeter Domini sacerdotes, ab episcopo ejusdem videlicet loci electos, nullus audeat praedicare, sive sit monachus, sive laicus, qui cujuslibet scientiae nomine glorietur."

[36] Concilium Triburiense (895), cap. 27: "Si quis monachus pro lucro animae vel animarum suo monasterio exire et aliud proposuerit intrare consentientibus episcopo, abbate et fratribus, consentimus et concordamus, quia id fecisse multos sanctos legimus. Si vero fuga regularis disciplinae elapsus propositum sanctitatis calcaverit, omnimodis coercendus et ab omnibus et detestandus atque omni onere est gravandus, ut saltim rubore verecundiae confusus et onere paupertatis afflictus redeat, quem relicta singularitatis professione inimicus tenebat."—*MGH*, *ibid*, p. 213.

[37] Conventus Lemovicensis (848); "Ainardus princeps seu abbas monasterii sancti Martialis, et omnes canonici, prostraverunt se subito ad pedes ejus, postulantes dare sibi licentiam se fieri monachos in eodem loco. Rex vero Deo gratias agens, cum magno gaudio petitionem eorum adimplevit et omnes episcopos et primores eorum voluntati inclinavit. Sed Stodilus episcopus Lemovicensis eum hoc graviter ferret et inflexibilis solus maneret; tandem rege cogente consensit."—Mansi, XIV, 917.

[38] Concilium Meldense-Parisiense (845-846), cap. 59: "Ut monachus de monasterio sine consultu vel praesentia episcopi aut vicarii eius ad hoc regulariter deductus non eiciatur..."—*MGH*, *ibid.*, p. 411.

[39] Concilium Romanum (853), cap. 10: "Sacerdotes namque constitui non oportet nisi in ecclesiis, aut speciali monasteria deputentur; ne necessitas in saecularibus domibus illis habitandi occurrat, alioquin a propriis epis-

If the monastery lost its abbot through death, it was incumbent upon the local bishop and the count-proprietor of the monastery to protect it until another abbot had been placed in charge.[40] It was the bishop's duty to prevent the abbots from forcing those to remain in monasteries who obviously did not have vocations.[41] But almost directly contrary to this was another conciliar decree which demanded that those who had been offered to the monastery from their infancy were not to be allowed to depart upon reaching adolescence.[42]

In other ways, also, the bishops espoused the monastic interests. They showed a new note of independence toward the weakened emperors by requesting them to protect the monasteries placed under their "*tuitio*" and not to permit them to fall into alien hands.[43] It was the practice of a large number of the monasteries to put themselves under royal protection, since it seemed less dangerous to their own interests to do so.[44]

copis aut in episcopia aut in monasteria habitandi et conversandi pro exercendo officio constituantur; in quibus mulieres conversari nulla ratio permittit."—Mansi, XIV, 1003.

[40] Capitulare Carisiacense (877): "Si abbas vel abbatissa obierit, episcopus in cuius parochia monasterium illud est, una cum comite illud monasterium custodiat, usque dum vestra iussio inde fiat."—*MGH*, *ibid.*, p. 355.

[41] Concilium Romanum (853), cap. 32: "Sicut enim qui monasteria elegerunt a monasteriis egredi non permittuntur; ita hi qui inviti sine justae ostensionis crimine monasteriis sunt intromissi, nisi volentes non teneantur, quia quod non petunt non observant."—Mansi, XIV, 1007.

[42] Concilium Wormatiense (868), cap. 22: "Si pater vel mater filium filiamque intra septa monasterii in infantiae annis sub regulari tradiderint disciplina, non liceat eis, postquam ad pubertatis pervenerint annos, egredi, et matrimonio copulari. Hoc ergo omnino devitandum est: quia nefas est, ut oblatis a parentibus Deo filiis voluptatis fraena laxentur. Igitur (ut praediximus) non liceat eis susceptum habitum unquam deserere..."—Mansi, XV, 873.

[43] Synodus Regaticina (850), cap. 16: "Suggerendum est beatissimis imperatoribus, quia hi qui monasteria et sinodochia sub defensione sacri palatii posuerunt, ideo fecisse probantur, quod a nullo melius quam a summis potestatibus protegenda crediderint; et si ea contra decreta institutorum personis quibus non licet dederint, ipsi impugnatores efficiuntur..."—Mansi, XIV, 937.

[44] Lesne, *Histoire de la Propriété*, II, II, 26: "A tout prendre en dépit de l'abus fait souvent par le souverain des monastères qu'on lui cédait, il paraissait avantageux aux moines que leur établissement prît le caractère

The bishops were to take the lead in restoring the monasteries which for one reason or other had been destroyed. Failure to do so brought the severe penalty of excommunication upon such a bishop.[45] Violence was not to be used for changing the condition of a monastery, but all of its rights were to remain secure.[46] The temporalities of the monasteries which had been squandered were to be returned by the guilty bishops.[47] The monasteries or oratories whose construction had been approved could not be razed against the will of those who had erected them.[48]

Only the episcopal court was able to try the cases of monks committing crimes, not the civil courts.[49] Nor were the monks permitted by the bishops to accept civil positions, such as

d'un monastère royal. Ni l'attribution de tant d'abbayes en bénéfice, au préjudice à la fois du spirituel et du temporel des communautés, ni même l'example de monastères royaux cédés en toute propriété à une église ou à un laïque, ne détournaient les fondateurs et propriétaires préoccupés d'assurer l'avenir religieux de leur maison, d'en attribuer la propriété au monarque."

[45] Synodus Regaticina (850); cap. 14: "...omnia monasteria, quae ab episcoporum sunt potestate, protinus restaurentur...synodum monasteria, quae sub sua potestate neglecta fuerant, aliqua ex parte recuperasse repertus non fuerit, excommunicetur."—Mansi, XIV, 937.

[46] Widonis Capitulatio Electionis (889), cap. 3: "Sancimus etiam, ut neque in episcopatibus neque in abbatiis vel senodochiis aut ullis Deo sacratis locis ulla violentia aut novae conditionis gravamina imponantur, sed secundum antiquam consuetudinem omnes in suo statu suoque privilegio perpetuo maneant."—*MGH*, *ibid.*, p. 104.

[47] Concilium Ticinense (Cisalpinorum Episcoporum) (855): "Quidam autem episcopi et rectores monasteriorum res ecclesiarum suarum subtractas et aliis personis largitas esse queruntur; et ideo ecclesiasticas utilitates nequaquam se implere posse dicunt. Quae ut restituantur, vestram regiam majestatem imploramus: quia si hi, qui eas pro animarum suarum remedio ecclesiis contulerunt, praemium merentur, sine dubio damnatione digni sunt, qui eas subtrahere moliuntur."—Mansi, XV, 18.

[48] Concilium Romanum (853), cap. 21: "Monasterium vel oratorium canonice constructum a dominio constructoris invite non auferatur..."—Mansi, XIV, 997.

[49] Additio tertia (capitulis) (late ninth century), cap. 59: "Nemo audeat monachum vel sanctimoniales feminas ad civile judicium accusare, sed ad Episcopum. Et ipse ex lege vel canonibus consentanium sententiam proferat."—Mansi, XVI, 582.

that of tax-gatherer.[50] Those in a condition of servitude who had entered an abbey were ordered by the bishops to obtain their freedom before being permitted to receive orders.[51]

The spiritual advantages of the exchange of prayers with the monastic communities was recognized by the bishops in one council, in which they joined the monks in a society for mutual spiritual assistance.[52] It was not uncommon for councils to be held in the abbeys. In 845, for example, Fleury was chosen as the site for the synodal gathering of bishops and abbots. Theodulph, commendatory abbot during the time of Charlemagne, had built an imposing church for the abbey and it seemed a natural location for such synods.[53] As an element forging unity between them, the translation of the relics of saints served the bishops and the abbots as an occasion for frequent concurrent action.[54]

Since the seventh century the monks took an increasingly greater part in the diocesan ministerial activities. In the beginning the rule applied that all were under the jurisdiction of the local bishop. Privileges gradually withdrew them somewhat from this exclusive episcopal jurisdiction, and devolved somewhat into the hands of the religious superiors. The presence of the monks in the parishes was never too popular with the bish-

[50] *Ibidem,* cap. 46: "Clericus vel monachus neque exactor publicarum rerum, neque conductor, aut vectigalium vel curationis domus, vel procurator litis, vel fidejussor in talibus causis fiat."—Mansi, XVI, 580.

[51] Concilium Triburiense (895), cap. 29 and 29a—*MGH, ibid.*, p. 228; Cf. also Bernard, *Etude sur les esclaves et les serfs d'Eglise en France du VIe au XIIIe siècles* (Paris, 1919), pp. 98 ff.

[52] Synodus apud Saponarias (859): "...In ultimo capitulo synodi Tullensis vicarias inter sese preces condixerunt episcopi et abbates; ut singuli pro cunctis per singulas hebdomadas feria quarta missam celebrarent; et post cujusque obitum pro defuncto in sedibus septenae missae, totidemque vigiliae persolverentur..."—Mabillon, *Annales,* III, 73.

[53] Cf. Rocher, *Histoire de l'Abbaye Royale de Saint-Benoît-sur-Loire,* p. 82: "...Charles-le-Chauve...vint à Saint Benoît (Fleury) en 845, et résida dans le monastère...(le monastère) était...occupé par les évêques et les abbés venus de diverses provinces pour assister au synode. Ce lieu fut choisi de préférence, sans doute, à cause du calme de sa solitude; son église, monument remarquable du au génie et à la munificence de Théodulphe, était assurément digne d'être le siège de cette importante assemblée."

[54] E.g., "Historia Translationis S. Viti," *MGH, Scriptores,* II, pp. 581-582.

ops, since it was more difficult to effectively manage a corporation than an individual. Therefore these prelates held to the thesis mentioned first by Gregory the Great,[55] namely that parish activity was incompatible with the religious profession. Hincmar (806-882), Archbishop of Rheims (845-882), was especially vociferous in propagating this view.[56] The practice could not have been exceptional, since monks were found to be active even in the diocesan curia. If operative in the very center of the diocesan administration, they certainly also functioned in the more remote parish activities, such as administering to the people.[57] Whether or not the monks were accepted in parish work, the fact remained that they had participated in it and could be credited with making the faith an accepted and permanent part of the country's *mores*.[58]

Although there was much cooperation between the bishops

[55] Cf. *supra*, Ch. IV.

[56] Amann-Dumas, *op. cit.*, p. 285: "Les évêques avaient lutté avec énergie contre cette pratique; au IXe siècle, Hincmar jugeait que le ministère paroissial était incompatible avec la profession religieuse. Cependant, dès cette époque, l'usage courant admettait que des moines pussent administrer des paroisses avec le consentement de l'évêque; mais ils devaient, comme les autres prêtres paroissiaux, se rendre annuellement au synode et restaient soumis du droit de visite de l'évêque;" Imbart de la Tour, *Les Paroisses Rurales*, p. 129, "Les fonctions curiales étaient exercées par l'abbe, le prévot ou un de leurs délégués. On sait que ces usages se sont maintenus jusqu' à nos jours. Mais ils n'étaient pas très répandus encore au IXe siècle...En réalité, les évêques se souciaient peu de voir des communautés monastiques à la tête des paroisses. Une corporation obéit moins aisément qu'un homme. Chanoines ou religieux pouvaient trouver toujours dans leur règle, leurs traditions, leur esprit même, les moyens efficaces de résister au gouvernement de l'épiscopat;" Cf. Moreau, *Les Abbayes de Belgique*, p. 295; Lemarignier, *Etude sur les privileges d'Exemption*, p. 12.

[57] Fournier, *L'Origine du vicaire général et des autres membres de la Curie Diocésaine* (Paris: Séminaire des Missions Etrangeres, 1940), p. 32.

[58] Moreau, *Histoire de l'Eglise en Belgiquc*, I, p. 175: "Si les évêques de diocèse et le clergé séculier furent les principaux agents d'évangélisation dans les anciennes villes romaines et dans les vici et castra, c'est principalement aux monastères que les populations rurales durent leur foi chrètienne...Les moines se trouvent ainsi en contact perpétuel avec les paysans, très ignorants des choses religieuses, et ayant conservé, nous l'avons vu, un bon nombre de supersitions païennes...Tandis que les moines allaient ainsi aux gens de la campagne, les gens des campagnes venaient à eux..."

and abbots, there were also some occasions in which friction arose between them. One of these was an objection on the part of the bishops that conspiracies were being formed by monks against them.[59] Both the bishops and the abbots were admonished not to indulge in vulgar stories and jokes; they were to have spiritual reading at table wherever possible.[60] Abbots who had gathered in a synod complained of the oppressions of the bishop of Le Mans, who disregarded the privileges they had received and violated their rights. Four metropolitans sanctioned the objection and confirmed the privileges of the abbey.[61] Wenilon, the Archbishop of Sens, in violation of the privileges and exemptions of the monastery of Saint-Colombe granted first by Louis the Pious, attempted to press the monks of the abbey under his jurisdiction. With the aid of the famous Loup de Ferrières and Pardulus, Bishop of Laon and intimate friend of Charles the Bald, King of the West Franks (843-877), there was issued a new charter which confirmed the old and added severe anathemas for violations of it.[62] A certain Bishop Gibertus invaded a monastery and absconded with its goods, also expelling the monks. As a punishment, the bishop was

[59] Concilium Wormatiense (868), cap. 74: "Conjurationis et conspirationis crimen et ab exteris legibus est omnino prohibitum. Si qui ergo clerici vel monachi reperti fuerint conjurantes aut conspirantes, aut insidios ponentes episcopis aut clericis, gradu penitus abjiciantur."—Mansi, XV, 73.

[60] Additio tertia (capitulis) (late ninth cent.), cap. 41; "Ut episcopi et abbates ante se joca turpia facere non permittant; sed pauperes et indigentes secum ad mensam habeant, et lectio divina ibi personet..."—Mansi, XVI, 579.

[61] Synodus Valentina (855): "Adfuit huic conventui Rainaldus ejus loci abbas, patribusque exposuit monasterii, fratrumque suorum oppressiones et perturbationes quae patiebantur ab episcopo Cenomannensi, qui hoc monasterium, regum Francorum titulis et privilegiis subinde ornatum, ecclesiae Cenomannicae subjicere moliebatur...quae previlegia tum immunitatis tum liberae electionis patres illius synodi intemerata permanere sanxerunt..."—Mabillon, *Annales*, III, 190.

[62] Brullee, *Histoire de l'Abbaye royale de S. Colombe-les-Sens*, (Sens, 1852), p. 70: "...le Roi (Charles the Bald) donnait, en faveur du monastère de Sainte-Colombe, une charte datée du palais royal de Compiègne...toutes les exemptions, privilèges, et donations en faveur de...Saint-Colombe... sont confirmée sur les plus terribles anathèmes."

excommunicated.[63] In the year 881, Pope John VIII (872-882) had to warn the Bishop Anspertus to release two monks from imprisonment who had journeyed to Rome and had been put in chains when seen to be visiting the city.[64]

Two conflicts are recorded as having arisen between Lupus, the abbot of Ferrières, and Wenilon, the Bishop.[65] A controversy over stipends given to a church whose possession was disputed arose between the Abbot Leo of St. Zeno's monastery and canons from the nearby church.[66] Although examples of such conflicts could be enumerated at some length, their very enumeration indicates their comparatively exceptional nature. However, it was probably to prevent such acts of injustice from occurring in the future that Pope John VIII wished to determine very exactly who should be considered as subjects of the bishops in a diocese. In an enumeration of the same, abbots significantly received no mention.[67]

Where the universal law did not exist in this period, the privileges became the canon law of the monasteries which possessed them.[68] During this period the privileges were granted

[63] Mabillon, *Annales*, III, 206 (anno 879).

[64] *Ibid.*, p. 215 (anno 881); Epistolae Joannis Papae VIII ad Anspertum Archiepiscopum Mediolanensem: "Inobedientiae eum arguit, praecipitque, ut Rhodoaldum, et Warlenum monachos, quos injuste in carcerem conjecerat, ad eorum monasterium honorifice remittat."—Mansi, XVII, 190; Jaffé, *Regesta Pontificum Romanorum*, I, 416 (n. 3329 [2550]); *MPL*, CXXVI, 916.

[65] Mabillon, *Annales*, III, 73 (anno 859).

[66] *Ibid.*, p. 121 (anno 865).

[67] Vita et Epistolae Joannis Papae VIII (872): "Joannes sedit annos decem, dies duos...Hic decreto suo statuit...clericos et sanctimoniales, pupillos et viduas sub tutela episcoporum esse decrevit..."—Mansi, XVII, 1.

[68] Tellenbach, *Church, State, and Christian Society at the Time of the Investiture Contest*, p. 21: "When the point has been grasped that to the Middle Ages *Libertas* simply means subjective right, and that law is nothing more than the sum of all individual *Libertates*, the meaning of a privilege as a reduction to writing of this right becomes fully comprehensible. A privilege does not—as one might suppose from the modern use of the term—create exceptions to a generally prevailing law; rather, it is the precise formulation of an actual concrete subjective right, that is, of a *Libertas*."

with easy abandon. Many came from the Pope.[69] Others came from the bishops and the emperor.[70] Many privileges were granted and confirmed in councils.[71] Most of these were generous and precise in their concessions. Some treated of the immunity of the monastic temporalities.[72] Others granted the right of free elections.[73]

[69] Letonnelier, *L'Abbaye Exempt de Cluny et le Saint-Siège* (Ligugé-Paris, 1923), p. 19: "Au VIIIe et IXe siècles, ces examples [of privileges] deviennent de plus en plus nombreux. Les plus célèbres sont ceux de Nicolas Ier pour l'abbaye de Saint-Calais en 863 (Mansi, XVII, 355), de Jean VIII pour l'abbaye de Fleury en 878, (Mansi, XVII, 503) du Pape Nicolas pour l'abbaye de Vézelay en 865 (Quartin, Cartul. de l'Yonne) et celle de Pitheires soumises au Saint-Siège par Gérard de Roussillon."

[70] Examples of these are numerous. E.g., Privilege to monastery of Corbie—Mansi, XVIII, 73 (Concilium Moguntinum); to St. Theuderus—Mansi, XVIII, 105; To Carus Locus or St. Marcellus—Mansi, XVIII, 49 (Concilium Cabilonense [886]); etc. Cf., e.g., Schmitz, *Histoire de l'Ordre,* I, ch. 3-5.

[71] E.g., Synodus Sistericensis (859)—Mansi, XV, 542; Concilium Moguntiacense (888)—Mansi, XVIII, 66; Concilium apud Vermeriam (869)—Mansi, XV, 735; Synodus Suessionicensis (866)—Mansi, XV, 735; etc.

[72] Boutaric, "Le Régime Féodal, son Origine et son Etablissement," *Revue des Questions Historiques,* XVIII (1875), p. 368: "Les effets des immunités se sont faits sentir en partie jusqu'en 1789; ces actes sont donc trés intéressants à étudier, car ils ont exercé une influence capitale... Les termes varient, mais ils sont toujours explicites, et ces variants mêmes procurent les lumières nouvelles. Les rois ont mis une telle précision, une telle clarté à l'étendue des concessions qu'ils entendaient faire par les immunités:" Cf. Concilium Moguntiacense (888), cap. 6: "Ne cui liceat res vel facultates ecclesiis aut monasteriis, vel xenodochiis, pro quacumque eleemosyna cum justitia delegatas retentare, alienare, atque subtrahere"—Mansi, XVIII, 66.

[73] E.g., Additio tertia (capitulis) (late ninth century), cap. 6: "Monachorum siquidem causam qualiter, Deo opitulante, ex parte disposuerimus, et quomodo constitutum fuerit, ex se ipsis sibi eligendi abbatis licentiam dederimus, et qualiter Deo opitulante, ex parte disposuerimus, et quomodo constitutum fuerit, ex se ipsis sibi eligendi abbatis licentiam dederimus, et qualiter Deo opitulante quieti vivere propositumque suum indefesse custodire valeant ordinaverimus, in alia scedula diligenter adnotari fecimus, et ut apud successores nostros ratum foret et inviolabiliter conservaretur confirmavimus:"—Mansi, XVI, 576; Cf. also Lesne, *Histoire de la Propriété,* II, II, 129: "La libre élection des abbés, qui était jadis la règle constitue au IXe siècle un privilège. Les moines qui ont perdu le bénéfice de l'ancienne coutume, cherchent à recouvrer, à force d'instances auprès des

Fleury's privilege of free election had an unusual history. King Charles the Bald visited Fleury in 845 upon the occasion of the death of its abbot, Boson. To fill the vacancy left by Boson's demise, Charles chose Raoul (Rudolph), Archbishop of Bourges, who already possessed numerous other abbeys besides this latest acquisition. The imposition of a commendatory abbot was not a new experience for Fleury, for as early as Charlemagne's period the emperor had reserved to himself the right of choosing the abbot of this community, having given it to Theodulph, Bishop of Orleans. History reports that the choice of Raoul was a happy one, for he was solicitous for the well-being of the community and used its great riches to found other monasteries. However, this represented a departure from the Benedictine Rule and an untold number of other abbeys underwent material and spiritual deteriorations as a result of the commendatory system. That Charles was aware of the incongruity of the royal imposition, especially since Benedict of Aniane had evidenced it a few years before, is plain, for he granted to Fleury the right to choose its own abbots, which privilege was to take effect upon the death of Raoul.[74] Similarly, Charles the Bald granted the Abbey of Flavigny to Bishop Adalguire.[75]

At times, when the privileges were not forthcoming, the monasteries fashioned their own, and passed them off as genuine.[76] But not to be outdone, the bishops did exactly the same in order to gain access to monastic rights or goods.[77] A tradi-

rois, le droit d'élire leur chef religieux et l'administrateur de leur temporel."

[74] Rocher, *Histoire de l'Abbaye Royale de Saint-Benoît-sur-Loire*, I, 85.

[75] De Charmasse, *Cartulaire de l'Eglise d'Autun* (3 vols, Autun, 1865), I, 11: "...sub serenitatem nostram deprecatus est ut Flaviniacum nostri juris abbatiam ubi beatissimus Christi Martyr Praejectus corpore requiescit, ad quam et Coriniacum aspicit, sancto Nazario Concederemus eamque aeternaliter et inviolabiliter ipsi episcopatui concederemus..."

[76] E.g., Fragmentum Historicum de Concilio Aquisgranensi (816)—*MGH, Constitutiones et Acta publica imperatorum et Regum*, Tom. I (ed. Ludwicus Weiland, Hannoverae, 1893), p. 632; Concilium Floriacense Spurium (839)—*ibid.*, p. 856.

[77] Deschamps, "Critique du Privilège Episcopal Accordé par Emmon de Sens à l'abbaye de Sainte-Colombe," *Le Moyen Age*, XXV (1912), p. 144: "On sait que les évêques de leur côté ne se privèrent pas d'exécuter des

tion, regardless of how it began, was strong enough to constitute a claim, and this claim was indisputable.[78] In all these grants, however, the bishops still retained to themselves the rights of blessing and ordination.[79] On the other hand, the proprietor, all through this period, was always to be understood as having first rights in the naming of the abbot and in the directing of the monastic policy. His power was greater always than that of the bishops, who through the abbatial blessing gained inroads into the abbeys in their elections and organization.[80] But it occasionally happened that the monks were able to insert into their charters the right of choosing their own consecrating bishops.[81]

From the sporadic and extremely locally operative nature of the legislation of this period one can delineate only a general notion of the situation existing in the bishop-abbot relations. Certain trends were quite apparent, however. The abbots,

chartes fausses à l'aide desquelles ils réclamaient la possession des abbayes..."

[78] Cf. De Lasteyrie, *L'Abbaye de Saint-Martial des Limoges* (Paris, 1901), 1901), p. 60: "Les abbés de Saint-Martiale avaient le suzeraineté du Château qui, d'après la tradition, leur aurait été donné par Louis le Pieux. Cette tradition, nous l'avons montré plus haut, repose sur un diplôme apocryphe; mais le fait même de cette suzeraineté n'est pas contestable."

[79] Letonnellier, *L'Abbaye Exempt de Cluny et le Saint-Siège*, p. 19: "En resumé, on peut dire que le premier exemple d'exemption n'est pas antérieur à la seconde moitié du VIIIe siècle. Même après cette époque, si l'on examine les privilèges les plus étendus, on peut voir qu'ils laissent encore les monastères sous la dépendance des évêques diocesains, et sous leur juridiction pour les cérémonies d'ordination et des bénédictions des autels et des églises."

[80] Lévy-Bruhl, *Elections Abbatiales*, p. 65: "...l'usage se répandit à partir du sixième siècle qu'il convenait de donner au nouvel abbé une bénédiction particulière. Cette bénédiction donnée par les évêques, était entre leurs mains une arme puissante qui leur permettait de paralyser les élections... L'abbé, nommé par le propriétaire devait, sans doute être béni par l'évêque, mais la volonté du propriétaire était toute-puissante. C'est seulement plus tard, au cours de la lutte entreprise par l'Eglise contre la propriété laïque, que l'évêque exerça sur le choix des abbés dans les monastères appartenant à des particuliers, une véritable collaboration."

[81] Imbart de la Tour, *Les Paroisses Rurales*, p. 100, "[In the ninth century] Quelques monastères pourtant firent insérer dans leurs chartes d'immunité une clause leur réservant le choix du prélat consécrateur."

bishops, and counts were principally the holders of honorary titles (*honores*), and these carried with them the right over the temporalities of the bishoprics or abbacies. The abbots realized an advancement in their position with respect to the bishops, but probably only as a result of the temporal acquisitions gained by the abbeys over which they were placed. The bishops still guarded the observance at the monasteries, but their effectiveness was stayed by the opposition of the abbots who were sufficiently influential to balk the bishops' authority when it becomes oppressive. Abbeys were becoming the centers of power and wealth rather than the bishoprics, and the office of bishop suffered a loss of prestige as a result. Because of the invasions, the elements of unity and order occasioned ever-present aspirations which were only imperfectly attainable. Privileges there were in abundance, but even these did not guarantee a complete assurance of the acquisition of permanent liberties, since the emperor or the proprietor could remove them almost as easily as he had granted them.[82]

The Church was in its monastic life ripe and ready for a complete reform.

[82] Lesne, *Histoire de la Propriété*, II, II, 129, "Les rois violent ces privileges aussi facilement qu'ils les confirment."

CHAPTER XI

TENTH CENTURY EUROPE AND CLUNY

The Church of tenth century Europe continued to display the pattern of profligacy into which it had lapsed through the unfortunate events and conditions of the previous period. But what might have been hoped by contemporaries to be a transient stage was, by lack of reform, becoming a habitual one.[1] The very institutions to which Christians might justly turn for strength and comfort in the practice of their faith had become so steeped in the vices of the age, that they proved in many cases to be more of a hindrance than a help. A thoroughgoing reform was badly needed, and the stage for such a reform was set by a council at Trosly (909) in the county of Soissons, northern France.

The council was called by Hervé, Archbishop of Rheims, who met with his suffragans to discuss the general state of the Church and to urge the return to a better practice of the faith. The various chapters of the council were shot through with pessimistic descriptions of the evils of the day. Chapter three spoke plaintively of the "lapse" rather than the state of the monasteries. It deplored the destruction wrought by the pagans, the presence of laymen in the monastic communities, and the participation of the monks and nuns and canons in secular activities prohibited by the sacred canons of the Church.

> De monasteriorum vero non statu, sed lapsu, quid dicere vel agere debeamus, jam pene ambigimus.

[1] Pignot, *Histoire de l'Ordre de Cluny depuis la fondation jusqu'à la mort de Pierre le Vénérable* (3 vols., Autun and Paris, 1868), I, 102: "La ruine des monastères, l'ignorance, la grosièreté, la vie licencieuse d'une grande partie du clergé, la simonie exercée par des hommes violents et dissolus, l'affaiblissement du respect envers la papauté, le pillage et les incendies des invasions normandes, la multitude d'êtres faibles et sans protection, moines, serfs, femmes et enfants, qui perissaient par les armes ou mouraient de misère, étaient, il faut en convenir, autant de fléaux qui menaçaient dans ses bases mêmes la civilisation chrétienne." Pignot's work will hereafter be cited as *Histoire de Cluny*.

Dum enim, mole criminum exigente, et judicium a domo Domini incipiente quaedam a Paganis succensa vel destructa, quaedam rebus spoliata, et ad nihilum prope sint redacta, si tamen quorumdam adhuc videntur superesse vestigia, nulla in eis regularis formae servantur instituta. Sive namque monachorum, seu canonicorum, seu sint sanctimonialium, propriis et sibi jure competentibus carent rectoribus, et dum contra omnem ecclesiae auctoritatem praelatis utuntur extraneis, in eis degentes, partim indigentia, partim malevolentia, maximeque inhabilium sibi praepositorum faciente inconvenientia, moribus vivunt incompositis . . . saecularia exercent. Prohibent quippe sacri canones, ne aliquis laicus de religione praesumat. Itemque et canonum praecipiunt instituta, simulque eorum pedissequa regum capitularia, sicut in libro primo capitulorum imperialium continentur, capitulo vigesimo octavo, "Ut clerici et monachi, si inter se negotium aliquod habuerint, a suo episcopo, judicentur, et non a saecularibus. Fas enim non est, ut divini muneris ministri temporalium potestatum subdantur arbitrio. Item: Ut laicis quam vis religiosis, nulla fit de rebus ecclesiae disponendi facultas. Item: Ut loca, quae semel Deo dicata sunt, aut monasteria sunt, maneant perpetuo monasteria, nec possint ultra fieri saecularium habitacula." Nunc autem in monasteriis Deo dicatis monachorum, canonicorum, et sanctimonialium, abbates laici, cum suis uxoribus, filiis, et filiabus, cum militibus morantur et canibus . . . etc.[2]

According to Mabillon[3] (1632-1707) the greatest necessity on the part of the monasteries was the restoration of regular abbots, whose incumbency had become a rarity in this period, as was mentioned in the previous chapter. That the Council of Trosly was instrumental in initiating such a reform as was

[2] Concilium Troslejanum (Apud Troslejum in Pago Suessonico) ab Heriveo Remensi archiepiscopo, ejusque suffrageneis celebratum die VI Kalendas Julias, anno Christi DCCCCIX. Sergii Papae anno II. Caroli Simplicis regis XVII; cap. 3—Mansi, XVIII, 270.

[3] *Annales*, III, 289.

about to take place in the monastic beginnings of Cluny was attested by the same Mabillon.[4] The bishops were not forgetful of their own responsibility, not only for the state of the monasteries but also for that of the Church as a whole. "We are called bishops, but we do not fulfil the episcopal duty."

> Omnis pene ordo, omnisque status ecclesiae confusus ac temeratus est. Denique ne nobis, inquiunt, parcere videamur, qui aliorum errata corrigere debemus; Episcopi dicimur, sed episcopale officium non implemus. Ministerium praedicationis relinquimus; eos qui nobis commissi sunt videmus Deum deserere, et in pravis actibus jacere: tacemus, nec eis manum correctionis tendimus.[5]

Nor were they unmindful of the guilt to be attributed to the throne for its part in the decadence, and accordingly they warned the royalty to act effectively in order to undo the harm caused by the invaders.[6]

A stronger statement of alarm could hardly have been issued by an episcopal assembly. Much had to be done, but this Council, even the while its members accused themselves of having been negligent, showed only a strong regret that conditions were as they were, without setting up the machinery to implement their *placita*. The centralization of authority under Charlemagne and the uniform reform undertaken by Louis the Pious and Benedict of Aniane could not have been operative at this hour, or the bishops would surely have recurred to them as the means wherewith to begin the reform. It is not surprising that the bishops later grasped at the straw of hope thrown to them by Cluny and gave the latter their wholehearted support.

> But out of the excess of evil good was to spring. In proportion as the lay world allowed itself to be thus carried away, and as the bishops and their clergy suffered the feudal spirit and customs to encroach upon

[4] L. d'Achery collegit et cum eo J. Mabillon edidit *Acta Sanctorum Ordinis S. Benedicti* (9 vols., Venetiis, 1733-38) (cited hereafter as Mabillon, *Acta*), Vol. VII, p. XV.

[5] Concilium Troslejanum—Mansi, XVIII, 266.

[6] Concilium Troslejanum—*ibid.*, p. 267.

> them more and more, the ascetic life came to present an ever stronger and deeper atrraction for all truly devout minds. The 10th century which saw the chair of Peter filled by a succession of the most unworthy popes, saw also the foundation of Cluny, and the great monastic reforms initiated and spread abroad by the monks of this order.[7]

The importance of this movement of monastic and general Church reform warrants a brief word of exposition to clarify the canonical activity involved during the period of its genesis.

To recall an allegation made earlier, the tenth century can hardly be treated in itself without an understanding of the existing state of canon law, since much of the thought of this century reflects that of the immediately preceding period. The principle is surely applicable in the case of Cluny, which mirrored not only the traditional ideas of monasticism (differing from some of them, however) but also revived the ideals espoused and propagated some hundred years before by the great reformer from Aniane, Benedict. According to de Valous[8] the classic historical treatments of the beginnings of Cluny have underplayed the importance of the first reform under Benedict of Aniane with relation to its bearing on Cluny.[9]

[7] Halphen, "The Church from Charlemagne to Sylvester II," *Cambridge Medieval History*, III, 456.

[8] *Le Monachisme Clunisien des Origines au XVe Siècle*, Vol. 1 (Ligugé, 1935), "L'Abbaye de Cluny; Les Monastères Clunisiens."

[9] de Valous (*op. cit.*) has castigated two of the great historical classics of Cluny's origins, that of Sackur (*Die Cluniacenser in ihrer kirchlichen und allgemeingeschlichtlichen Wirksamkeit bis zur Mitte des elften Jahrhunderts* [2 vols., Halle, 1892] and that of Pignot (*op. cit.*, I, *loc. cit.*). Of Pignot he said: "Un autre grave reproche que l'on peut faire à Pignot est de n'avoir pas vu que les conceptions de Cluny sont le résultat des idées de réforme mises en honneur un siècle auparavant par saint Benoît d'Aniane et que c'est bien plus à la doctrine de ce dernier qu'à celle de saint Benoît qu'il faut recourir pour comprendre et expliquer les institutions monastiques clunisiennes. La grande abbaye bourguignonne et ses filiales ne peuvent être envisagées comme formant un tout isolé du reste des maisons ou groupements de maisons bénédictiones contemporaines. Elles constituèrent au contraire un élément du vaste ensemble de mouvements de réforme à source d'inspiration commune des Xe et XIe siècles. Pour avoir méconnu ou ignoré ces divers mouvements monastiques qui souvent influèrent sur Cluny

However much the authors treat or ignore the prior reforms, the fact is undeniable that a continuity of development existed between the reform of Benedict of Aniane and that of Cluny in the person of Berno (850-927), the first Abbot of Cluny. This is admitted by all scholars today.[10]

Berno, according to Mabillon,[11] became a monk in the Abbey of Gigny, rather than in the Abbey of St. Martin of Autun, where, if he was ever a member of this community at all, he was affiliated only after taking the habit at Gigny. A later

autant qu'ils subirent l'action de son prestige ou de sa puissance, Pignot a incomplètement éclairé son tableau; souvent il a même de ce fait abouti à le fausser en expliquant tel ou tel point de la discipline clunisienne ou en comblant telle lacune par une prescription de la règle de saint Benoît quand il aurait fallu en chercher les raisons dans un passage des capitulaires de 817 du à l'initiative de saint Benoît d'Aniane ou d'un des coutumiers monastiques contemporains de la reforme clunisienne." (p. III). He notes likewise of Sackur, "Sackur, dont l'ouvrage est célèbre à juste titre et le fruit de recherche méritoires, se place surtout au point de vue de l'ordre de Cluny et de son expansion dans la chretienté. . . . Sackur n'a pas ignoré, à l'instar de ses devanciers, la pré-réforme de saint Benoît d'Aniane, mais il l'a exécutée de propos délibéré en deux pages (4-5), et pour faire la part plus belle à Cluny, il a également passé sous silence les tentatives antérieures de restauration monastique qui se sont suivies depuis Charlemagne jusqu'à l'époque de derniers Carolingiens." (pp. IV-V).

[10] Cf., e.g., Smith, *Monastery of Cluny* (London, 1920), p. 8: ". . . thus the chain runs from Monte Cassino to Glanfeuil, from Glanfeuil to St. Savin's, Poitiers, from St. Savin's to St. Martin's, Autun, from St. Martin's to Baume, and hence to Cluny;" Symons, *Regularis Concordia—The Monastic Agreement of the Monks and Nuns of the English Nations* (New York: Oxford Univ. Press, 1953), p. XLVII; "Benedict of Aniane had left his mark on the whole of western monasticism, and his ideas underlay, in a general way, all the continental reforms of more than a century later;" Graham, *English Ecclesiastical Studies*, p. 1: "The customs which the monks of Baume brought to Cluny were those of Benedict of Aniane." The monk John, biographer of Odo, second Abbot of Cluny, indicated as much when he said: Euticius (Benedict of Aniane) instituted those customs which have hitherto been observed in our monasteries."—*MPL*, CXXXIII, 93. Naberhaus (*op. cit.*, p. 75) wrote: "Wenn durch Odo von Cluny Frankreich im frühen Mittelalter Führer der Kultur Europas geworden ist, weil adeliges Blut, monastische Frömmigkeit und karolingische Renaissance diese Kultur herbeigeführt haben, so ist dies wohl auf Benedikt zurüchzuführen, da Cluny in seiner Reform nichts Neues ist, sondern nur die Übernahme der Gedanken Benedikts von Aniane."

[11] *Annales*, III, 310 ff.

account, which differed from Mabillon's assertion that Berno was sent from Gigny to Baume to reform this abbey, indicates that, since the Abbey of St. Martin was flourishing in this period, Berno rather adopted some of the customs of Benedict of Aniane, which this abbey had received from St. Savin of Poitiers, and carried them to Gigny.[12] From Gigny, apparently, Berno as abbot went to Baume, one of the monasteries most lacking in discipline, and reformed it, implanting there many of the traditions of Benedict of Aniane, with which he was imbued. At Baume, Berno was able to revivify the formation introduced by the earlier reformer, and, becoming well-versed in the life himself, to continue this formation through his new monastic reform.

These early peregrinations of Berno are under somewhat of a cloud, however,[13] so that Jean de Valois[14] presented a somewhat different development, putting the founding of Gigny after that of Baume.[15] He showed with Mabillon that Berno, at an unknown date, entered the monastery of St. Martin of Autun. This monastery was restored in 870 by the count Badillon, a lord of the court of Charles the Bald, and led a flourishing and edifying Benedictine life. New monks came from St. Savin-sur-Gartempe near Poitiers, which was still living the reformed Benedictine life instituted there by Benedict of Aniane. After this new reform had been brought into

[12] *Gallia Christiana*, IV, 1122: "Ritus autem ejusmodi haud aliunde Berno accepisse censendus est quam a vicino Eduensi S. Martini coenobio, quod religione tum florentissimum erat, eo derivata per coloniam eductam e S. Savini monasterio apud Pictones, uno ex illis monasteriis quae Benedicti Anianensis imbuta fuerant institutis."

[13] Schmitz, *Histoire de l'Ordre*, I, 130: "De la vie de Bernon on connaît fort peu de chose..."

[14] "Sur quelques points d'histoire relatifs à la fondation de Cluny," *Millenaire de Cluny* (Mâcon, 1910), p. 200.

[15] *Op. cit., loc. cit.*: "De là, tout naturellement, on en vint à regarder la fondation de Gigny, non seulement comme antérieure à Baume, ce que tous les historiens s'obstinent à répéter, mais encore, comme accomplie par Bernon, en se faisant moine. Ce qui aurait eu lieu après la mort de son père; et la chose n'est aucunement prouvée...La fondation de Baume, antérieure à celle de Gigny, ruine toutes ces hypothèses, ou, pour mieux dire, ces invraisemblances." Schmitz (*Histoire de l'Ordre*, I, 130) follows the same pattern.

St. Martin from St. Savin, monks, one of whom was Berno, went to Baume and reformed that abbey according to the methods propagated by Benedict of Aniane. They chose Berno as their abbot. The abbey flourishing, Berno felt free to found another monastery on the territory owned by his family at Gigny. That Baume was subject to Gigny, so Valois explained, was not strange, nor did it date Gigny's foundation as prior to that of Baume, for Berno regarded Gigny with a specially gracious consideration, and hence placed it above Baume, even though it was founded later.[16]

Sackur rejected this exposition on the basis of insufficient evidence.[17] A later author, Evans, preferred Sackur's opinion, which seemed the more likely one to hold.[18] But since in either case, whether it was at Baume or at St. Martin that Berno caught the spirit of the first reformer, a link was formed between Cluny and the earlier reformer, and this conclusion is now the common acknowledgment of all.

[16] De Valois, *art. art.*, p. 207: "...le secret attachement qu'il portait, de façon toute naturelle, à ce qui était chez lui oeuvre personnelle..."

[17] *Die Cluniacenser*, I, 37: "Durchaus zweifelhaft ist nun das Verhältnis des Autuner Klosters zu dem Mutterstift Clunis, der Abtei Baume in der Diocese Besançon. Dass Beziehungen zwischen Baume und St. Martin bestanden haben, wird nicht nur von verschiedenen Seiten überliefert, es ist auch durchaus wahrscheinlich angesichts der Tatsache, dass die in Baume befolgten Vorschriften die des hl. Benedict von Aniane waren, wie wir noch sehen werden. Während aber nach einer unserer Quellen Baume von Autuner Mönchen reformiert wurde, die einen von ihnen, Berno, zum Abt wählen, erfahren wir von anderer Seite, dass Berno, ein reicher und vornehmer Burgunder, noch Laie war, als er mit sienem Vetter Laifinus auf eigenem Grund und Boden die Abtei Gigny im Sprengel Mâcon gründete, und reichlich austattete. Erst nachher sei er in Gigny Mönch und Abt geworden und schlieslich auch in den Besitz von Baume gekommen. Dass Baume später von Gigny abhängig war, bestätigen auch die Urkunden, aber wenigstens eine von ihnen begünstigt die Auffassung, dass die Widerherstellung von Baume vor die von Gigny fällt und dass Berno, der bereits während des Aufbaues dieser Abtei den Abttitel führe, vorher anderwarts das Mönchskleid genommen hatte."

[18] Evans, *Monastic Life at Cluny*, 910-1157 (London, 1931), p. 3: "The other account of his (Berno's) life, that makes him a monk of Saint-Savin near Poitiers, sent with seventeen others to restore the abbey of St. Martin at Autun, and thence sent to reform Baume, seems less worthy of credence, since in later history Baume was dependent on Gigny."

Against the canonical legislation of the day[19] Berno as abbot ruled the two abbeys of Gigny and Baume simultaneously. In order to assure the fullness of freedom from extraneous influence in instituting a strong monastic life in these two houses, he traveled to Rome and obtained a grant of full immunity for both communities, with regard both to tithes and to the authorities outside of the Holy See.[20]

His success in ruling these two communities was probably the leading element which moved William II, Duke of Aquitaine and Count of Auvergne (d. 926), to invite him to Mâcon to discuss plans for the founding of a new monastery on the basis of donations of land under his patrimony.[21] After some discussion on the location of the new enterprise, terms were finally agreed upon, and in 910 William added his signature to the charter bringing Cluny into existence.[22] For purposes of ratification, William himself journeyed to Rome and contributed the first payment of dues to John XI (914-928), as recognition of Cluny's subjection to the pope alone.[23]

[19] Amann-Dumas, *L'Eglise au Pouvoir des Laïques*, p. 321: "Le droit canonique interdisait qu'un même abbé dirigeât plusieurs monastères. Cette prohibition avait été rappelée par le pseudo-Isidore qui l'avait appuyée de textes faux. On n'y avait plus égard: les plus puissants des ducs et des comtes cumulaient un grand nombre d'abbayes. Nul ne pouvait songer à blâmer un abbé régulier de faire la même chose dans l'intérêt de la discipline." Although appearing in the Pseudo-Isidorian decretals, the prohibition also appeared in earlier legislation, e.g., in the Council of Agde (506), cap. 38—Bruns, II, 154. Cf. also Mabillon, *Acta*, VII, 66; the Council of Trosly (909), cap. 3—Mansi, XVIII, 270.

[20] Mabillon, *Acta*, VII, 66. Cf. also, Sackur, *Die Cluniacenser*, I, 37; Evans, *Monastic Life at Cluny*, p. 3.

[21] Evans, *op. cit.*, p. 4.

[22] William was reluctant to relinquish the grounds chosen by Berno because of the premium he placed on them as his choicest hunting grounds, but Berno silenced them with the remark: "Drive your hounds hence, and put monks in their places; for you know which will serve you better before God—the baying of hounds or the prayers of monks."—Evans, *op. cit.*, p. 4. Cf. Mabillon, *Acta*, V, 94.

[23] Jaffé, n. 3584 (2744), (Bull of John XI confirming the statute of Cluny): "Monasterii Cluniacensis libertatem bonaque, petente Odone abbate, confirmat, et privilegia instituat ea lege "ut dentur per quinquennium decem solidi." Cf. also, *MPL*, CXXXII, 1055; Pignot, *Histoire de Cluny*, I, 34.

The charter of Cluny indicated rather the intentions of William regarding the abbey than any actual deed of law, since it would have needed Church sanction to permit the full liberty conceded by it. Among its provisions were included the insistence that the Benedictine Rule be followed by the abbot and monks who would possess the abbey. William reserved to himself the right of choosing the first abbot, which was not a difficult choice for him, since he had personally invited Berno to come, and naturally expected him to institute a regular discipline in the community. After Berno's death, the members of the community were able to elect their own abbot without interference from any other authority. In temporal things the abbey was to be completely immune from external powers, whether such powers derived from secular or from ecclesiastical sources. Not even the Pope could disturb the monastery in its temporal regime, although Cluny was theoretically subject to him, and placed under his protection. The manifestation of this protection was a token payment of annual dues, as mentioned above.

Perhaps its most important grant[24] was that of being completely free of outside interference in its government. The abbot and monastery were to possess the abbey and its property, which were to be in no way vulnerable to the authority of another. Other abbeys before Cluny had received immunity from the interference of external powers. Bobbio and Fulda had been placed under the direct protection of the Holy See. But in these former cases such privileges were exceptional and limited to a single monastery because of its excellent discipline or contributions to the Church. In Cluny's case the original charter became the proto-type after which were modeled the many charters of the monastic foundations begun or reformed by Cluny.

The deed was further sanctioned with the invoking of a dire curse upon anyone who dared to violate its provisions. Because of the charter's importance, its actual wording should in part be attended to.

[24] Smith, *Monastery of Cluny*, pp. 12 ff.

. . . Eo siquidem dono tenore, ut in Clugniaco in honore sanctorum Petri et Pauli monasterium regulae construatur, ibique monachi juxta Regulam beati Benedicti viventes congregentur, qui res ipsas perennis temporibus possideant, teneant, habeant, (atque) ordinent, ita dumtaxat, ut ibi venerabile orationis domicilium votis ac supplicationibus fideliter frequentetur, conversatioque caelestis omni desiderio et ardore intimo perquiratur et expectatur. Sedulae quoque orationes, postulationes . . . tam pro me, quam pro omnibus, sicut eorum memoria superius digesta est. Praecipimus . . . ut . . . nostra donatio ad perpetuum refugium, qui pauperes de saeculo egressi . . . ut supplementum fiat abundantis illorum. Sintque ipsi monachi cum omnibus praescriptis rebus sub potestate et dominatione Bernonis abbatis, qui, quamdiu vixerit . . . presideat. Post discessum vero ejus, habeant iidem monachi potestatem . . . secundum placitum Dei atque Regulam sancti Benedicti promulgatam, eligere quem maluerint Abbatem atque Rectorem, ita ut nec nostra, nec alicujus potestatis contradictione contra religiosam dumtaxat electionem impediantur. Per quinquennium autem Romae ad limina Apostolorum, ad luminaria concinnanda decem solidos praefati monachi persolvant, habeantque tuitionem ipsorum Apostolorum, atque Romani Pontificis defensionem, et ipsi monachi corde et animo pleno praelibatum locum pro posse et nosse suo aedificent . . . Placuit etiam huic testamento inseri, ut ab hac die nec nostro, nec parentum nostrorum, nec fastibus regiae magnitudinis, nec cujuslibet terrenae potestatis jugo subjiciantur iidem monachi ibi congregati; neque aliquis Principum saecularium, non comes quisquam, non episcopus quilibet, non Pontifex supradictae sedis Romanae . . . Non distrahat, non minuat, non procamiet, [sic] non beneficiet alicui, non aliquem Praelatum super eos contra eorum voluntatem constituat . . . Si qui forte (quod absit . . .) aliquam concussionem inferre tentaverit, primum quidem iram omnipotentis Dei incurrat, etc.[25]

Pignot noted that[26] the exemption from all jurisdiction did not constitute common law, nor even did it reflect the tenor of the Rule of St. Benedict. The latter law-giver had left to the diocesan bishop the right of surveillance over the election of the abbots and over the monks, a right thus far not abandoned—even by Benedict of Aniane. In the eventuality that an unworthy abbot was chosen, St. Benedict the lawgiver provided that the bishop use his spiritual authority to unseat him, and the community was to attend to the counsel of neighboring abbots and even the Christian people to choose one who might better serve as the head of the monastery.[27] However, since the monasteries were looked upon as rich prizes by many bishops, who might be tempted to impound their temporalities, the Rule of St. Benedict offered many dangers to the community's well-being. The one way of averting this jeopardy was to place the abbeys under the protection of the pope, and thus to provide for the safeguarding of the regular life.[28]

Though Berno was well established in Cluny, when he foresaw his approaching death he feared that his efforts might be undone by the monks' choosing a successor who would fail to continue the policy he had initiated. Ignoring both the provision of the Rule of St. Benedict, and the *placita* of Wil-

[25] A. Bernard and A. Bruel, *Recueil des Charles de l'Abbaye de Cluny* (6 vols., Paris, 1876-1903) (Cited hereafter as Bruel), I, 124 (112).

[26] *Op. cit.*, I, 21, ff.

[27] *Rule of St. Benedict*, Ch. 64.

[28] Pignot, *Histoire de Cluny*, I, 22: "La dignité épiscopale était le but de l'ambition et des intrigues des laïques ou des clercs; on y vit élever, par la protection des rois, des ducs et des comtes, des gens de guerre, des gens mariés, ayant femme, enfants et concubines, des clercs sortis à peine de l'enfance, dépourvus d'instruction, de moralité, d'intelligence, n'appartenant à l'Eglise que par leur habit. Comment pouvait-on compter sur leur zèle pour maintenir la vie chrétienne dans les seuls asiles où elle eût trouvé un refuge? De là, les exemptions demandées au profit des monastères par leur fondateurs, exemptions qui étaient devenues générales au dixième siècle, et que les papes accordèrent comme le seul moyen de sauver la regularité, et avec elle l'idéal de la vie chrétienne."

liam's charter, he chose his own successor, Odo (879-943), whom he knew to concur in the desire to extend the influence of this reform. Likewise, Berno not only chose Cluny for his burial, but in his will he gave over to Cluny some of the property from Gigny. This act of alienation was not only unusual, in that it took wealth from one monastery to bring it to another, but it also violated the current canonical legislation as sanctioned by past councils and reiterated in the recent bull of Pope Formosus (891-896), forbidding all alienations of property on the part of the religious establishments.[29] The testament was challenged by Widon, Abbot of Gigny. Abbot Odo (927-943), successor to Berno, carried the matter to Rome for a settlement. Pope John X, who had equal authority over both monasteries since they were each under his protection, wrote to King Rudolph II of Burgundy (d. 937), to Guy, Archbishop of Lyons, to Stateo, Bishop of Chalon, to Berno, Bishop of Macon, to Gislebert, Bishop of Vergy, and to others to carry out the provision of the will.[30] Widon, opposed by these, consented to the provisions of the testament, conditioning his acquiescence on the fact that, if the Cluniac monks decided to follow the common canonical practice rather than to rely on their special privilege and papal protection, then the possession was to devolve to Gigny, from which it had been taken.

Thus Cluny began its existence upon a foundation not entirely consonant with the current law and practice, but rather in line with particular usages as based upon those of Benedict of Aniane, and upon the particular expediencies of the new foundation—all of which permitted it better to devote itself to the monastic discipline. There was being formed a tradition which was to mold the later development of the monastery. Founded by a layman, it owed much to the emperor and the nobles, and depended largely upon the temporal power to sustain it. Placed under Rome, it was removed from all diocesan

[29] Jaffé, n. 3497 (anno 893); cf. also Pignot, *op. cit.*, I, 129.

[30] Jaffé, n. 3578 (2741) (anno 928); Cf. also Mabillon, *Annales*, III, 393. Marrier—Des Chesne (*Bibliotheca Cluniacensis* [Mâcon, 1915], p. 2) erroneously attributed this last work to Pope John XI (931-935).

control. It possessed a unique canonical status, which was clearly underlined by the practices which will receive closer consideration in the following pages.

CHAPTER XII

BISHOPS AND CLUNIAC ABBOTS (910-950)

Abbot Berno undertook Cluny's government with a hand perhaps as free from external interference as any abbot before his time had had. Cluny could choose its own abbots; it was relieved of the fear of encroachment from all outside powers with regard to its temporalities, and claimed an almost nominal submission to the Holy See, which had been weakened by many disintegrating influences. Cluny was still not completely exempt from the bishop in his exercise of spiritual power over the abbey. It was to realize this exemption only at the end of the tenth century.[1] As to any potential external disturbances from lay powers, Cluny could not have been better located, since it was situated on the border between France and Germany, and safely distanced from the power of either monarch. In these peaceful conditions, Cluny developed its own customs, based upon the practices of Benedict of Aniane, as is affirmed by the Cluniac monk John, biographer of Abbot Odo.[2]

Berno ruled, besides Baume, Gigny and Cluny itself, the monasteries of Déols, Massay and Mouthier-en-Bresse.[3] Although this conflicted with the canonical practice of the day, the policy added greatly to the reform pretensions.[4]

Odo followed Berno as abbot in 927. Under his regime the number of dependent foundations numbered seventeen.[5] Aymard

[1] Schmitz, *Histoire de l'Ordre*, I, 131.

[2] Joannes (Monachus), "Sanctus Odo Abbas Cluniacensis," *MPL*, CXXXIII, 54: "Ipse enim pater Euticius institutor fuit harum consuetudinum quae hactenus in nostris monasteriis habentur." Ibidem (note), "Euticium seu Euticum hunc non alium esse a Benedicto abbate Aniancensi ostensum est supra." Modern authors agree that Euticius must be identified as Benedict of Aniane.

[3] *Gallia Chrsitiana*, IV, 1122; II, 142; II, 148; Sackur, *Die Cluniacenser*, I, 63-64.

[4] Mabillon, *Acta*, VII, 66; Amann-Dumas, *L'Eglise au Pouvoir des Laïques*, p. 321.

[5] Graham, *English Ecclesiastical Studies*, p. 7.

began his short reign in 943 after Odo's demise. It seems that only two monasteries came under Cluny's jurisdiction while he was in office.[6] During the terms of these first abbots Cluny had assuredly assumed a moral leadership in Europe which gave it the prestige necessary to affect also the canonical field through its relations with external powers, and also in the very customs formed within the monastic sphere itself. The present chapter will discuss the canonical developments stemming from the unique organization of Cluny. From concrete individual incidents it will be seen why Cluny was to take the lead in the formation of canonical evolution regarding the monastic life in the first years after its foundation.

Much of Cluny's success can be attributed to the active assistance of the bishops without which the reform would have been rendered, if not impossible, at least extremely difficult. To their assistance likewise can be attributed Cluny's complete coup d'état in the struggle for monastic autonomy. This is evidenced in the actual consignment to Cluny of abbeys, newly founded or revived, by the bishops; in the granting by them of privileges to the Cluniac houses; in the bishops' confirmation and sanctioning of donations and exemptions emanating from the secular powers, and in their many small manifestations of friendliness, which all facilitated Cluny's struggles to maintain a physical existence and to form a stabilized monastic policy of reform, which was itself the nucleus of canonical customary law.

Berno, the first abbot, was mainly interested in establishing the motherhouse of Cluny. No apparent episcopal resistance was shown to the charter of William of Aquitaine, and Cluny had a free rein to pursue its intended course. Shortly after its foundation, Berno, Bishop of Mâcon (928-936), openly proclaimed his friendly interest in the Cluniac movement.[7] Before abbot Berno's death, Bishop Turpio of Limoges, impressed with the talents and sanctity of the future abbot of Cluny, Odo, asked him to write several treatises on spiritual subjects.

[6] Smith, *The Monastery of Cluny*, p. 91.

[7] "In quantum possumus solaciari."—Bruel, I, 373 (p. 350); Cf. also Smith, *op. cit.*, p. 52.

Odo acquiesced in his petitions, but only with the permission of his abbot, Berno, as required by the Rule of St. Benedict.[8]

According to Mabillon,[9] Berno is to be remembered for two things, the founding of Cluny and the institution of the famous second abbot of the monastery. The incidents relative to this latter occurrence are illustrative of one of Cluny's privileges, that of choosing its own abbot. Foreseeing his approaching death, Berno invited the neighboring bishops and sought their advice about the choice of a new abbot, besides asking them to witness his own resignation. This was thoroughly in keeping with the Benedictine Rule,[10] although, as indicated above, Berno had himself indicated his preference. When the choice fell upon Odo, the latter resisted the vote, and accepted only when he was threatened with excommunication by the bishops.[11] The actual abbatial blessing was given by Berengar of Besançon.[12]

The procedure in Cluniac elections followed the pattern in vogue in the individual houses, slight differences being notable from one monastery to the next. The Cluniacs met to choose their abbot, installed him and then called upon the bishop consecrator to confer the blessing on the abbot. The consecrator could be any bishop upon whom the predilection of the abbot and monks fell, and this very privilege was one of the principal ones possessed by Cluny. Vézelay required its abbots to go to Rome to receive the blessing directly from the Pope, while Saint-Martial of Limoges accepted a bishop for the purpose designated by the Pope.

The consecrating or some other bishop first of all ratified the election of the new abbot before a meeting of the monastic chapter. He solemnly asked the chapter members three times

[8] Reg. LVII: "If there be skilled workmen in the monastery, let them work at their art in all humility, if the Abbot giveth his permission." Cf. also "Sancti Odonis Collationum, Libri Tres," *MPL*, CXXXIII, 518.

[9] *Acta*, VII, 66.

[10] Reg. LXIV.

[11] "...et superatus tandem Episcoporum excommunicatione, ordinatus est abbas paullo ante obitum Bernonis..." Mabillon, *Acta*, VII, 127. Cf. also Mabillon, *Acta*, VII, 193.

[12] Sackur, *Die Cluniacenser*, I, 65.

if there was any objection from the chapter constituents to the proposed candidates. Silence signified the absence of such objections. The blessing then followed. There seemed to be no canonical precept that demanded the confirmation of the abbot by the bishop, but such a confirmation seemed to be a matter of convention, and served mainly to publicly proclaim the act accomplished by the abbey exclusively.[13]

Bishop Berno in 929 confirmed the possession by Cluny of four churches whose possession had been disputed in the time of his predecessor, Hildebald, who according to Pignot, on scanty evidence,[14] consecrated the first abbey church at Cluny. These were the churches of Saint-Martin de Langres, Blanot, Jalogny, and Cropte. He also granted to Cluny the right to the tithes which in the charter were rightfully claimed to be his own.[15] Rudolph of Burgundy, a secular prince, reaffirmed the decree of Bishop Berno of Mâcon which granted to Cluny the rights over these tithes, and no one was to attempt to divert these to his own use.[16] In the original confirmation by Berno, at the end of the document, appear the signatures of Berno and a number of witnesses. After the same occurs the note that the charter was negotiated publicly.[17] This formula and similar ones which attest their being publicly authorized were in vogue at that time, and added a note of solemnity and

[13] de Valous, *Le Monachisme Clunisien*, I, 99; Cf. also Pignot, *Histoire de Cluny*, I, 195.

[14] Pignot, *op. cit.*, I, 34. Cf., on the consecration of the church of Cluny, De Valois, "Fondation de Cluny," *Millenaire de Cluny*, p. 209, (note): "...Que l'ancienne église ait été, comme le prétend Pignot, consacrée par Hildebald, évêque de Mâcon, c'est possible, mais on n'en a aucune preuve. Ce qui paraît certain, c'est que l'église consacrée en 910—si elle l'a été par un évêque de Mâcon, n'a pu l'être que par Géraud, dont l'évêque Bernon fait mention dans son accord de 929 avec Cluny." Cf. also *Gallia Christiana*, IV, 1048 ff.

[15] "...placuit tam mihi quam omni nostrae congregationi ut quicquid vel ad episcopum vel ad archidiaconem de ipsis ecclesiis pertinet, excepto hoc quod ad synodales eulogias vel ad paroctam (paratam) debetur, totum habitatoribus predicti loci concedamus, ita ut ipsas ecclesias vel decimas, vel tenere, vel dare, sine ullius contradictione valeant..."—Bruel, I, 373 (p. 350).

[16] Smith, *op. cit.*, p. 50.

[17] "...apud Matisconensem urbem publice."—Bruel, I, 373 (p. 350).

firmness to the document. Violators of the contract were made answerable to the public officials, since the notice of the act had been publicly made to all.[18] For this reason many of the charters that were issued in favor of Cluny bore the seal of having been publicly witnessed, and included mention frequently of the names of bishops, of the abbot, or of officials in the diocese, with the titles of the offices they held. In the case of a dispute, such a form was preferable to a mere private one, which could be disparaged by doubtful spectators. The document was honored in either forum, the civil as well as the ecclesiastical, for at this time a sharp line had not been drawn between the two forums.

When in 933 several Cluniac brothers wished to build and maintain a chapel at Salustriac, they called upon Bishop Berno to consecrate it, and asked rights over the tithes as an endowment for its support. Consulting with the chapter of canons, he gave the brothers permission to accept and use the tithes of this church, including also the ones from all the land given by the king in Salustriac and the surrounding country which belonged at one time to St. Peter's Massiacus, half likewise to the tithes from Bulon, and in addition other tithes from Salustriac and Bulon which yielded to St. Julian's Rocca, to which the new chapel was subject. Although the tithes were granted in their entirety, the bishop still retained a measure of control over the church, by imposing a nominal tax of 2 *denarii* in "*eulogiae*" and 12 *denarii* in "*paratae*," which were to be paid at the time of the synodal meeting by the priest in charge of the chapel. So solicitous was the bishop for the good of the monks and the servicing of the chapel, that he asked his successors to maintain the terms he had established in the contract.[19] The *eulogiae* constituted a small gift of what-

[18] Pignot, I, 25: "*Actum publice*...n'était point une simple donation, une libéralité dont l'une des parties était libre d'user dans un sens plus ou moins conforme aux intentions du donateur; c'était un contrat contenant des stipulations réciproques, obligatoires, révocables en cas d'inexécution; c'était un acte passé en présence du peuple...et cette publicité solennelle lui imprimait ce caractère d'authenticité...plaçant les contrats sous le sceau du pouvoir public."

[19] Bruel, I, 408 (p. 393); Cf. also, Smith, *op. cit.*, p. 51.

ever kind, in this case money to be presented to the bishop, while the *paratae* covered the expenses involved in receiving bishops and archdeacons in their visits to these small rural churches.[20] They corresponded to the more usual *Cathedraticum* and *procuratio*. Here, as in most cases, the bishop, as the donor, expressed the hope that he and the monks benefited might share in each others' prayers and good works.

It should not be thought queer that so much importance be placed on the privileges granted to the Abbey of Cluny itself, since the same or similar privileges were granted to the monasteries dependent upon or reformed by Cluny. With the possession of each new house, an added amount of power was given to the Abbot of Cluny, who held the other houses under his control, placing therein co-abbots or priors who were subject to him. The congregational plan made uniform the customs and privileges extant in each house. It is not far from true what Mabillon noted concerning this work of Odo, namely, that what Benedict of Aniane had initiated in France and what Pachomius before him had begun in the East, was perfected under Odo, the second Abbot of Cluny.[21]

When Cluny reformed a monastery, however, this did not automatically make it a dependent of Cluny, nor did it add to its temporal stature. The reformed houses actually could remain autonomous and unaffiliated with Cluny, although they did, of course, reflect the customs and spirit given them by Cluny.[22] The new abbeys, whether annexed to Cluny or remaining autonomous, and many of which had been built by the counts and other nobles, received through the concession of these benefactors the same rights as Cluny, or rights analogous to those of Cluny. Hence it was not a question of Cluny's imposing such rights by the mere fact that a new house became affiliated with Cluny in the congregational plan, or had been reformed by Cluny. The charters of dependent monasteries and of many reformed independent ones modeled their charters after those of previous times, often after Cluny's, and

[20] Smith, *op. cit.*, p. 52, (note).
[21] Mabillon, *Acta*, VII, 136.
[22] Evans, *Monastic Life at Cluny*, pp. 10 ff.

hence it is not mere coincidence that many are similar one to another.

As an example of this one may point to the charter of the monastery of Romainmoutier, at Orbe in Upper Burgundy, which was placed under the Cluniac system by Adelaide, a Burgundian countess. The charter placed the monastery under the control of Odo, who was to rule as abbot over both houses. It granted the abbey whatever privileges had been given to Cluny itself by the Holy See, which was to be its protector. The monks could elect their own abbot according to the Rule of St. Benedict, but not without the consent of the other abbey. Personnel and likewise temporal goods could freely be exchanged in aid of the other abbey, if such need arose and if it seemed necessary and useful in the judgment of the Abbot of Cluny. All accrued alms or offerings of whatever kind were to be retained by the abbot of the monastery and the monks in order to be used for charitable purposes. No taxes were to be levied against the monastery, and it was not to be subject to any external power in temporal things, not even to the Roman Pontiff himself.

> . . . notum sit, quod ego Adeleydis, dono dei comitissa . . . monasterium quod Romanis vocatur . . . de meo jure et dominatione ipsa ego jam dicta Adeleydis in dominium et providentiam monachorum per omni transfundo, id est Odonis venerabilis . . . abbatis, omniumque fratrum . . . sub ejus regimini Cluniacensis coenobii degentium, ipsum monasterium . . . reformare. . . . abbas, dum advixerit, et . . . monachi idem monasterium ita possideant, tot quamvis apostolicae Sedi, sicut et Cluniacum delegatum sit; semper tamen velut una congregatio sub uno agant atque disponantur abbate; in tantum ut cum ipse discesserit, non illis aut istis liceat sine communi consensu abbatem sibi praeficere; nec privati, quod absit, isti alium nisi ipsum, quem illi habuerint, substituere praesumant; quoniam valde injustum esset, si illi qui forte velut filii Romanis monasterio succreverint, socialitatem Cluniacensium, qui veluti patres locum resuscitant,

> aliquando discederint. Sane in ordinando Abbate constitutio sancti Benedicti semper emineat . . . De fratribus vero vel hinc illic vel inde huc pro utilitatem transmutandis, sive etiam de subsidiis, quae forte uni loco plusquam alteri abundaverint, vicissim ex altero in alterum transferendis in potestate Abbatis fit. Et ut inter eos germanior societas perseveret, ipsas quoque divinae servitutis aut eleemosynarum seu cujuslibet boni operis sanctiones ita communiter teneant, ut quod pro bonae memoriae Willelmo, vel certe aliis, ut vivis, aut defunctis apud Cluniacum geritur, nobis atque nostratibus proficiat . . . Placuit etiam huic testamento inseri, ut ab hac die nec nostro, nec parentum nostrorum, nec fastibus regiae magnitudinis, nec cujuslibet terrenae potestatis, jugo subjiciantur iidem Monachi ibi congregati; neque aliquis Principum saecularium, non Comes quisquem, nec Episcopus quilibet, non Pontifex supradictae urbis Romanae, per Dominum et in Domino, omnes Sanctos ejus, et tremendi judicii diem contestor et deprecor, invadat res ipsorum Dei servorum, non distrahat, non minuat, non procamiet, non beneficiet alicui, non aliquem Praelatum super eos contra eorum voluntatem consituat . . .[23]

The mention of William of Aquitaine leads one to believe that a copy of the document written by him was in the hands of the donor of this abbey, and laid before the donor as a model form. In this and other donations, consultations could then have been held with the representatives of Cluny to make sure that uniformity would exist in the rights and exemptions of new additions to the Cluniac congregation. One has only to compare this cited charter with that of the previous chapter to notice the similarities. Therefore, what was granted to the monastery in the diocese of Mâcon became extended to other dioceses, not directly by episcopal sanction, but by the will of the donors, with only the passive permission of the bishops for the stipulations annexed to the charters. Many things

[23] Mabillon, *Acta*, VII, 132.

could have been responsible for the ready acceptance of such charters by the bishops. A reform was necessary, and to oppose a Cluniac monastery could have seemed like opposition to the reform itself. Nobody questioned the efficacy of the reform undertaken by Cluny, and its prestige carried much weight before possible opponents. The Popes supported the movement, and to oppose Cluny seemed like opposing the Pope. Then, too, when powerful nobles donated churches or monasteries to Cluny, there was small thought on the part of ecclesiastical power to oppose the civil power, especially in so far as the action by the latter was contemplated with charitable motives.

In 938, Bishop Berno's successor, Maimbod (937-962), granted a charter almost identical with the one given by Bishop Berno in 929. Offering as his reason the great damage wrought by the invaders, Maimbod reduced the dues of the *eulogiae* to one *denarius* for each church, and to 5 *denarii* for the *paratae*, besides remitting completely the said dues with regard to other churches.[24] Like his predecessor, Maimbod expressed his friendship with Cluny and indicated the concurring of the cathedral chapter of canons with his action.[25]

Odo had another episcopal benefactor in Turpio of Limoges, the same one who requested him to write the spiritual treatises. In this neighboring diocese of Limoges, through the efforts of Turpio and his brother Aimo, Abbot of St. Martial of Limoges, Odo was made Abbot of Aurillac in 928. The abbey had been steeped in vices as a result of the exploits of two former abbots, who had themselves been protected from interference from the outside by a grant of immunity accorded them by papal indulgence. The bishop and his brother disregarded this immunity, and Odo as abbot went ahead with the reform, setting over the abbey a co-abbot, Arnulf. Aimo, pleased with the results obtained by Odo, placed the Abbey of Tulle under his guidance, and thereby superseded the rights of

[24] Bruel, I, 484 (p. 467).

[25] *Loc. cit.*: "...quia Cluniacensis coenobii congregationem speciali nobis familiaritate conjunctam...ut ipsorum bonis operibus...perticipemur. Siquidem, tempore predecessoris nostri, beatae memoriae Bernonis episcopi, tam ipsius quam nostrorum omnium consensu..."

St. Savin's monastery in Poitiers, which had held Tulle under its jurisdiction. Rudolph II of Lower Burgundy (d. 937) backed the move by disclaiming the rights of St. Savin's and by turning them over to Odo as the new abbot, the latter in turn appointing a co-abbot to rule in his stead. Bishop Turpio likewise aided in the reformation of two other monasteries in the Limoges diocese, St. Martial and St. Augustine, which were placed under another abbot, Martin, of St. Cyprian's in Poitiers.[26] Besides these monasteries, Odo in 937 reformed St. Peter le Vif, in Sens; and St. Julian's, in Tours, which had been endowed by Archbishop Teotolo of Tours. Odo likewise restored St. Paul's outside the Walls and other Roman and Italian monasteries.[27] Maimbod's relations were so friendly with abbot Odo, that on one occasion he is found asking Odo to witness a transaction made with a certain Aycardus and his wife concerning a piece of land in the villa Artiduno.[28]

In 936 Odo was asked by Raymond Pontius of Toulouse, the nephew of Berno, Cluny's first abbot, to take over a monastery called Chanteuge[29] and recently built for him. Odo, however, being in Italy at the time, appointed Arnulf of Aurillac as abbot. The monks were given first of all freedom from external jurisdiction and, after Arnulf's death, freedom also to elect their own abbot. Another abbey, called St. Pontius, was founded by Count Raymond III (d. 950) in Narbonne, and this was given to Arnulf and his monks. The bishop of the diocese asked Arnulf to reform another house, St. Chaffre du Monastier, which was completely devoid of monastic life.[30]

In an incident which is redolent of the perversity of the time, Odo was called upon to reform the abbey of Fleury.

[26] Mabillon, *Vetera Analecta* (3 vols., Parisiis, 1723), II, 349; Sackur, *Die Cluniacenser* I, 81; Smith, *The Monastery of Cluny*, p. 58; Pignot, *Histoire de Cluny*, I, 147.

[27] Smith, *op. cit.*, pp. 58-59.

[28] Bruel, I, 642 (p. 598).

[29] Smith, *op. cit.*, p. 59.

[30] M. Marrier (ed.), *Bibliotheca Cluniacensis* (Matiscone, 1915), p. 25. Cf. also Sackur, *op. cit.*, I, 86, and Smith, *op. cit.*, p. 59. Odo was responsible for the reformation and restoration of a large number of other monasteries, all of which need not be recorded here. For an enumeration of these, cf. Evans, *Monastic Life at Cluny*, pp. 10ff.

Accompanied by a group of bishops and counts, Odo approached the abbey. When the approaching party came into sight, the monks threatened them with a show of arms, and all turned back except Odo, who mounted a donkey and rode forward. The bishops entreated him with "Where are you going, Odo, do you wish to die?" The abbot however, patiently went ahead, winning the confidence of the monks with his meekness, and initiated a reform which was the fountainhead of another reform movement of such dimensions as to parallel Cluny itself.[31]

By still another diocese Cluny was petitioned to institute a reform. In 936 Abbot Bernard of the monastery of Saint Allyre, asked Arnold, Bishop of Clermont (912-936), and Count Raymond to invoke the clergy and the nobles to advise the restoration of the monastery. The reform was conditioned on the permission to permit the monks from Cluny to revive the ancient observance.[32]

Towards the end of Odo's tenure, the Bishop of Mâcon, Maimbod, in 941 received a grant of land from a certain Girberga, wife of Rotardus, which he gave to Cluny along with some other possessions to maintain the monks. It was to serve as a burial place for Rotardus and his wife, for whom the monks were to offer their prayers. According to the terms of the donation, in line with a practice in vogue during that period, a threat against violators was annexed at the end. The threat of excommunication, common in the earlier documents, became mitigated in this one, which simply threatened spiritual and temporal retribution. In this particular charter violators were designated as falling under the yoke of divine disfavor, and were compelled to pay one libra of gold in reparation.

> . . . Igitur ego, in Dei nomine Maimbodus, episcopus ecclesiae Matisconensis, et Girberga, uxor Rotardi, pro remedio predicti Rotardi et pro redemptione ani-

[31] Cf. Mabillon, *Acta*, VII, 180; *Gallia Christiana*, VIII, 1545; Pignot, *op. cit.*, I, 158; Sackur, *op. cit.*, I, 90.

[32] Mabillon, *Annales*, III, 405; 448; Sackur, *op. cit.*, I, 85; Pignot, *op. cit.*, I, 164.

> mae prememoratae Girbergae, loco sepulture donamus ad predictum locum aliquid de rebus nostris, donatumque in perpetuum esse volumus. Si quis vero, quod futurum esse non credimus, aliquam calumniam contra hanc donationem generare presumpserit, primitus iram Dei omnipotentis incurrat, et insuper cogenti fisco auri libra I coactus exsolvat, et hac donatione semper firma et inlibata permaneat, stipulatione subnixa.[33]

Odo's fame spread far and wide. Not only in his immediate vicinity, but also as far as Rome and Spain, Odo's name was held in great veneration. The pope regarded him as one of the great moral powers of the century.[34]

Cluny's third abbot, Aymard (d. 965), was chosen by the monks in 942 in accord with Odo's expressed preferences. For the conferring of the blessing, Rotmund, Bishop of Autun (935-968), was called in. The election was confirmed by Rudolph, the Burgundian duke.[35]

During this period bishops were called in to defend the rights of the abbeys against potential usurpers. In the reign of Aymard a certain vassal named Charles, dispossessed son of Louis the Blind, sorely dissatisfied with his limited possessions, usurped certain lands of Cluny to increase his holdings. Two months after the donation of the land of Thoissy-sur-Saone to Cluny, in the same year as the election of Aymard (942), there was convoked a meeting at which assisted various nobles, Sobbon (927-949), and Guy (928-949), Archbishops of Vienne and Lyons respectively, and Aymo, Bishop of Valence, besides other lords and prelates. At the meeting a protest was raised against the unjust aggrandizement undertaken at the expense of Cluny by this and other lords and bishops of the territory. The bishops added their names to the protest and

[33] Bruel, I, 534 (p. 520).

[34] "Postmodum vero abbas ordinatus, Franciarum, Aquitaniarum, Hispaniorumque partium, atque Romanae urbis circumstantium Coenobiorum, effectus ext dux et pater dulcissimus."—Marrier, *Bibliotheca Cluniacensis*, 15. Cf. also Pignot, *op. cit.*, I, 178.

[35] Mabillon, *Annales*, III, 426.

placed the lands owned by Cluny under their own protection.[36]

Burchard, Archbishop of Lyons (949-956), when petitioned by James and Frotier, two monks who had been sent to him by Abbot Aymard, and after conceding that the instability of the times and the aftermath of the invasions had diminished the revenue of the churches, exempted the Cluniac churches of St. Martin and St. Aband of Ambierle in Ronnais from all preceptive offerings to the bishop, except one token offering made once a year.[37]

Likewise at that time the Bishop of Autun, Rotmund (935-968), desisting from his propensity of enriching the children born to him in a marriage entered into before his assumption of Orders, was asked by the priest Edward to give to Cluny an oratory which had been conceded by Rotmund's predecessor, Valon, to a certain priest. Edward's reason for asking was based on the assurance that the oratory would be serviced better by the Cluniac monks than if left alone. Acquiescing in the plea, Rotmund exempted the oratory from all subjection to the episcopal rights, retaining only the right to a nominal payment of dues made annually on St. Peter's feast day.

> . . . Aydoardus . . . noster honorabilis levita . . . volebat religiosis fratribus Cluniacensis coenobii . . . quidam injuste et contra fas eandem quasi successores invaserant; visum est autem prefato Aydoardo ut predictam capellam presignatis fratribus rationabilius traderet, quo inibi condignum Deo officium celebraretur aptius, et census (censum) condignum debitum sue ecclesie [sic] restitueret honestius. Est vero prefata capellula sita in comitatu Matisconensi omni episcopali debito immunis . . .[38]

The donation was further granted immunity and was signed by the bishop and two abbots, Haldebod, and Gerald, besides others.[39]

Manasses, powerful Archbishop of Arles (914-962), repentant of taking sides with one of the parties under his relative,

[36] Pignot, *op. cit.*, I, 217.

[37] Pignot, *op. cit.*, I, 218.

[38] Bruel, I, 474 (p. 460).

[39] Cf. Pignot, *op. cit.*, I, 218.

Hugh, King of Italy (926-947), was led to give Cluny a very important piece of land in Juilly in Chalonnaide, the while he asked prayers for the repose of his soul and that of his mother.[40]

Aymard's rule was comparatively brief, and it seems that only two monasteries were added to Cluny during his reign. One of these was Sauxillanges (Celciniacus), which was founded by Count Acfredus in 927, and given to Cluny by Stephen, Bishop of Clermont (945-976), in 950. Stephen, together with his father and father's wife, asked Aymard to send monks to the monastery. The usual privileges were given, and no taxes, services or dues were to be required of the monks, nor was the bishop to hold any jurisdiction over the monastery. That the bishop thought his powers insufficient to guarantee such rights was shown by his asking Louis IV of France (936-954) to confirm the possession of the monastery.[41]

The donations made to Cluny in the first half of the tenth century ran into the hundreds. One can gain some idea of the number of these in the report that between 910 and 980 there were 630 such donations, which enables one to understand Cluny's increase.[42] The first donations, as might be expected, included land near the abbey in the diocese of Mâcon, while later ones extended throughout the territory of Mâcon into Chalon, Lyons and Bresse, and over the Loire and Rhône rivers as far as the Provence. A similar order of donations surrounded the outlying abbeys and priories founded or donated to Cluny, or dependent on it.[43] Although the donations were numerous, still much of the wealth was spent for purposes of hospitality, and did not enrich the Cluniac monks personally. For the entire rule of Bernò, and well into Odo's reign, Cluny had to struggle to maintain itself, and it was only later that it became powerful in virtue of the wealth and possessions considered in themselves.

[40] Bruel, I, 726 (p. 681); Cf. also, *Gallia Christiana*, I, 93 (Instrumenta); Pignot, *op. cit.*, I, 218.

[41] Bruel, I, 792 (p. 743); Smith, *The Monastery of Cluny*, p. 91.

[42] Pignot, *op. cit.*, I, 212; de Valous, *Le Monachism Clunisien*, p. 325. The most complete collection of records of these donations can be found in Bruel's volumes.

[43] Pignot, *op. cit.*, I, 212.

Although Aymard had a short tenure, he was favored by the bishops with donations just as Berno and Odo had been before him. Maimbod, Bishop of Mâcon, exchanged land with him,[44] and Guy, Archbishop of Lyons (928-949), gave him several plots of land.[45] Gerald, a certain archbishop, although not ceding territory owned by the diocese, and hence not needing the sanction of the chapter of canons, gave all his personal possessions to Cluny and became a monk there.

> Igitur ego Geraldus, indignus archiepiscopus . . . offero per saeculi abrenunciationem et habitus commutationem . . . omnes meas res quas in presentiarum habere vel possidere videor et qu[a]e mihi de paterna successione in hereditatem obvenerunt . . . trado et transfundo, Cluniacum denique monasterium hujus facti delego . . .[46]

Likewise, Maimbod of Mâcon gave personal possessions to Cluny which, by not being undersigned through the canons, had to be identified as goods belonging to himself personally.[47]

Just as bishops had served as witnesses of such donations as early as Berno's reign over Cluny,[48] so also in Aymard's reign a certain Einricus, in place of Bishop Amon, subscribed his name to a royal precept confirming the Cluniac possession in 943.[49] In the same year a similar precept of Conrad (937-993) was signed in like manner.[50] Again, a certain Bishop Peter witnessed a donation of land by the priest Hubert to Cluny in 943, in the presence of the abbot Vulfardus of Inde along with

[44] Mabillon, *Annales*, III, 441 (anno 944).

[45] Bruel, I, 670 (p. 623) (anno 945).

[46] Bruel, I, 724 (p. 677); Mabillon, *Annales*, III, 442; *Acta*, VII, 104.

[47] Bruel, I, 707 (p. 661).

[48] In 926 a donation made to Cluny included in the body of the charter, rather than at the end, an actual reference to bishops who were to act as witnesses: ". . .et coram domnis episcopis Anscherico et Geroldo." To this the editor of the charter added that Anschericus (926-928) was probably the Archbishop of Lyons, and Gerald (886-926) the bishop of Mâcon. Cf. Bruel, I, 270 (p. 263).

[49] "Signum domni Chuonradi piissimi regis. Einricus, notarius, ad vicem Amonis episcopi, recognovi. . ." Bruel, I, 627 (p. 584).

[50] Bruel, I, 628 (p. 585).

the monks and others.[51]

This period may well be termed an "era of good feelings" between the bishops and the abbots. This spirit remained even later in central and southern France, but from the north there came to the Cluniac centralization a more hostile element, which was later to stand clearly revealed.[52] The bishops had ceded many of their rights to the Cluniac monasteries. They no longer possessed the right of visitation; the local bishops could no longer assume the right of blessing the abbots or of ordaining the monk-priests; they could not expect customary donations or taxes as in former times, had little control over the rural parishes, and did not receive the tithes, but only small token offerings at rare intervals. These were probably not long-term arrangements according to the plans of the original abbots and monks of Cluny, but rather temporary expediencies, without which the movement could not have succeeded.[53]

With charters in their possession that were filled with immunities and privileges of all kinds, the abbeys did not easily give up the rights to which they had become accustomed. These very immunities became the magnets of donations, for the people were more disposed to give when they were assured that the donations would go to the direct benefit of the monks, rather than when they were being diverted to the needs of prince, proprietor or bishop. The abbeys under the Cluny system, just as under that of Benedict of Aniane, formed a tight net, and even in those not directly dependent upon Cluny there existed a spirit and practice imitative of Cluny. Customary law and privileges, with regard to Cluny at least, summed up the canonical position of Cluniac monasticism in this period, and controlled the relations between bishop and abbot.[54]

[51] Bruel, I, 635 (p. 592).

[52] Guy de Valous, "La Domaine de l'Abbaye de Cluny aux Xe et XIe Siècle," *Annales de l'Académie de Mâcon*, 3 serie, XXI (Mâcon, 1920-1921), p. 313.

[53] de Valous, "La Domaine de l'Abbaye de Cluny," *loc. cit.*

[54] Cf. Pignot, *op. cit.*, I, 21.

CHAPTER XIII

BISHOPS AND NON-CLUNIAC MONASTIC CURRENTS

ARTICLE 1. CENTRAL EUROPE

Besides Cluny and the monasteries which were founded or made dependent upon it in the early years of the 10th century, there were others which, although influenced by Cluny, can be considered separately. These also were closely associated with the bishops and in various manners, principally again, as in the case of the bishops' transactions with Cluny, in the building, the restoring or the confirming of the monasteries. Instances of these episcopal acts regarding monasteries are not lacking in the years between 900 and 950.

Europe was just recovering from the wounds inflicted by the invasions, and hence the bishops set about reviving the ancient monasteries and attracting monks to live once again the monasticism of former days. Aganus, Bishop of Chartres (931-941), deploring the lack of divine services in the once thriving monastery of Saint-Pierre-en-Valley in his diocese, decreed (ca. 940) that it should be restored and receive the pontifical benediction, in order that the divine office might be prayed there at all times. From the document of the restoration it seems that he intended this for the canons regular, however.[1]

When Alveus, Abbot of the monastery of Saint-Pierre, which had been devastated by the Northmen but afterwards was revived when given over to the canons by Bishop Aganus, de-

[1] *Gallia Christiana,* VIII (Instrumenta), 288: "Ego Aganus...episcopus Carnotensis ecclesiae, super quodam monasterio nostro pene diruto, in honore S. Petri dicato, condoluimus...illudque a fundamento reaedificare, et canonica institutione clericorum cunctorum graduum inibi Deo servire, sanctam exercendo religionem jussimus. Tempore siquidem pacis jam olim splendide locus ille viguit in canonicis Domino militantibus...ibi...celebretur canonicali authentico in psalmis, hymnis et canticis spiritualibus perpetuali ritu observandum." The chart is entitled, "Aganus episcopus Carnotensis monachis sancti Petri clausam vincarum restituit," but the word "monk" was applied at that time also to the canons regular. Cf. also *Gallia Christiana,* VIII, 1109.

cided in 950 to again restore a good observance according to the Rule of St. Benedict, he sought aid from the pious Bishop Rogenfold. Going to Fleury, which was flourishing under the reform that had been instituted by Odo of Cluny,[2] he lived there three years as a member of the community. When he returned to Saint-Pierre he was accompanied by twelve religious and the abbot Wulfade, and he there inaugurated the new Benedictine monasticism and affiliated the abbey with that Order.[3]

Rembert, a monk of Sens, when elected abbot, decided to bring the abbey back to a regular observance, even though some of the community begged him to permit them to pursue their decadent ways. Adelbero, Bishop of Sens, was in favor of the restoration, and gave him a helper in Agendal, prior of Gorze. Together, Rembert and Agenald inculcated a new discipline, asking all who did not care to follow it to leave. All but four of the monks cast their lots with the reform, and the monastery thereafter witnessed an edifying monastic life. Adelbero confirmed all the donations and privileges extended to the monastery by his predecessors, and petitioned further confirmation from King Otto I (936-973) of the privileges granted by Childeric III (743-752). The date of the restoration was 938, while the confirmation by Otto was made in 949.[4]

When the same Adelbero in the year 941 observed the decadence of the regular canons inhabiting the monastery of St. Arnulf, and received no favorable response after having warned them to lead a more edifying life, he replaced them with Benedictine monks.

> Idcirco ego indignus Adelbero, sanctae sedis Metensium episcopus, operae pretium duxi, et qui diu mihi commissa in torporis negligentia cuncta duxeram, saltem aliqua quae corrigere valerem et congruebat, sagaci providerem industria. Itaque monasterium cunctis notum, scilicet beati Arnulphi, in quo videba-

[2] Mabillon, *Annales*, V, 503.

[3] Rocher, *Histoire de l'Abbaye royal de St. Benoît-sur-Loire* (Orleans, 1865), p. 129.

[4] *Gallia Christiana*, XIII, 1385.

> tur coadunatio clericorum, utque veridice dicam, et sub testimonio totius ecclesiae, Acefalorum sub specie canonicorum regulae existere, succrevit ardor summi desiderii, ut qui illorum mores et vitam incorrigibilem noveram (namque et hoc experientia diversarum ammonitionum antea cum nostris experieram suffraganeis) quo potioribus et vitae praestantissimis ipsius loci praebendam converterem disciplinis: hujus si quidem deliberationis summa fuit, ut eos inde expellerem, et Deo authore, vitam instituerem monasticam, nisi se ipsos sanctae illius subderent vitae. Sed hoc quasi despectui habentes, ut erant uniti coetu, maluerunt esse pares in imperfectionem consensu. Denique consultu nostrorum clericorum, scilicet abbatum utriusque ordinis atque fidelium laicorum, praefecimus ibi abbatem, Arbertum nomine cujus institutionibus in reliquum adventantes, inibi eodem quo definivimus ordine, scilicet monastico erudientur . . . etc.[5]

The replacement was further sanctioned by the decree of the King of Germany, Otto I, in 941, when he approved the institution of the Benedictines in the monastery.[6]

In 936 Rotbert, Bishop of Trier (931-956), found the monastery of Metlac (Mediolacense) despoiled of its necessities and in a state of poor observance. He therefore sent a letter to the monastery of St. Cornelius at Inde (Cornelimunster) and asked that they send someone who might be able to restore the monastery of Metlac to its former state of temporal and spiritual prosperity. A monk, Rotwicus, was sent, and the reform was carried out. He likewise commended the new abbey and a new abbot to King Otto, and asked that its old possessions and rights be restored. In 942 he consecrated the abbatial basilica of St. Maximus, and in 945 petitioned the restoration of the Abbey of St. Servatius of Utrecht (Trajectensis) from Otto.[7]

Gauzlin, Bishop of Toul (922-962), went to Fleury to study

[5] *Gallia Christiana*, XIII, 386 (Instrumenta).

[6] *Loc. cit.*

[7] *Gallia Christiana*, XIII, 396.

the monasticism there in order to spread the reform movement to his own diocese. Returning to his see with a copy of the Benedictine Rule, he reformed St. Evre's,[8] and appointed Archembald, of Fleury, the abbot in 934. Evidently to assure the success of the reform, the bishop held the abbot under his jurisdiction, and the abbatial election depended upon his approval for validity.[9]

In 948, not satisfied with having restored St. Evre's, he insisted on providing the necessities of life for monks who would inhabit it. He therefore sought to ascertain from Archembald, the abbot whom he had placed over the monastery, what would suffice to maintain the monks, and thereupon proceeded to fulfil their needs. Moreover, seeking the consent of the faithful, the clergy and the laity alike, he added to the prebends of the monks a church situated in the villa Colombier.[10] He later restored St. Mansuy's with Archembald's help.[11]

In 949, Bishop Roricon of Laon (949-976) reestablished the Abbey of St. Vincent.[12]

The church of St. Augustine in the diocese of Limoges had been founded by Bishop Romricio, but subsequently was destroyed by the Danes. In 934 Turpio (905-944), the bishop, along with Martin, the abbot, restored it and animated it with a robust discipline. The sanctity and high intentions of Bishop Turpio were noticeable in the document of restoration, which indicated his great efforts to raise up a new religious spirit from the ruins caused by the invasions.

> Mundo jam senescente religio defectum incurrit et ita irreligiositas seu injustitia abundavit, ut ipsi nos, qui prae caeteris Domino adhaerere debueramus, in cujus sorte esse noscimur . . . simus lupi verspertini . . . Lumen vero cordis amississe probatur, quisquis ille sit . . . qui adhuc novellus et rudis erat, non pepercit; et sibi credit parci, si in peccatis perseverare

[8] "Gesta Episcoporum Tullensium," c. 31—*MGH, Scriptores*, VIII, 639.

[9] Smith, *The Monastery of Cluny*, p. 44; Sackur, *Die Cluniacenser*, I, 176.

[10] Mabillon, *Annales*, III, 455; *Gallia Christiana*, XIII, 453 (Instrumenta).

[11] "Miracula Sancti Mansueti," *MGH, Scriptores*, IV, 508.

[12] Wyard, *Histoire de l'Abbaye de Saint-Vincent de Laon* (St. Quentin, 1858), p. 115.

voluerit et surgere per poenitentiam noluerit. Quam ob rem ego Turpio, Lemovicum omnium episcoporum extimus, de sede quam mihi Dominus regendam tuendamque immerito committere dignatus est, religionem auferri conspiciens, valde pertimui. In memet autem reversus, diutinis precibus a Domino auxilium petens, implorabam ut ipso juvante, sancta religio, quae usque ad nos illibata pervenerat, nostris temporibus non deperiret, sed successoribus inviolata succederet. Incidit deinde mihi, Deo opitulante, consilium bonum, ut credo et confiteor, quatenus claustrum construerem, et ibi fratres boni testimonii adgregarem, qui in commune sine aliqua proprietate degentes, absque ullo strepitu saeculari divinae servituti incumberent. Hoc vero quod nos, utpote turbis saecularibus admixti, explere nequimus, saltim hi, qui intra claustrum morarentur, strenue et absque impedimento carnali peragerent. Scriptum est enim: Si primitiae sanctae, et massa; quod et feci, consentientibus tamen nostris consanguineis seu optimatibus in Lemovicensi pago degentibus, domno scilicet Aymerico abbate, Aymono abbate, Petro praeposito, etc. Volo autem, atque inhianter cupio, ut absque inopia et sine aliqua perturbatione Deo servire studeant; quod ut decentius fieri possit, do illis villam, quae vocatur Bacalaria, quae decem in se mansos continere probatur . . . Oratorium praeterea, in quo Deo militant, ipsis committo, ut ipsi praevideant, qualiter horae operis Dei significentur, nemoque eos contristet in domo Dei. Ministerium etiam cantorum, necne lectorum, librorumve, sive omnium, quae ad sacrum mysterium pertinent, vel ibidem Deo offeruntur, ipsis committimus. Claustrum et omnia interiora ipsi provideant, et dominentur. In hoc autem quod ego illis do vel committo, sive etiam deinceps daturus vel commissurus sum, nullus habeat potestatem nec licentiam dominandi, nisi his, quem sibi propter Deum et secundum vitae meritum pars melior praeesse poposcerit, post tamen proprium episcopum.[13]

It is obvious from the last words of the charter that the generous bishop also retained a measure of control, but the nature of the *"post tamen proprium episcopum"* is not too clear, and could refer to two things: 1) the *potestas dominandi*—a general right to watch over all monastic affairs or 2) the election, in which case his approval would have been needed in confirmation of the election of the abbot. Since the election of the abbot seemed to be the dominant note in the immediate context, it seems that the phrase in question points rather to the bishop's right to approve of the election, as a token of his power over the community, which in other things was inoperative. This is in contrast to the charters granted to the Cluniac foundation, which were modeled after that of William of Aquitaine, and accordingly precluded the monastery in all things from the control of the local bishops, although, of course, the necessity of having a bishop administering to the monastery in the episcopal functions of Order always remained. Bishop Turpio was undoubtedly anxious to see to the continued success of this monastery which he protected, and hence he held on to the right of overseeing the vote since the expression *"proprium episcopum"* seemed to refer to nobody else than himself and his successors.

According to Mabillon,[14] Aymo was the abbot of St. Martial, Stephen his successor and a brother of the bishop. Turpio, therefore, not only saw to the appointment of the presiding abbot of the monastery, but likewise made sure that in the abbatial chair would be one who would carry on the ideals he had introduced.

It should also be noted that in the charter no mention was made of papal protection; the authority in the abbey and the possession of goods are restricted to the abbot and the proper bishop. Since the abbey was not placed under the congregational system of Cluny, and since the papacy in its exercise of power was at a very low ebb, the bishop was evidently placing full responsibility for the maintenance of good observance

[13] Mabillon, *Annales*, III, 391; *Gallia Christiana*, II, 167 (Instrumenta).
[14] *Annales*, III, 39.

in the abbey upon the person of the abbot together with his own in his acts of surveillance. His action could hardly be interpreted as being a rebuke to the Cluniac system, since his personal friendship with Odo was such as to preclude a conclusion of this kind. It was a smaller current of reform, however, not directly commingled with the Cluniac current, but undoubtedly prompted and influenced by that movement.

On various sides there appear other evidences of episcopal aid in the constitution or re-establishment of monasteries, if not also in their actual foundation, at least by way of approval and confirmation of the foundation itself. The confirmation was important in that it added a note of official recognition to the foundations, and encouraged the newly founded monasteries in the name of the Church to seek vocations in the diocese. In 912 Anselm, Bishop of Orleans (912-938), subscribed his name to the document of the Prince and Abbot of Marmoutier (*Majus Monasterium*), a monastery of canons regular, and to the letters of Hugh, Count of Paris, and Marquis of Orleans, giving the Abbey of St. Symphorian, and the churches of St. Laeta and St. Sulpicius to the canons of St. Samson, in 938.[15]

Arnold, Bishop of Clermont (912-936), in 912 approved the letter of foundation of the monastery of Bourg (*Burgidolensis*). This is undoubtedly the same person who subscribed the original charter of Cluny under the name Ermoldus, and the foundation charter of St. Vincent de Cantella in 936 under the name of Arnoldus, *episcopus Arvernorum* (Clermont).[16] In addition to Arnold's name in the latter charter appeared those of Gerontius (910-948), Archbishop of Bourges (*Bituricensis*) and Turpio, Bishop of Limoges, besides those of several abbots, Odo, Erericus, and Walo.[17]

Arnulfus I, Count of Flanders (d. 964), restored the monastery of St. Peter of Blandin (*Blandiniense*) in the county of Ghent, acting with the permission of King Louis, and that of Transmaro, the bishop, "*ad cujus dioecesim locus iste pertinebat.*" Consulting his friends and others among the faithful, he

[15] *Gallia Christiana*, VIII, 1427.

[16] *Gallia Christiana*, II, 254; II, 6 (*Instrumenta*).

[17] *Op. cit.*, II, 6 (Instrumenta).

sought to restore to the monastery a part of the revenue which Amandus, the saintly bishop-founder of St. Peter, had petitioned for and received from the kings and others. This included the property (*census*) and several farms (*mansiones*) which the abbot and monks were to possess on the condition that they serve God exactly—"*adamussim*"—in the manner in which the monks under the monastery's founder had done. They were to follow the Rule of St. Benedict, and could elect their own abbot.[18]

Abbo, Bishop of Soissons (909-937), in 909 was present at the council of Trosly, which decried the decadence of the times, and he subscribed his name to the decrees of the council. Impelled, perhaps, by the ideals voiced in that council, he petitioned Charles the Simple (898-923) to confirm the privileges of St. Maurus of Fosses, which was granted in 920.[19]

In the charter of foundation of the Abbey of St. Thierry (*Thiernensis*), in the diocese of Clermont in the early tenth century, there was included a petition for confirmation of the abbey by apostolic privilege and royal approval, as well as an appeal for support through the authority of the Bishop of Clermont, Stephen (945-976), and for a donation from one of the nobility, William by name.[20] The Abbey at Tulle was restored in 933 by King Rudolph II of Burgundy, and recognized by Bishop Ansegisus in the diocese of the same name.[21]

In the diocese of Le Puy (*Aniciensis*), the monastery of St. Theofredus was restored and recognized in signature by Bishop Gotischalchus (936-962), Bishop Gerontius of Bourges (*Bituricensis*), Bishops Gegonis and Wido, besides the Abbots, Bernard and Dalmatius.[22] In the diocese of Poitiers, Alboinus (937-962), the local bishop, in 946 confirmed the donations made ten years previously by Bishop Froterius (905-936) to

[18] Mabillon, *Annales*, III, 423 (anno 941).

[19] *Gallia Christiana*, IX, 345.

[20] "Ego in Dei nomine Wido laudo et confirmo, confirmari opto apostolico privilegio, regali praecepto, auctoritate Stephani Arvernensis ecclesiae pontificiae, et donatione carissimi senioris mei Willelmi..."—*Gallia Christiana*, II, 120 (Instrumenta).

[21] *Gallia Christiana*, II, 203 (Instrumenta).

[22] *Gallia Christiana*, II, 259 (Instrumenta).

the monastery of St. Cyprian, and showed himself favorable to the foundation.[23] Eirus, Bishop of Saintes (*Santonenesis*), in 942 recognized the charter of the monastery of St. Jean-d'Anfely.[24] In 908, Emperor Louis III confirmed the Abbeys of Lobbes (Laubach) and Fosses for the church of Liege and its bishop, Stephen.[25]

At times the bishops favored the monastic life in order to maintain a source to draw upon for the badly needed vocations, as well as to secure these vocations at home in their own dioceses. The diocese of Verdun had been without monasteries in the first half of the tenth century, and as a result many of the clerics who wished to join monastic communities were compelled to leave for neighboring dioceses. Deploring this, Bishop Berengarius (940-959) upon consulting with the clerics and church officers, constituted in the church of Sts. Peter and Paul a congregation of clerics who lived the monastic life, and who would thereafter reside in his diocese when called to that vocation.[26]

The bishops were generous to the monasteries with donations and open manifestations of friendship. Monasticism needed these aids, at least in the period of foundation, for the work of resurrecting the monasteries was a task which could not be shouldered by good will alone, but required material helps, and these in substantial quantities. Resistance from the bishop, who could, if he so willed, channel all the donations of the faithful into the non-monastic needs of the diocese, might have spelled out a fateful doom for more than one monastery.

In 933, after fifteen years of service to his diocese, Waldricus (Gaudry), Bishop of Auxerre (918-933) (*Autisiodorensis*), was buried in the basilica of St. Germain, where he had lived from his earliest years as a monk and later became "archimandrite" (abbot). He had always showed himself benevolent to the monks of his diocese.[27] Archbishop Hogero of Bremen (909-915) had during this period been most diligent and severe in

[23] *Gallia Christiana*, II, 328; 329; 341 (Instrumenta).
[24] *Gallia Christiana*, II, 464 (Instrumenta).
[25] *Gallia Christiana*, III, 146 (Instrumenta).
[26] *Gallia Christiana*, XIII, 1179.
[27] Mabillon, *Annales*, III, 383.

maintaining Church discipline, and made periodic visitations not only of the churches but also of the monasteries, where he enforced the monastic observance according to the vows of the monks.[28]

The Bishop of Autun, Hervé (920-929), in 921 confirmed a donation made by Theotbald, Abbot of Conclus, in favor of two friends of the bishop, which gift they could enjoy during their lifetime.[29] Achardus, Bishop of Langres (*Lingonensis*) (948-967), in 948, at the petition of Abbot Archembald, granted several churches to St. Benoît of Fleury along with the *paratae* and every "*obsequium*" except that of the *eulogiae*.[30]

Girfredus, Archbishop of Besançon (932-953), in 945 gave certain plots of land to the Abbey of Tournon (*Trenorchiensis*) and its Abbot, Aymino. These plots were intermingled with those of laymen, who inflicted grave damages upon the monks of the abbey, since the laymen had received these very lands as benefices. The monks, therefore, of St. Mary's, St. Filibert and St. Valerian, and the "*missi*" of Syminus, Abbot of St. Valerian, petitioned the archbishop to grant it to them in his annual census. After consulting with his clerics, the archbishop consented to grant this, since he believed it opportune to give some measure of aid to the monks who were helping to bring the faith to the people in this rural area.[31]

A very interesting benefactor to the monasteries was a certain bishop, Keonwaldus, who journeyed throughout Germany, giving generous gifts of gold to monasteries which he visited, the gold having been given to him by the King of the Angles, Ethelstan (925-940). His purpose was to have his name inscribed in the monasteries, and to be remembered in their suffrages. Coming to the monastery of St. Gall, in 949, he left

[28] Mabillon, *Acta*, VII, 25.

[29] De Charmasse, *Cartulaire de l'Eglise d'Autun* (3 vols., Autun, 1865), I, 61.

[30] The redactor of this notice added to this: "In charta Guilenci episcopi res sancti Johannis Reomanensis confirmantis haec lego: Privilegium Achardi episcopi de ecclesia corpus Sancti, de ecclesia Montis Bertaldi, Berfontis et Asneriis, Riceii et Nuidis. Unde patet has omnes ecclesias huic monasterio ab eo fuisse concessas."—*Gallia Christiana*, IV, 547.

[31] Mabillon, *Annales*, III, 443.

there a large gift, and asked the monks to pray for his king, for a certain Wigbarth, for himself, and for five others. Mabillon recorded that some even believed that he made monastic profession there.[32]

The bishops were called upon at times to witness the business negotiations of the abbeys. The importance of this is not to be overlooked. Episcopal sanctioning of such negotiations added a note of legality and security to the contracts entered into by the monks, and likewise indicated a healthy state in the relationship which existed between the monks and the bishops. When Walafrid, Abbot of Sorèze (*Soricinius*) in the diocese of Aux (*Ausciensis*) in 904 sold the Abbey of Cella Modulfi with the churches to Count Garcia, Bishop Arimando (879-906) of the diocese witnessed the transaction, and added his name to the document.[33]

In the year 910, Gerontius, Bishop of Bourges (910-948) (*Bituricensis*), undersigned a trading contract involving several plots of land, made between Robert, Abbot of St. Martin's Abbey, and canons.[34] In 913 the same bishop undersigned the charter of the monastery of Dol. In 926 he not only gave his consent but also helped the monks of Vierzon—formerly of Dover—in every way to transfer their monastic residence to the *Castrum Virzionense* (Vierzon) for purposes of greater security. In 936 Gerontius helped with the construction and endowment of a monastery which was being built by a certain Airaldus and his wife Rothilde. The new construction was to be an addition to a church dedicated to St. Vincent in the county of Bourges (*Bituricum*) for canons, who called their new monastery Cantella. The same bishop conferred many benefits on the monastery of Issoudun (*Exoldunese*), including twenty churches and the body of St. Peternus, which the monks were thence to revere and care for. In 938 he undersigned the charter of Goteschalchus, bishop of Le Puy (*Aniciensis*) for the restoration of the regular discipline in the monastery of St. Theofredus.[35]

[32] Mabillon, *Annales*, III, 370.

[33] *Gallia Christiana*, I, 170 (Instrumenta).

[34] *Gallia Christiana*, II, 34.

[35] For charter of Vierzon (St. Peter's), cf. *Gallia Christiana*, II, 135; for

Contracts of trade were entered into also between the bishops and the monks, at times for the mutual benefit of either party, and again on the occasion of pressing monastic necessities. An interesting exchange occurred between Gimera, Bishop of Carcassone (903-931), and Erifonsus, Abbot of Mount Olivet, in 925. In the exchange the bishop went to great lengths to extend every privilege regarding the property given to the monks in exchange for their grant to him.

> . . . ut ab hodierno die inantea habeatis potestatem de ipsis ecclesiis cum illorum decimis sine aliquo censu vos et successores vestri et quidquid exinde agere, facere vel judicare volueritis in Dei nomine habeatis potestatem cum omni voce oppositionis nostrae. Sane, quod fieri minime credimus esse venturum, quod si, ego Gimera Episcopus, aut mea congregatio, aut aliquis successorum meorum qui contra hanc procambiationem venerit ad irrumpendum, aut supposita persona ulla, aut nos venerimus (qui inferant) inferam vel inferent vobis aut parti vestrae quantum apud vos aut successores vestros ipsas ecclesias cum illarum decimis sine aliquo censu adeo tempore melioratus fuerint, componat vobis tantum et aliud tantum quantum ipsas res valere potuerint, et hoc quod repetit non valeat vendicare, sed inantea ista procambiatio firma et stabilis permaneat omni tempore. Facta charta procambiationis idus Junii anno vigesimo octavo regnante Carolo rege . . . Gimera humilis episcopus . . . etc.[36]

In 911 a charter very similar to this one was made by Arnustus, Archbishop of Narbonne (896-912), giving certain grants to the church of St. Paul of Narbonne, which were to be possessed for all time by the monks and clerics serving it.[37]

Bishop Gimera and Abbot Erifonsus negotiated another exchange in 931 under conditions similar to the first.[38] In 950 Honoratus, Bishop of Marseilles (948-(?)), with his clerics,

the transfer of the monks, cf. *ibidem*, p. 134.

[36] *Gallia Christiana*, VI, 421 (Instrumenta).

[37] *Gallia Christiana*, VI, 14 (Instrumenta).

[38] *Gallia Christiana*, VI, 422 (Instrumenta).

gave permission to the monks of St. Victor to take possession of lands (*ad inquirendam terram*) which, although possibly within the claim of the bishop, were nonetheless to be left free for the monastery to possess.[39]

From the monastic communities came many of the bishops during this period. Relations between the bishops and the monks reached the most personal note when the episcopal sees became occupied by members of the religious life. This was not a new phenomenon of the tenth century, since it could be found in the West almost with the very beginnings of monasticism. It is noteworthy, however, that it appeared in this period, for it indicated the caliber of the monasticism not directly linked with Cluny in view of the fact that monks and abbots were thought worthy of receiving the high office of bishop.

In 940, Rangefridus, formerly the Abbot of St. Egidius, became Bishop of Avignon (*Avenionensis*).[40] Rostagnus, formerly monk and prior to Cella Gordanica in Aniane, became Archbishop of Arles and, under John VIII (872-882), vicar of the Holy See over all the other bishops of France. He was later said to have possessed the Abbeys of Goudargues, Cruas and Aniane, which he held until 913.[41] Waldric, a noble, was placed over the Abbey of St. Germain d'Auxerre, and given the title of Archimandrite (Abbot). When in 918 the Bishop of Auxerre died, Waldric was chosen to succeed him.[42]

In 931 two monks were made bishops, Walbertus, Abbot of Corvey, to the See of Noyon (*Noviomensis*) and Ingrannus of St. Medard, to the See of Laou (*Laudunensis*).[43] Gerlannus, a monk of St. Germain, in 938 replaced the deposed bishop of the See of Auxerre.[44] From Fulda were consecrated two monks to the episcopacy, Frederic, in 938, and his predecessor in the See of Mainz, Hildebert.[45] In 937, Transimarus, abbot of St.

[39] *Gallia Christiana*, I, 108 (Instrumenta).

[40] *Gallia Christiana*, VI, 483.

[41] *Gallia Christiana*, VI, 835; I, 548.

[42] V. B. Henry, *Histoire de l'Abbaye de Saint-Germain d'Auxerre* (Auxerre, 1853), p. 118.

[43] Mabillon, *Annales*, III, 379; *Gallia Christiana*, IX, 990.

[44] Mabillon, *Annales*, III, 408.

[45] Mabillon, *Annales*, III, 410.

Vedastus (*Vaast*) in Arras, became Bishop of Noyon.[46] In the same year Bernuin, monk of St. Crispin, was made bishop of the See of Senlis (Silvanectensis).[47] Witfridus, Abbot of Sithiu (later known as St. Bertin), in 935 became bishop of the See of Therouanne (Tarvannensis).[48]

In 920 the see of Liege (Leodiensis) was vacant and the place was contested by two candidates, Hilduin, a cleric, and Richarius, the Abbot of Prüm. The Duke of Lorraine, Gislebertus, favored Hilduin, but the king, Charles III, favored Richarius. Acting quickly, the duke presented Hilduin to the Archbishop of Cologne, Herimannus, who proceeded with the consecration. Clerics of the diocese brought the matter to the attention of the Pope John X (914-928), who excommunicated Hilduin, and designated Richarius.[49]

Bishops, on the other hand, were not averse to taking the habit of the monk and giving up their dioceses. The general acceptation of the monastic life by the Church as a whole and its fulfilment of a need of the times is patently illustrated in the applications by bishops for reception of the habit of the monk. If a bishop entered a monastery, a favorable future for that religious house seemed assured, for it served to draw others into the monastery and thus lent the monastic vocation a healthy publicity, which contribution to the monastery's well-being was indeed a welcome factor.

In 950, Mabbon, Bishop of Saint-Paul-de-Leon, became a monk in the Abbey of Fleury, and presented to the abbey a relic of St. Paul, the bishop of Leon, and other precious treasures.[50] Gerald, Archbishop of Mâcon (according to Mabillon's testimony), became a monk of Cluny in 945, and donated all his goods to the abbey.[51] In 912, Argrinus, Bishop of Langres, having relinquished his see, became a monk in the Abbey of

[46] *Gallia Christiana*, IX, 991; Mabillon, *Annales*, III, 404.

[47] *Gallia Christiana*, X, 1388; Mabillon, *Annales*, III, 404.

[48] *Gallia Christiana*, X, 1536.

[49] M. Bouquet, *Recueil des historiens des Gaules et de la France* (19 vols., Paris, 1869-1879), VIII, pp. CVII-CVIII.

[50] Rocher, *S. Benoît-sur-Loire*, p. 130.

[51] Mabillon, *Acta*, VII, 104; *Annales*, III, 442.

St. Benignus in Dijon.[52]

The monks of the Abbey of Trudo in the diocese of Metz in 945 chose Bishop Adelbert as their abbot, since he had been friendly and shown himself helpful to them.[53] Stephen, bishop of a see near Metz, in 903 was also Abbot of Lobbes, which had been united to the bishopric by the King Arnulf (896-899), and of the Abbey of St. Michael on the Meuse. Documents do not show, however, whether the monasteries were secular or regular.[54] A certain Bishop Salomon, of the See of Constance (891-920) was in 920 also Abbot of St. Gall.[55] The bishop of Autun had in 928 under his power the abbey of Flavigny (*Flaviniacense*) and committed a pro-abbot to serve in his stead.[56]

Though the councils are few in this period, there is some evidence that bishops and abbots attended together, but whether the abbots came by precept or invitation is not altogether clear. One of these was the Council of Mouzon (*Mosomense*), held in 948, in which the bishops conferred with the abbots and other learned men in attendance.[57] In 911, in a council held in Fontcouverte near Narbonne (*Villa Fons-coopertus*), Savaricus, abbot of St. Paul, signed the decrees of the council in place of the bishop Armannus, who was either blind or sick, but it was not determined whether the abbot was or was not required to attend the council.[58]

With the increase of monastic establishments came the necessity of setting norms of monastic behavior in the diocese. The councils of this period were few. Hence one must conclude that such behavior was controlled by the immediate mandate of the bishop, wherever privileges were lacking. In the infrequent councils that were called, there were included on the conciliar agenda matters of monastic import and interest. The Council of Coblenz (*Confluentinum*) in 912 ordained that monks

[52] Bouquet, *op. cit.*, VII, p. CV.
[53] Mabillon, *Annales*, III, 446.
[54] *Gallia Christiana*, III, 836.
[55] *Gallia Christiana*, V, 950.
[56] Mabillon, *Annales*, III, 365.
[57] Mansi, XVIII, 417.
[58] *Gallia Christiana*, XIII, 10; Mansi, 18, 313.

located in the parishes were to be subject to the bishops in all things and were to exhibit the proper acts of respect toward them.[59]

The Synod of Altheim ruled that monks who had become bishops by a canonical election, and thus were absolved from the monastic rule, had the right to inherit possessions. But whatever was his or what he gave to the monastery was to remain in the power of the abbot under whose jurisdiction he had served while a monk. What he received later was to be restored to the cathedral where he was consecrated a bishop.[60] This decree seemed to reflect the practice elsewhere and earlier, for Bishop Hervé of Autun, in 920, had signed away all his goods to the cathedral in token of his consecration to the episcopacy for that see.[61]

Between 912 and 915 Gauthier, Archbishop of Sens (887-923) (*Senonensis*), called a diocesan synod, in which he issued several decrees concerning the bishops and abbots. He ordered that abbots and conventual priors who did not report to the bishop, or who excused themselves by means of some pretended canonical impediment, were to be suspended from entering a

[59] Concilium Confluentinum, Cap. 6: "De Ecclesiis monachorum. Hoc quoque statutum est, quatenus ecclesiae quorumcumque monachorum in singulis parochis sitae, episcoporum, ut decet, divinitus subdantur regimini, eisque debita obsequia in exercendis ecclesiasticae curae negotiis sollicite exhibeant. Ipsi proculdubio monachi episcopis suis in omnibus obediant." —Mansi, XVIII, 343.

[60] Synodus Altheimensis (936), cap. 2: "Statum et rationabiliter secundum sanctos Patres a synodo est confirmatum, et Monachus quem canonica electio a jugo regulae monasticae professionis absolvit, et sacra ordinatio de Monacho Episcopum facit, vel ut legitimus haeres paternam sibi haereditatem postea vi revendicandi potestatem habeat. Sed quidquid acquisierat, et habere visus fuerat monasterio relinquat, et Abbatis sui qui fuerat secundum regulam S. Benedicti arbitrio. Postquam enim Episcopus ordinatur ad altare ad quod sanctificatur et titulatur secundum sanctos canones quod acquirere poterit, restituat." Mansi, XVIII, 362; Mabillon, *Annales*, III, 396.

[61] Bulliot, *Essai Historique sur l'Abbaye de Saint Martin d'Autun* (2 vols., Autun, 1849), I, 162: "En 920, l'abbé prend part du sacre de l'évêque d'Autun Hervé, fils de Manassès de Vergy, comte de Chalon; il signe avec les prélats assistants, le testament par lequel le nouvel évêque, comme s'il mourait du monde, fait en leur présence abandon de tous ses biens à sa Cathédrale."

church for eight days, and were to be subject to an even greater penalty if they repeated this neglect in later years.[62] In those places where priories or monasteries formerly existed, the religious houses could be restored only if sufficient faculties existed to warrant their restoration.[63] In the established houses, the divine services were to be celebrated.[64] Monasteries could not demand a pension or gifts from those monastic houses which were dependent upon them, unless the bishop permitted it.[65]

It appears from these decrees of the synod held by Bishop Gauthier that a rigid check was maintained over the monasteries by the ordinary of Sens. There is no distinction drawn between the types of monasteries, hence these episcopal precepts included in addition the canons regular and also the Benedictine monks.

In England, where monasticism was less developed at this period than on the continent, a close relationship between bishops and monks was manifested in the Constitutions of the Archbishop of Canterbury, in which he exhorted the monks, few though they were, to live in accord with their vows, and not to become vagabonds, but to remain in a single monastery. The zeal of the apostles was to be their ideal.[66] One notes that

[62] Constitutiones ex Concilio Galteri Archiepiscopi Senonensis, Cap. 1: "Statuimus, ut abbates et priores conventuales, qui nec venerint, nec se excusaverint, praetendendo canonicum impedimentum, per octo dies ab ingressu ecclesiae suspendantur, et poena, quantum ad hoc conciliis statuta est, sub cominatione majoris poenae, si aliis annis supra his culpabiles inveniantur."—Mansi, XVIII, 323; Hefele-Leclercq, *Histoire des Conciles*, IV, 733.

[63] *Ibidem*, Cap. 10: "Statuimus ut in locis sive prioratibus, ubi conventualis congregatio solet esse, si facultates illius ecclesiae suppetant, conventus ibidem restauretur."

[64] *Ibidem*, Cap. 11: "Item quod in domibus sive locis, ubi solebant esse prioratus, si facultates locorum sufficient, monachi vel canonici regulares ad divinum servitium ibidem celebrandum reducantur."

[65] *Ibidem*, Cap. 12: "Monemus abbates et priores conventuales, quod tot servitores in abbatiis et prioratibus sibi subditis instituant, si ad hoc sufficiant facultates locorum, quot ibi deservire solent: et ne pensionem sive censum ab eisdem exigant, quem non solent exigere ab antiquo, nisi forte alicui ex justa causa ab episcopo suo permittatur."

[66] Constitutiones Odonis Archiepiscopi Cantuariae (943), Cap. 6: "Sexto

nothing was said about the duties of the monks to the bishop, and hence it seems, in the absence of such legislation, that the relations between the two were harmonious.

From a fragment of an unidentified Rule of a certain Grillaicus, which relied, perhaps, on an earlier decree,[67] one learns that those monks who wished to become solitaries had to receive the permission of the bishop before doing so. In addition, the permission of the abbot and of the other members of the community had to be received. With all the foregoing accomplished, the future solitary had to set himself apart from his confreres in the monastery for one year, or, if not yet a monk, for two years, and was not to depart from the cloister except for entering the church. When he successfully completed this test, the bishop was to bless his cell. If he was a priest, he was permitted to have within his cell an oratory consecrated by the bishop, and the cell was to be near enough to the church to allow the solitary to take an active part in the Masses and the choir services of his brethren.[68]

The judicial function of the bishop regarding the monks is exemplified in the following instance.[69] In 933, a certain Witardus and the Abbot of St. Jean of Mount Olivet along with the monks gathered in the presence of Aimeric, Archbishop of Narbonne (927-977), and Count Pontio, as judges to have a

capitulo hortamur monachos et omnes qui votum Deo voverunt, ut in omni humilitate et obedientia die noctuque hoc adimplere studeant, permanentes in timore Dei in ecclesiis ubi se voto constrinxerunt. Non sint vagabundi, neque gyrovagi, qui nomen monachi desiderant, officium autem ejus contemnunt; sed secundum exempla apostolorum, per habitum humilitatis, laboribus manum, et lectione sacra, et continuis orationibus se exercentes parati, praecinctis lumbis, ardentibusque lucernis, patremfamilias expectent, ut veniente eos faciat in aeterna requie sine fine permanere." —Mansi, XVIII, 393.

[67] Concilium Francofurtense (794), cap. 12: "Ut reclusi non fiant nisi quos ante episcopus provinciae atque abbas comprobaverint, et secundum eorum dispositionem in reclusionis loco ingrediantur."—*MGH*, Legum Sectio II, *Capitularia*, tom. I, *Capitularia Regum Francorum*, p. 167.

[68] Mabillon, III, *Annales*, 287 (Anno 900).

[69] For an insight into the functioning of the bishop's judiciary position, cf., e.g., Duby, "Recherches sur l'évolution des institutions judiciaires pendant le Xe et le XIe siècle dans la Bourgogne," *Le Moyen Age*, LII (1947), 15-38.

decision rendered concerning the ownership of some bread, wine, and other articles. The abbot complained that Witardus had taken these from the land which was owned by the abbey according to a privilege received from Rome, which granted all to the monastery. Witardus, when questioned concerning the law to which he appealed, answered that he followed the Salic Law.[70] The decision, however, on the basis of the produced privilege, was rendered in favor of the abbot and the monks.[71]

From this testimony, scattered though it be, and at times even inconsistent, it is nonetheless clear that outside of the Cluniac reform current the bishops were more prone to follow the traditional pattern of relations between themselves and the abbots, by retaining always some rights of control over the abbey. It was the rare bishop who opposed monasticism as such, and most of them looked to the cloistered monks as an mportant element in stabilizing Europe, which had been convulsed by the invasions. The bishops in this secondary current seemed always to suspect possible lapses on the part of monasteries begun or confirmed by them, into habits of laxity in line with the spirit of the times, and hence they reserved some authority to themselves in their demand that certain tokens of subservience be shown them by the abbot and the monks. When the monastery had been instituted by the bishop, he merely held on to the then prevalent right of proprietor to choose the abbot himself, or required his approbation of the election as a condition for its validity. In other cases the bishop made regular visitations or requisitioned the help of observant communities for instructing a stricter observance of the monastic life. For the churches given over to the monasteries, the payment of almost all the taxes was remitted, though certain small payments, such as that of the *eulogiae* remained in force, and thus the bishop was afforded a measure of control over the churches of the monks.

It was the trend of this period to transform the monasteries

[70] Regarding these laws cf., e.g., Stickler, *Historia Juris Canonici Latini, Institutiones Academicae,* Tom. I, *Historia Fontium* (Taurini: Libreria Pontif. Athenaei Salesiani, 1950), p. 436.

[71] *Gallia Christiana,* VI, 423 (Instrumenta).

which once had been in the hands of canons, whether secular or regular, into Benedictine houses. The provisions of the Benedictine Rule for the elections of abbots, along with the ascendance of the Cluniacs, pressured the bishops who had to deal with non-Cluniac monasteries to relax their complete control over abbatial elections, although where there was no monastic congregation to maintain high ideals, the bishop, principally for security's sake, undertook the function of guarding the inner monastic discipline.

The unique position of Cluny was brought into clearer focus by comparison with these other streams of monastic reform, since outside of the Cluniac houses only rare mention was made of the bishop of Rome. The primary concern of the bishops, undoubtedly influenced by the spirit of the Council of Trosly (909), was to see that monasticism once again should take hold, in order that the people might unite themselves within a stabilized realm of spirituality, and settle down to a peaceful and exemplary Christian life.

In the few instances of episcopal legislation, the bishops seemed to recur to Chalcedon's precept, which subjected the monks and the abbot to the bishop. If this was not evinced in actual and express decrees, it was reflected in the paternal nature of the episcopal asseverations. There were as yet no evidences of strife between the bishops and the abbots. The first problem the bishops faced was the restoring of Europe to its pre-invasion *status quo*. After this task had been successfully initiated, and after monasticism had again taken root, the bishops turned their attention from the spiritual and primary nature of monasticism to its secondary and temporal character, and therein sensed a threat to their diocesan hegemony. The relations between the bishops and the abbots, harmonious and concordant in their earlier stage, became in their later stage tense and official between these same authorities.

ARTICLE 2. MONASTICISM IN ITALY, SPAIN, ENGLAND

Since the Kingdom of Italy and the territory of northern Spain were parts of the Carolingian empire, the legislation of the latter affected them also. With the disruption of the centralized power after the death of Louis the Pious (840), that legislation was suspended, and these two countries needed thenceforward to fend for themselves. It seems unnecessary to attempt a systematic investigation of the monasticism in Italy during this period. Though Italy was delivered from the Saracens in 915, the devastation continued in the central portion for more than a century. Some Benedictine houses did remain, but their activity was not impressive. The northern sector of the country sustained attacks from the Hungarians, and could not compose itself to peaceful living until the latter half of the tenth century. These were for Italy, therefore, times of confusion. Monasticism indeed did not disappear, but it lacked a vigorous animation.[72]

Odo of Cluny came to Rome to help reform several of the monasteries. In the process of this work he received the title "arch-abbot" over all the Roman monasteries from Leo VII (936-939). A few other houses showed some activity—Subiaco, Monte Cassino, St. Vincent, Farfa—but these also manifested no remarkable life. It is not until later that the monastic life came to such a state as to warrant serious study concerning bishop-abbot relations.

Central Spain was still under the power of the Arabs in the early tenth century, and although the latter permitted the monastic state to continue, it could not have existed in too organized a state. Although other Rules persisted until after our period, the Benedictine Rule was not propagated extensively until early in the tenth century, and the most ancient document of the *Dialogues* of St. Gregory only dates to 938.[73] Reports from this country on the bishop-abbot relations are too few to warrant attention.

England also was still recovering from the invasions, and underwent new life only with St. Dunstan (924-988) about the middle of the tenth century. England was influenced much by the monastic activities on the continent. Flanders, as being

[72] Schmitz, *Histoire de l'Ordre*, I, 164.

[73] Schmitz, *Histoire de l'Ordre*, I, 164. For a coverage of Spanish monasticism in the late ninth and early tenth century, cf. Urbel, *Los Monjes Espanoles en la Edad Media* (2 vols., Madrid, 1934), Vol. II, part 4, "Los Monjes en los Siglos de la Reconquista," pp. 253 ff.

nearest to the Island, played a large part in the reform movement in England, and particularly through the Abbey of St. Bertin. In 944, many monks fled from Flanders in objection to the reform of St. Gerard of Brogne (d. 957), and received help from King Edmund (940-946), thereafter settling in St. Peter's in Bath.[74] Moreover, during the period of calm and peace under Edgar the Peaceful (959-975), after so many years of strife, Dunstan, Archbishop of Canterbury (960-988), could inaugurate his reform of the Church, secular and monastic. Monastic properties which had been annexed by the crown were returned, and lands in the hands of the feudal lords were repurchased for the Church. Dunstan had previously been exiled by Edgar's predecessor, Edwy (955-959), and had learned much of the monastic reform of the Cluniac houses. In 946, Ethelwold, Abbot of Glastonbury, traveled to the continent to study the monastic customs under the reform movement in order to bring them back to England.

When Odo, the predecessor of St. Dunstan, was told in 942 of his promotion to the See of Canterbury, he claimed that an ancient custom demanded that whosoever was to be archbishop of Canterbury had to be a monk. He therefore went to Fleury, already reformed by Odo of Cluny, and brought its customs back with him to England.

About the same time, Oswald (d. 992), who had taken the habit at Fleury, returned to England, and became bishop of the important See of Worcester. At this time the canons were expelled and replaced by monks.[75]

The monasticism at this date in England seemed to be *sui generis*. The secular and monastic states were intermingled in such a way that they were almost indistinguishable one from the other. Mabillon contended that the See of Canterbury was held by monks from the time of St. Austin up until the tenth century, which could have accounted for Odo's actions.[76]

[74] Grierson, "Relations between England and Flanders before the Norman Conquest," *Transactions of the Royal Historical Society* (4th Series, Vol. XXIII) (London, 1941), p. 89.

[75] Pignot, *Histoire de l'Ordre*, I, 161.

[76] Mabillon, *Acta*, VII, XXXVI-XXXVII: "Per totum illud intervallum temporis, quod ab Augustino Anglorum Apostolo ad saeculum 10 effluxit,

Other places showed the effects of the invasions, and revealed many unexpected situations. In the ninth century, an abbot held jurisdiction over monks who dwelt in the episcopal church, which was also the *Sedes Episcopalis.*[77] Again, diocesan clerics were found chanting the office together with the monks.[78]

In the monastery of Evesham, Abbot Egwin (d. 717) was succeeded in turn by eighteen abbots, the last of whom was Edwin. Athelm, a secular prince, procured the abbey upon the demise of Edwin and together with the Bishop by the name of Osulf and another layman, Ulfric, dispersed the monks and replaced them with secular canons. In the year 960, under the impulse of King Edgar (959-975), St. Ethelwold restored the monks. Upon King Edgar's death, however, Elfere, Duke of Mercia (d. 984), once again introduced secular canons, the occupancy of Evesham alternating between canons and monks for many years thereafter.[79]

It seems, therefore, that whatever the exact conditions of England in this period the bishoprics were still largely mo-

numquam intermissa est haec monachorum possessio ac sedes in illa ecclesia (Canterbury)...Sub finem saeculi decimi monachis suffectos clericos, iisque amotis a Rege Aethelredo restituos fuisse monachos apparet ex hujus Regis privilegio apud Spelmannum relato, quo Aethelredus instigante Archiepiscopo, monachos ejusdem Ordinis, quem huc attulit sanctus Augustinus, et in Christi ecclesia posuit, se restituisse testatur, nempe sub annum 1003.

[77] Mabillon, *Annales*, III, 37: "In insula Britannia Lindisfarnensem ecclesiam (circa 854) hoc anno regendam post Eanbertum accepti Eardulfus episcopus, Osberte regis anno quinto...Lindisfarnensem ecclesiam incidebant etiam tunc monachi, quibus sub episcopo praeerat Eadredus abbas mirae apud Deum sanctitatis, nec exiguae nobilitatis apud homines...hinc confirmatur id quod alias diximus, in cathedralibus monachorum apud Anglos ecclesiis, praeter episcopum extitisse quandoque abbatem, qui monachis sub episcopo praeesset."

[78] Mabillon, *Annales*, III, 157 (about 870): "Is clericos simul cum monachis in ea ecclesia psallere gravate ferens, id tamen corrigere distulit usque ad tempora pacis et tranquillitatis...clerici tam in ecclesia Cantuariensi, quam in aliis, monachatu non suscepto, cum monachis permixti permanserunt. Semper tamen monachi Cantuariensis ecclesiae dominatum retinuerunt."

[79] Mabillon, *Annales*, III, 457; Sir William Dugdale, *Monasticon Anglicanum, a History of the Abbies and other Monasteries, Hospitals, Frieries, and Cathedral and Collegiate Churches, with their Dependencies in England and Wales* (6 Vols in 8 Parts, London, 1817-1830), II, 2.

nastic. With some of the more important bishops taking the habit at Fleury on the continent, the customs of this latter house were introduced into England, and were the touchstone of the reform there.[80]

[80] Cf. Schmitz, *Histoire de l'Ordre*, I, ch. 14, "L'Angleterre benedictine;" cf. also Smith, *Monastery of Cluny*, pp. 44 ff.

CHAPTER XIV

CANONICAL COLLECTIONS

Another very important element in the formation of the canon law of this period was reflected in the various canonical collections, some spurious and others authentic, but all of them contributing to the canonical legislation. This chapter will deal with some of the most influential of these, which were the so-called Pseudo-Isidorian decretals, the collection of Regino of Prüm, that of Abbo of Fleury and the *Decretum* of Burchard of Worms. Attention will be paid, not to the authorities from which the material is drawn in the collections, since these are not of any especial concern here, but rather to the content of their collections, and to the pictures they present in the selections and rubrics of monasticism in its relations with the bishops.

The Pseudo-Isidorian Decretals were composed in the middle of the ninth century. Their purpose was not simply to deceive the people—although this was manifestly achieved—but to reform the discipline of the Church, and to defend it against the abuses of the period, particularly that of the violations against ecclesiastical rights perpetrated by laymen. The bishop's position was augmented over against that of the metropolitans, the *chorepiscopi*, and other clerics and laymen. Monks were aggregated in this latter class, and had to give place to the priority of position granted by the decretals to the bishops.[1]

The so-called Pseudo-Isidorian group of forgeries comprised

[1] Cf. Kurtscheid-Wilches, *Historia Iuris Canonici*, I, *Historia Fontium*, I, 134; Naz, "Décrétales (Fausses)", *Dictionnaire de Droit Canonique*, IV, 1062 ff.; Fournier-LeBras, *Histoire des Collections Canoniques*, I, 127 ff.; Van Hove, A., *Commentarium Lovaniense in Codicem Iuris Canonici*, Editum a Magistris et Doctoribus Universitatis Lovaniensis (5 vols., Vol. I, *Prolegomena*, 2. ed., Mechliniae, Romae: H. Dessain, 1945), Vol. I, pp. 306-307 (hereafter cited *Prolegomena*); Stickler, *Historia Iuris Canonici Latini, Institutiones Academicae*, Tom. I, *Historia Fontium* (Taurini: Libreria Pontif. Athenaei Salesiani, 1950), pp. 117-127 (hereafter cited *Historia Fontium*).

four separate collections; the *Hispana Augustodunensis*, the *Decretals of Isidore Mercator*, the *Capitula Angilramni*, and the *Capitularia of Benedictus Levita*. Probably all four emanated from a common workshop.[2]

These forgeries had a wide influence in Europe after their publication. The extent of their dissemination is suggested by their occasional citation in the period of the ninth and tenth centuries, which citation was not without its influence in the period covered in this work.[3] The manuscripts of the *Capitula Angilramni* number about thirty-seven, and appear usually as appendices to Ps.-Isidore. Those of the False Capitularies do not appear in their entirety, though two almost complete ones of some antiquity have been found, and three more of the late tenth and eleventh centuries. Other manuscripts are fragmentary. About ninety-three codices of the Ps.-Isidorian Decretals have come down to us, and eighty are known to be genuine.[4]

Hincmar, Archbishop of Rheims (845-882), knew of the *Capitularia Angilramni*, although he was somewhat hesitant in using them. His nephew, Hincmar of Laon, quoted from them in an argument with his uncle and metropolitan in 870. Regarding the False Capitularies of Benedictus Levita, portions were inserted in the Capitulary of Quierzy in 857,[5] in the *Capitula Missis Tradita* in 860,[6] and in others.[7] From then on they appeared in councils until the beginning of the tenth century and the Council of Trosly in 909. Bishop Isaac of Langres at the end of the 9th century made use of them to compose

[2] Zeiger, *Historia Iuris Canonici* (2 vols., Romae: Apud Aedes Universitatis Gregorianae, 1947), I, *De Historia Fontium et Scientiae Iuris Canonici*, 48; Fournier-LeBras, *op. cit.*, I, 183-201.

[3] The matter which is to follow is taken largely from Fournier-Le Bras, *op. cit.*, I, 201-233. Cf. also, Zeiger, *op. cit.*, I, 48-51; Kurtscheid-Wilches, *op. cit.*, I, 143-145; Van Hove, *op. cit.*, pp. 300-311; Stickler, *op. cit.*, pp. 117-146.

[4] Kurtscheid-Wilches (*op. cit.*, I, 143) listed 75 as the number of such manuscripts on Ps.-Isidore, but this must be amended in the light of more recent scholarship done by Schaefer Williams, "The Pseudo-Isidorian Problem Today," *Speculum*, XXIX (Oct. 1954), n. 4, pp. 702-707.

[5] *MGH, Cap. Reg. Fr.*, II, 290-291.

[6] *Ibid.*, p. 300.

[7] *Ibid.*, pp. 307, 309, 326.

his statutes. About the same time, Rudolph, Archbishop of Bourges, drew texts from them. They appear still later incorporated into the *Collectio Ansegisi.*

Hincmar already in 852 reproduced texts from the False Decretals in his diocesan statutes, and in other works authored by himself. His adversaries also made use of them against Hincmar, such as his nephew, the other Hincmar. Loup de Ferrières used them in a letter in 858. The French Councils of Troyes in 867, Douzy in 874, Fimes in 881, also made use of them, and the Council of Trosly in 909 cited Isidore in its 4th and 5th canons. In the German councils—Cologne in 887, Tribur in 895—mention was made of a part of Ps.-Isidore. Regino of Prüm (d. 915) used some portions, although very few, in his collection. In the tenth century they had a wide diffusion in France and Germany, although not without opposition. Abbo of Fleury (ca. 945-1004) cited them in a defense of Arnold, Archbishop of Rheims (d. 1021), in 991 at a council held at Sainte-Basle, but he was opposed by Arnold, Bishop of Orleans, who refused to recognize the genuineness of the texts. Abbo did not use the False Decretals in his canonical collection, perhaps because it might have weakened the position which he expounded, although this cannot be strictly proved.

About 882, the author of the canonical collection called "*Anselmo Dedicata*" (dedicated to Abbot Anselm of Milan) used the False Decretals abundantly. Another collection of lesser importance in the manuscript T.XVIII of the *Bibliotheca Vallicelliana* in Rome appeared in the 10th century. Bishops Atto of Vercelli (d. 961) and Ratherius of Verona (d. 974) spoke of the use of these Ps.-Isidorian texts, though other important collections made little or no use of them.

The Holy See used them rarely in the beginning. Pope St. Nicholas I (858-867) seemed influenced by the collection, at least by fragments of it. Hadrian II (867-872) quoted a long portion of it in a letter to bishops meeting together at Douzy in 871, but this seemed his only use of them. John VIII (872-882) utilized one of the apocryphal decretals in a letter of his. Gregory V (996-999) in 998 also mentioned portions of a false letter taken from Ps.-Isidore.

Since the false decretals shared a common purpose and are thus attributable to authors of one and the same mind and intent, there will be no attempt to treat them separately. Many of the sources used by them were genuine, while others were fictitious. Moreover, since during the period in which they exerted their influence little attempt was made to distinguish the spurious from the genuine—for their authenticity went largely unquestioned—likewise no effort seems indicated for establishing the sources of the citations or their genuine or spurious character. Rather, since they exerted a common impact upon canonical thought, they will be treated *in globo*. Only two of the collections will be analyzed, the *Capitularia Benedicti Levitae*, and the *Decretals of Isidore Mercator*. The *Hispana* has not been available for inspection, since it exists only in manuscripts, and the collection of the *Capitularia Angilramni* offers no pertinent matter.

Monks, according to Pseudo-Isidore, could take part in clerical activities, but were to be sharply controlled by episcopal authority. They were held to the same requirements for the reception of orders, such as the observance of the interstices, as were the secular clerics. Monks could do pastoral work only with the permission of the abbot, and at the request of the bishop. They were not to give up their monastic vows, nor were they to be permitted to enter the married state. Once entered into the clerical state, the monks were to remain in the power of the bishop, and if they proved contumacious toward him they could be excommunicated.

The monasteries of nuns were to have their spiritual needs administered by monks appointed for this work by the bishops. But neither these monks nor their abbots could disturb the inner monastic discipline once established in the nuns' monastery. Visits to the monasteries of nuns were to be made only for purposes of the ministry, and all cautions were to be observed during the ministry, after which the monks were to leave immediately.

Monks were to be appointed to see to the upkeep of the rural and urban churches entrusted to the monasteries, the choice of these monks falling to the abbot, and their approval to the bishop. Any monk involved in such clerical work was not to perform other ecclesiastical or civil acts without the authorization of the bishop. No monk could preach in public, even though he was suited for the work, unless his designation was approved by the bishop. Faculties given to a cleric for the convenience of the monastery could not be interfered with by any bishop, or by diocesan law.[8]

The monasteries were permitted to receive and control temporalities. Offerings made to monks caring for a parish in the diocese could not be taken from them. If the bishop wished to grant one of the parish churches to monks for their regular residence, he could do this with the consent of his chapter. He could donate certain things for the sustenance of those monks if it did not prove too great a burden to the diocese.

The bishop was even permitted to construct a monastery in his diocese, but was limited regarding the amount of the diocese's money he could expend for this end. It was a duty of the bishop to see to it that a part of the donations given to the churches be granted to monasteries. No one, not even a king, could alienate or change in any way the temporalities of the monasteries, the violation of which law entailed suitable penalties. If such property was sold, the sale was not valid. Whatever price had been paid was to be restored, and the sold property was to be returned to the monastery. Even the abbots could not alienate any property of the monastery, or enter into obligations concerning it, without the permission of the bishops and their explicit signature.

Any person who despoiled monastic property was not only to be punished by means of episcopal sanctions but also was to see to it that the damages were repaired and the monastery restored to its former favorable condition. Donations given to secular churches in the diocese could not be alienated, except for some charitable reason such as the endowing of monasteries. Monasteries which were granted immunity were especially protected from outside usurpation. In order to preserve the

[8] Hinschius, *Decretales Pseudo-Isidorianae et Capitula Angilramni* (Lipsiae, 1863), pp. 343, 346, 439, 521, 530; "Benedicti Capitularium Collectio," *MPL*, 97, 707 (Liber I, can. 27); 803 (Lib. III, can. 12); 865 (Additio II, can. 19); 894 (Additio IV, can. 33).

internal harmony of a monastery, the abbot was not to dispose of any of the monastic goods in favor of individual subjects, for this could give rise to quarrels and enmities. A special penalty awaited him who made off with monastic goods, for he fell prey to an ecclesiastical interdict until they were restored. It was the bishops' duty to see that these rules were observed regarding monastic temporalities.[9]

Abbots and monks were in all things to be subject to their bishops. The latter were to ascertain the state of discipline in the monasteries of monks and canons, and to learn their Rules, in order to control their separate types of life. Abuses of the abbots were to be corrected by the bishop, and every abbot had to appear before the bishop at the latter's notice once each year.

Bishops were to accompany the *missi* in inspection tours of the monasteries, to see that these were housed in suitable places, that all the necessaries were provided within the monastery so as to render excursions outside the cloister unnecessary, that the buildings were suited for the monks, that a proper cloister was provided for them, and that the discipline of the community be kept on a monastic and edifying level. Since some bishops had shown negligence in their duties of surveillance over the monasteries, they were to be reproved, and were to be reminded to attend to their charge in the future. The bishop of the city was to provide for the monasteries in his territory. Monks were not to conspire against their bishop. They were not to become engaged in secular affairs, nor were they to travel about without the permission of their bishops. Violations were subject to punishment with excommunication.

Monks were to be counselled on how they had to lead their lives in order to please God. No occasion could be allowed to give rise to vagrancy. Without an episcopal letter no monk was permitted to journey about. If one was corrected by the bishop and yet did not desist from such a practice, he was to

[9] Hinschius, *Decretales Ps. Isidorianae*, pp. 359, 395, 398, 401, 439, 657; "Benedicti Capitularium Collectio," *MPL*, 97, 726 (Lib. 1, can. 209); 736 (Lib. 1, can. 279); 751 (Lib. 1, 376); 751 (Lib. 1, can. 386); 768 (Lib. II, 167); 833 Lib. III, can. 275); 851 (Lib. III, can. 419).

be coerced by means of physical chastisement (*verberibus coerceri*). Any accusations launched against monks were to be brought before the bishop, not before the civil courts. Proper punishments could be imposed by the bishops for violations. Monks could not form rebellious groups, and as part of them sign a document in common attesting to their ill will. Nothing left room for such a suit, and it was to be brought before the synod of bishops and exhibited there. The publicity thus attached to the uncharitable action paved the way for the official reprimand. No cleric or monk or abbot could appear at civil litigations without the command of his proper bishop.

Commendatory letters were to be issued to monks before they could permissibly travel, for they were to go nowhere outside the monasteries without the approval of their bishops. The bishops could not force upon monks any servile work, and could not violate the rights of the monasteries which had been constituted for them by the councils. Those who were constituted in authority over the monasteries were not to exceed the measure of their authority, that is they were simply to see that the monks acted in full accordance with their Rules. Those who acted contrary to the Rules were to be excommunicated.[10]

Many of the monastery's domestic affairs also fell under episcopal authority. The various hours of the monastic office chanted by the monks had to follow the rules laid down for the metropolitan cathedral. The suffragan bishops were to regulate their subjects according to like norms. A monk who through his own will assumed monastic vows could not depart from the monastic life without incurring sin, for which he was to make public satisfaction if he entered military service or took a wife. Bishops were to see to it that the fugitive slaves

[10] Hinschius, *Decretales Pseudo-Isidorianae*, pp. 371, 439; "Benedicti Capitularium Collectio," *MPL*, 97, 708 (Liber 1, can. 29); 712 (Liber 1, can. 71); 720 (Lib. 1, can. 143) 745 (Lib. 1, can. 328); 750 (Lib. 1, can. 373); 751 (Lib. 1, can. 378); 764 (Lib. II, can. 124); 765 (Lib. II, can. 132); 765 (Lib. II, can. 139); 776 (Lib. II, can. 246); 804 (Lib. III, can. 12); 804 (Lib. III, can. 18); 817 (Lib. III, can. 155); 818 (Lib. III, can. 159); 824 (Lib. III, can. 210); 876 (Additio III, can. 44); 879 (Additio III, can. 59); 908 (Additio IV, can. 157).

who attempted to enter monasteries were returned to their masters, since non-compliance with this norm would militate against civic order and give rise to grave disputes. The abbots and monks who had charge of a religious community were to pursue their duties with all zeal and good example for their charges. Abbots could not live in dwellings outside of the cloister; they had to live with the monks. Abuses were to be corrected by the bishops.

If a monk had given up his vows and thereupon became reduced to lay status, he was to be deprived of his habit (*cingulo spolietur*) and his property was to remain with the monastery. Once a monk had quit the religious life, he was to be numbered among the faithful of that diocese, and his name was to be added to the curial census list. Once a monk had entered a monastery, he lost all control over the property he once owned, even though he had children of his own for whom he wished to provide the needed care. Monks could not leave a monastery to construct a cell apart from the community unless they had the permission of the bishop and of the proper abbot. An abbot could not preside over two monasteries at the same time. Any monk or nun who had once taken vows in a religious community and had later abandoned this life without permission was to be admonished by the bishop to return. If they spurned the warning he gave them, and did not return, they were to be deprived of communion with the church until death, and were not to be permitted to receive the sacraments until they had made due satisfaction.[11]

From the tenor of these decrees it is evident that the decretals of Ps.-Isidore were designed as a means for suppressing exemption, and for exalting the spiritual and temporal jurisdiction of the bishop over monasteries. Appearing in the middle of the ninth century, these directives were already counterbalanced by many exemptions granted to the French monasteries, which quite understandably added to the burdens placed

[11] Hinschius, *Decretales Ps.-Isidorianae*, pp. 408, 617, 650; "Benedicti Capitularium Collectio," *MPL*, 97, 745 (Lib. 1, can. 329); 746 (Lib. 1, can. 333); 751 (Lib. 1, can. 379); 762 (Lib. II, can. 108); 751 (Lib. 1, can. 381); 762 (Lib. II, can. 110); 765 (Lib. II, can. 140); 767 (Lib. II, can. 155); 841 (Lib. III, can. 337); 879 (Additio III, can. 62).

upon the bishop's shoulders by the metropolitans and laymen. Other currents, somewhat contrary to this one, were shortly to appear, however, in defense of the monastic rights.

The canonical collection of Regino of Prüm is entitled, "*Reginonis libri duo de synodalibus causis.*" The author, abbot of the monastery of Prüm in Germany, compiled this collection about the year 906. The work comprises both a collection of canonical decrees and a norm for procedure within the Church. The "Synodal Causes" were evidence of the gathering of the clergy and the people attendant on the episcopal visitations, and presented a set of norms to guide him in rendering judgments concerning the violations of church law. The obligations of clerics and laity were discernible from the interrogations listed in the formulary. Three appendices followed the work of Regino; they however were of later period. This collection with its appendices exercised a great influence on later works. The manuscripts of Regino's collection are not numerous, and they are found mostly in Germany. However, Burchard of Worms (d. 1025) made much use of the work, and other smaller collections utilized greater or lesser portions of it until the end of the 10th century.

There is here no ample treatment of bishop-abbot relations, although the duties of abbots and monks are partially discussed in the measure in which they would bear on their relations with the bishops. Monks who had undertaken ministerial work were not to attempt to bribe the clerics of another diocese (*parochia*) in order to have them secretly ordained in their own diocese. The penalty for so doing was excommunication.[13]

Monks ordained in monasteries and in the basilicas of martyrs were to remain under the power of the bishops; the former

[12] Cf. Fournier-LeBras, *Histoire des Collections Canoniques*, I, 244 ff.; Kurtscheid-Wilches, *Historia Fontium*, 151 ff.; Zeiger, *Historia Iuris Canonici*, I, 51-52; Van Hove, *Prolegomena*, pp. 317-318; Stickler, *Historia Fontium*, pp. 146-147.

[13] "Collectio Reginonis Prumiensis Abbatis," Lib. 1, Cap. 237, "De his qui per pecunias fuerint ordinati," *MPL*, 132, 235. The preferred edition of Regino's Collection is that of F. G. Wasserschleben, *Reginonis Abbatis Prumiensis Libri Duo de Synodalibus Causis et Disciplinis Ecclesiasticis* (*Lipsiae*, 1840).

were not to show themselves contumacious toward the latter. Monks violating this canon were subject to excommunication.[14]

Serfs (*mancipia*) when given to monks by their abbot were not to be manumitted by them. It would be unjust for such slaves to have leisure while the monks in the rural areas worked daily.[15] Archbishops travelling throughout the provinces were to have in their hands a list (*exemplar*) of the servants of the Church and when one was found worthy of ordination, his name was to be read to the people and to the priests and other clergy from the altar, and in this way given his liberty to pursue the process of ordination. This same process was to be followed with regard to a monastic servant, whom the laity deemed worthy of ordination and whom the abbots asked to receive ordination.[16]

Journeying clerics were to bear with them commendatory letters from their bishop. The same held for monks.[17]

Bishops were to make their visitations in the various monastic houses in their diocese for the purpose of inspecting the monasteries regarding their religious life. Whatever was found reprehensible was to be corrected by them.[18]

Monks who were found to have conspired against their bishop or deceived him were to be demoted from their grade. As actions like this were prohibited in civil law, so much the more should they be so in the Church.[19]

The abbots were to remain under the power of their bishops. If the abbots were active outside their Rule, they were to be corrected by the bishop. Once each year, at the notice of the bishop, they were to gather before him. Monks were subject to their abbots, in all obedience and devotion. If monks con-

[14] *Ibid.*, Cap. 252, "De clericis qui praeficiuntur ptochiis," *MPL*, 132, 239.

[15] *Ibid.*, Cap. 355, "De manumissionibus in Ecclesia," *MPL*, 132, 259.

[16] *Ibid.*, Cap. 399, "De ecclesiarum vero servis," *MPL*, 132, 269; Cap. 400, "De familiis monasteriorum," *loc. cit.*

[17] *Ibid.*, Cap. 429, "Ut clerici cum epistolis episcopi sui proficiscantur," *MPL*, 132, 275.

[18] Lib. II, Cap. 167, "Ut episcopus monasterium monachorum vel puellarum introeat," *MPL*, 132, 315.

[19] Lib. II, Cap. 428, "De conspirationibus," *MPL*, 132, 366; Cap. 429, "De eadem re," *loc. cit.*

tumaciously left the monastery and wandered about, in the meantime acquiring certain items on these journeys, the said items were to be taken from them by the abbots. The fugitive monks were, with the help of the bishop, to be brought back to the monastery in which their monastic life had its origin. Any abbot who aided a monk to leave and did not reveal it, or who received a foreign monk, made himself guilty of violating this canon.[20]

Bishops violated the mind of canon law by enlisting monks in their service and forcing them to do servile work. Likewise they violated the rights of the monasteries. Bishops having charge of monasteries were not to perform any actions of this sort if they were not prescribed by the Church canons, that is, they were simply to see that abbots were placed over the monasteries, their duties properly indicated for them, and the abuses corrected. If they went beyond this, for example by usurping monastic possessions, they were subjected to excommunication.[21]

The bishops were not to restrain clerics from entering the monastic life if they desired to do so. Since it was a higher life, no one should be prohibited from following his desires in this respect.[22]

One notices in this collection small if any advance over the false decretals, and the author may have been guided by them, although he used them only very rarely.[23] The reason may be that the purposes of the two respective compilers were different. The varying content of the two compilations reflects this strongly. With regard to monks, therefore, Regino represented no prejudicial position. Apparently he afforded only one major advance over the Ps.-Isidore in bishop-abbot relations, namely by making the monks directly subject to the abbot rather than to the bishop.

[20] Appendix I, Cap. 32, "Ut abbates episcopis, monachi abbatibus subsint. Et de monachis vagis," *MPL*, 132, 376.

[21] Appendix I, Cap. 33, "De discretione potestatis episcoporum quam in monasteriis habere possunt," *MPL*, 132, 376.

[22] Appendix I, Cap. 55, "De clericis qui monachorum propositum appetunt," *MPL*, 132, 348.

[23] Kurtscheid, *Historia Fontium*, p. 144.

The collection of Abbo, Abbot of the French monastery of Fleury, represented a definite effort towards monastic independence, for it defended what it acknowledged as exemption of the monks. Abbo's collection was compiled toward the end of the tenth century, about 996, and hence immediately after the period just considered. Yet, it is important to note his approach toward bishop-abbot relations, inasmuch as it summed up the mentality of the abbots of his time and was fully in sympathy with their struggle for monastic liberty. He made no use of the false decretals of Isidore, for these, it must be surmised, could have weakened his position.[24]

Abbo launched without delay into his discussion of monastic exemptions. Monastic exemptions, fortified as they were with a sanction of papal anathemas, were to be observed by all. It would be acting contrary to one's priestly intentions to ignore these exemptions and thus to render them nugatory. Such privileges and exemptions had been granted by the bishops' predecessors, and were to be retained in customary usage. Therefore they were to be not only acknowledged but also respected. Likewise, the immunities attaching to the monastic possessions were to be held in honor by all.[25]

The precepts of the kings, when in accord with the mind of the Church, were likewise to be respected by all. Whosoever sought to contradict such precepts showed his lack of love and fear for the kingship.[26] The abbot of a monastery was to be chosen not because of his rank in the monastery but rather according to the free choice of the monks. Once chosen the abbot was in his election to be confirmed by the bishop to whom the monastery was subject.[27]

The internal quietude of the monastery was to be respected in such a manner that it suffered no unnecessary disturbance from outsiders. No outside person could seek by alteration or diminution to dispose in any way of the contributions, the

[24] Cf. Fournier-Le Bras, *Histoire des Collections Canoniques*, I, 322; Zeiger, *Historia Iuris Canonici*, I, 52.

[25] "Canones Domni Abbonis Abbatis," Cap. 5, "De privilegiis," *MPL*, 139, 479.

[26] Cap. 6, "De praeceptis regalibus vel imperialibus," *MPL*, 139, 480.

[27] Cap. 14, "De electione abbatis," *MPL*, 139, 484.

revenues (*de redditibus*), the temporalities, or the charters of a monastery; these all called for his compliance. Difficulties between churches of the diocese and the monasteries were to be settled according to evangelical principles. When the abbot died, no one from outside the monastery was to be chosen to succeed him. Once the abbot was in power, no monk was to show opposition to him. Without the will of the abbot no monk could be deputed for the forming of new monasteries (*ad ordinanda alia monasteria*), or be forced to assume clerical orders. If it served a useful purpose to have a monk ordained, he was to be chosen by the abbot and offered by him for the reception of orders. If not enough monks could be offered for ordination, the bishop could approach other monasteries in his jurisdiction to solicit vocations.

For the performance of other ecclesiastical duties also, no one was to be pressed into service unless the abbot had chosen him for the task. Whoever was requisitioned from the monastery for clerical orders was not to return to live in the abbey. The bishops were not to examine the charters and other items in the monastery; any needed inventory was to be made by the abbot of the monastery, assisted by others of abbatial rank. The abbot enjoyed complete freedom for visiting the Roman Pontiff. When the bishop made his visitations in monasteries, he was in all charity to curb the duration of his stay, lest his visit prove an undue burden to the monks. Priests, even those who formerly were monks, were not to return except to join in the community prayer or, if invited, to celebrate Mass.[28]

Abbots were to be graced with ordination to the priesthood, in order to better rule their monks.[29] If an abbot was accused of a crime, he was not to be immediately deposed, unless the very nature of the crime demanded this. With reference to the prospective passing of judgment in a trial, it was not within the competence of the bishop of the city alone to do so, but rather a number of bishops had to be gathered together. On a

[28] Cap. 15, "De abbatis ordinatione, et de accessu episcopi ad Monasterium," *MPL*, 139, 484.

[29] Cap. 16, "De eo quod abbas sacerdos esse debet," *MPL*, 139, 486.

thorough examination of the circumstances of the case they could then pass judgment, either declaring the abbot guilty and worthy of punishment, or vindicating him as innocent and as worthy of confidence, honor and respect.[30]

Monks were to live in the full spirit of their Rule, but if they had lapsed from an edifying life, the bishop of the city had the duty of striving to correct them. If they ignored his warnings, the metropolitan was to be informed. His efforts failing, a public synod was to be called regarding the matter. If, however, they disparaged the synodal warnings, they were to forfeit all honors, or be excommunicated by all the bishops. This was to be expedited within the will of the king, or with the consent of those in whose charge the monks were placed.[31]

The monasteries were to be provided with what was needed for the livelihood of the monks. If the monastic community was within the holding of the king, the abbot was accountable to him; otherwise he was answerable to the bishop.[32] With regard to the Abbey of Fleury, the privileges of the monastery which had been granted by King Charles and by Archbishop Rudolph were to be observed. If, in a visitation by the *missi*, the abbot was found to have lapsed from compliance with the monastic rules, he was to be deposed by the two authorities, and another was to be substituted in his place. The privileges, however, were to remain intact.[33]

Any monk when presented for the reception of sacred orders was to be investigated thoroughly; once he was approved, the ordination could follow. The one who was ordained for the community was not to receive any special privileges; he was simply to celebrate the Holy Sacrifice of the Mass when that was opportune.[34]

Clerics who desired to share in the monastic life were to be accorded free entry and no prohibition was to be placed upon them, since it represented a higher state of life. Some monks

[30] Cap. 17, "De accusato abbate quid sit agendum," *MPL*, 139, 486.

[31] Cap. 18, "De monachis et sanctimonialibus, et regulariter vivant," *MPL*, 139, 487.

[32] Cap. 19, "De abbate ad regem pertinente," *MPL*, 139, 487.

[33] Cap. 20, "De rectore Floriacensi," *MPL*, 139, 487.

[34] Cap. 21, "De sacerdotio monachi," *MPL*, 139, 487.

had been called by the bishops to do servile work. This practice was to cease, for it was alien to the mind of the Church. The bishops were to correct abuses, to delineate certain duties for the abbots, and to see that a regular monastic life was in force. They were not to exceed their rights, nor to usurp any of the monastic goods.[35]

If any cleric had abandoned his duties, but wished out of vanity to appear a monk rather than a cleric, he was to be restrained by the Church until he had suitably satisfied for his vanity. In this decree all the bishops agreed (*ab universis episcopis dictum est: ita fiat*).[36]

Any person entering into a dispute with a monk was not to presume hailing him before a civil court; the hearing was to be before the bishop of the city. The bishop best knew how the monk must be defended, in view of being acquainted with the sacred canons in such affairs. Suitable punishments were invoked as a sanction against the violation of this decree.[37]

A definite trend toward independence seemed to pervade this compilation of Abbo of Fleury. However, even though Cluny had been well established in its liberties at this time, the note of subjection to the local bishop was still present and reflected in the collection of Abbo. The canons which dwelt upon this subjection were perhaps meant for other than Cluniac abbeys, for the collection's first thought and intent was perhaps one of the most liberally endowed monasteries of Europe. This was not the only trend, however, as will be apparent from the work of the next compiler.

In the first part of the eleventh century Burchard, Bishop of Worms in Germany (1002-1025), composed the work which is entitled the "*Decretum of Burchard.*" It was a complete and organized work, and hence more useful than the works of Regino of Prüm or of Abbo of Fleury, which covered only certain parts of Church discipline. Burchard was opposed to ex-

[35] Cap. 23, "De clericis qui monachi volunt fieri, et de insolentia episcoporum," *MPL*, 139, 488.

[36] Cap. 24, "De clericis qui propter vanitatem efficiuntur monachi," *MPL*, 139, 489.

[37] Cap. 26, "De monacho, vel sanctimoniali, in jus vocata," *MPL*, 139, 470.

emptions, and hence one finds little mention of them in his collection. He is one of the few bishops of his time who did not found a single monastery. Although he was opposed to the grant of exemptions by local bishops, he was not unfavorable to the reform activity of the monasteries. However, a mild tone of opposition to the rising power of monasticism is apparent in his work. In this, nonetheless, as in other matters which received attention in the collection, he adopted a moderate policy.[38]

In his first book Burchard treated of monks who became bishops. Having been freed from the monastic vows, they were free through inheritance to acquire goods. What had been acquired up until the time of the episcopal consecration was to be retained by the monastery and the abbot. Later acquisitions were to be dedicated to the altar under whose title he had been consecrated a bishop.[39] No monk could roam about without commendatory letters from his bishop.[40] No title of knowledge or skill made it permissible for a monk to preach without the permission of his bishop. Such work remained for the priests of God, who were under commission for its execution.[41]

Monasteries, if with the counsel of the bishops they had received their dedication, were to remain monasteries, not to be transformed into secular dwellings. Everything belonging to the monasteries was to remain in their possession. Violations were made punishable by the sacred canons.[42] Regular monasteries could not be sold or bartered by kings or by anyone else. Monasteries were permitted to exchange goods with one another, or even to sell certain things to one another. Abuses

[38] Cf. Fournier-Le Bras, *Histoire des Collections Canoniques*, I, 364 ff.; Kurtscheid-Wilches, *Historia Fontium*, p. 153; Zeiger, *Historia Iuris Canonici*, I, 52.

[39] "Burchardi Wormaciensis Ecclesiae Episcopi Decretum," Lib. 1, Cap. 231, "De eo qui ex monacho factus fuerit episcopus," *MPL*, 140, 645.

[40] Lib. II, Cap. 141, "De clericis et monachis, qui sine litteris episcopi sui vagantur," *MPL*, 140, 649; Cap. 142, "De eadem re."

[41] Lib. II, Cap. 158, "Nulli monacho non sacerdoti, vel laico, quantumlibet sint eruditi, licet praedicare," *MPL*, 140, 651.

[42] Lib. III, Cap. 19, "De monasteriis semel consecratis," *MPL*, 140, 676.

were punished with excommunication of the perpetrators, and the monasteries involved were to be restored to their former state and condition.[43] Neither bishops nor abbots could transfer land from one church to another, even if both the churches and the land were in their power. However, with the consent of both churches, such exchanges could be made.[44] If someone wished to change the location of a monastery from one place to another, with the end in view of bettering its status, this was possible with the permission of the bishop and the monks (fratrum suorum). He is to place a priest in the former location to care for the sacred ministry. Monks who were assigned in the parishes of the bishops were to be subject to them, obedient, and prompt in the fulfilling of their ecclesiastical duties.[46]

Those who once had embraced the monastic state were thereafter not to enter into military service or aspire to important positions in secular society. To attempt to do so, in violation of this canon, was to lay oneself open to excommunication.[47]

The canons who lived in monasteries were to live either as monks or as canons regular. The bishops were to know how many canons were living in the religious communities, and then had to see to it that all who were subject to the abbot embrace either the one way of life or the other.[48] There are two ways of becoming a monk: through the devotion shown by parents in offering their children (*paterna devotio*), and through one's own profession. To one who in either of these ways had become a monk, departure from the community

[43] Lib. III, Cap. 23, "Ut regularia monasteria nec vendi nec commutari possint," *MPL*, 140, 677.

[44] Lib. II, Cap. 24, "Ut non liceat alicui unius Ecclesiae terram, nisi cambiat, vertere ad alium," *MPL*, 140, 677.

[45] Lib. III, Cap. 26, "Ut monasterium ad meliorandum in alium liceat ponere locum," *MPL*, 140, 677.

[46] Lib. III, Cap. 240, "De ecclesiis monachorum," *MPL*, 140, 724.

[47] Lib. VIII, Cap. 4, "De illis qui semel in clero deputati sunt, aut monachorum vitam expetiverunt," *MPL*, 140, 793.

[48] Lib. VIII, Cap. 5, "Ut canonici qui in monasterio monachorum conversantur, aut monachice vivant, aut sub canonica regula constringantur," *MPL*, 140, 793.

was denied.[49]

Clerics who pretended to be monks and paraded as such were open to correction and also the command either to be true monks or true canons.[50] Anyone who had voluntarily made a monastic profession was bound to remain faithful to his vows, and was not permitted either to join the army or to take a wife. Public penance was the due punishment for him who violated this law.[51] No one was permitted to take monastic vows without the permission of his abbot. An unauthorized vow was deemed null and void.[52]

If an unknown person applied for acceptance in a monastic community he was not to be admitted immediately; rather, he was to be subjected to observation for a three-year period. If during these three years it was found that this person was a serf of some lord, and that the latter was still seeking him, such a one together with all that he had brought with him was to be returned to his master. If his condition as a serf became detected only after a lapse of this three-year period, the goods which had been brought with him into the community were to be returned to the master, but the monk himself was to remain.[53] If a cleric wished to become a monk, there was to be no opposition on the part of his bishop, who indeed had to realize that the life of contemplation was the higher one.[54] A slave could not be accepted in a community without the knowledge and permission of his master. Suspension accompanied the violation of this canon.[55] A fugitive monk, or one contemptuous of discipline, was to be returned to his community.[56]

[49] Lib. VIII, Cap. 6, "Quod monachum paterna devotio, vel propria professio faciat," *MPL*, 140, 793.

[50] Lib. VIII, Cap. 7, "De clericis qui se fingunt monachos esse," *MPL*, 140, 793.

[51] Lib. VIII, Cap. 8, "Quod spontaneum propositum monachi mutari non liceat," *MPL*, 140, 793.

[52] Lib. VIII, Cap. 9, "Ut monacho sine conscientia sui abbatis votum vovere non liceat," *MPL*, 140, 794.

[53] Lib. VIII, Cap. 20, "Ut aliquis incognitus, non cito in monasterio monachorum recipiatur," *MPL*, 140, 795.

[54] Lib. VIII, Cap. 21, "De clericis qui monachorum propositum appetunt," *MPL*, 140, 796.

[55] Lib. VIII, Cap. 24, *MPL*, 140, 796; Lib. VIII, Cap. 28, *MPL*, 140, 797.

[56] Lib. VIII, Cap. 26, "De fugitivis clericis," *MPL*, 140, 796.

A bishop had frequently to enter a monastery for purposes of visitation. If practices contrary to the monastic Rule were current, he was to correct them.[57] Abbots were subject to the power of the bishop; they invited his corrections if they lapsed into malpractices. Not merely once but many times during the year the bishop was to visit the monasteries to certify the presence of an edifying discipline. The monks, on the other hand, were to be subject to the abbots in all humility. Fugitives who on returning had goods in their possession were to hand these over to the abbot and the community, and bishops were to help in bringing such fugitives back to their monasteries.[58] Abbots were not to be compelled to attend synods, except for some reasonable cause.[59] Unless their erection was brought to the notice of the bishop and received his approval, new communities could not be erected in a diocese.[60]

One abbot could not alone rule over two houses.[61] Monasteries could likewise claim only one father.[62] An abbot who wished to resign his position through motives of humility could do so with the permission of the bishop. The monks were to elect someone from the same community to succeed him. The bishop could not force the abbot to retain his position. Relatives or friends of the departed abbot could not be chosen to fill the vacant abbatial seat except with the unanimous will of the monks.[63] The bishop was not permitted to impound the goods of a monastery, or to appropriate the monastery itself, if the abbot had committed a crime against him. In punish-

[57] Lib. VIII, Cap. 66, "Ut episcopus monasteria monachorum et sanctimonialium frequenter visitet," *MPL*, 140, 805.

[58] Lib. VIII, Cap. 67, "Ut abbates in potestate episcoporum consistant," *MPL*, 140, 806.

[59] Lib. VIII, Cap. 73, "Ut abbates ad synodum ire non cogantur, nisi pro rationabili re," *MPL*, 140, 807.

[60] Lib. VIII, Cap. 74, "Ut congregationes monachorum sine collaudatione episcopi fieri non liceat," *MPL*, 140, 807.

[61] Lib. VIII, Cap. 81, "Ut unus abbas duobus monasteriis praeesse non debeat," *MPL*, 140, 808.

[62] Lib. VIII, Cap. 82, "Ut monachi compatres non habeant," *MPL*, 140 808.

[63] Lib. VIII, Cap. 86, "Quod abbas pro humiliatione locum suum relinquere possit," *MPL*, 140, 809.

ment for the offense, however, the bishop was to send the abbot to another monastery, where he was to be subject to another abbot.[64]

Wherever it was possible, the order of the day was to be arranged by deans in accord with the Rule of St. Benedict, so that all risk of a sense of elation on the part of the abbot would be duly obviated. Monks were not to travel about, and all, even the abbot, were to receive the bishop's permission to go on a trip. Dissensions were not to be stirred up in the community, but if a dissension did arise, then at the ensuing trial monks were to answer only when questioned, remaining silent otherwise. No monk could presume to leave the monastery to take a meal or to partake in secular diversions without the permission of the abbot.[65]

Monks were to be kept far removed from secular transactions and occupations. They were not to enter into public disputations, were not to heed the lure of their concupiscence, were not to accept, give or sell gifts or other items, were not to dote on boisterous activities, and were not in any way to follow the habits of worldly men. All was to be in keeping with the Benedictine Rule, which prohibited this.[66] No cleric could be given the monastic tonsure against his will. Rather, under all due and constant caution this tonsure could be administered to a candidate only when he was of sufficient age, when he had the needed intention, and when he had the permission of his master or of his parents.[67]

Any abbot who within the demand of the Rule was not circumspect, humble, chaste, sober, merciful, and discreet, and who did not mirror forth the fulfillment of the precept in words and works, could be deposed from his office by the bishop of the territory in which the abbey was located together with the neighboring abbots, even though the whole monastery

[64] Lib. VIII, Cap. 88, "Quod non liceat episcopo abstrahere rem monasterii quamvis erga se peccaverit abbas," *MPL*, 140, 809.

[65] Lib. VIII, Cap. 89, "Ne monachi placita saecularia adeant," *MPL*, 140, 809.

[66] Lib. VIII, Cap. 90, "De negotio saeculari," *MPL*, 140, 809.

[67] Lib. VIII, Cap. 91, "De clericis injuste tonsuratis," *MPL*, 140, 809.

or congregation looked with favor upon his conduct.[68]

Monks who conspired against their bishop were to be degraded. This applied also for those who calumniated the bishop.[69]

Monks were not to be required to administer penance to seculars, but they could freely give or withhold its administration.[70]

Burchard thus adopted an attitude quite divergent from that of Abbo of Fleury, who was zealous in extolling the monastic exemptions. Burchard simply ignored them.[71] He did this in spite of the fact that some texts of exemptions were very well known at the time, and indeed were used for the procuring of other exemptions. On the other hand, he expended much effort in proclaiming the subjection of the monks to the bishop. The canon which excluded abbots from synodal meetings unless there was a definite reason for calling them seemed to reflect the design to keep the abbots and monks under submission by giving them no voice in the diocesan legislation. The bishops were given great liberties over monasteries inasmuch as entry was authorized many times (*non semel, sed saepius*) during the year. Though certainly Burchard was not hostile to monasticism, for he devoted a full book (VIII) to a consideration of the monastic life, yet it seems that he did not establish a single monastery in his diocese throughout his reign as a bishop. He did not make a definite decision concerning the place held by

[68] Lib. VIII, Cap. 96, "Qualiter indignus abbas a suo separetur officio," *MPL*, 140, 811.

[69] Lib. X, Cap. 68, "De clericis vel monachis conjurantibus vel conspirantibus contra episcopum suum," *MPL*, 140, 854; Lib. X, Cap. 69, "De eadem re," *MPL*, 140, 854.

[70] Lib. XIX, Cap. 142, "Quod monachi secularibus poenitentiam dare non debeant," *MPL*, 140, 1010. A suspicion of doubt existed concerning the authorship of this book of the collection of Burchard which goes by the name "Corrector." Fournier-LeBras, however, assert that it emanated surely from Burchard. Regarding the text quoted from the XIX Book, it is corrupted in Migne, and reads: "Liberi sint monachi ad dandam poenitentiam saecularibus." This, however, does not concur with the title, and Fournier-LeBras (*Op. cit.*, I, 395, note 1), contend that the reading should follow the sense indicated above.

[71] Cf. Fournier-LeBras, *Histoire des Collections Canoniques*, I, 390.

monks in parishes; he simply pointed out the necessity of their submission to their bishop. In Chapter 142 of the 19th Book he indicated that the monks were not to exercise confessional jurisdiction over anyone at random, but this seemed to apply only to the monks who resided in the monasteries, and certainly not to the monks who labored in parishes. He placed no hazard in the way of clerics wishing to enter the monastic orders, but he exerted personal pressure over some important members of his clergy to change their minds when they revealed their intention of leaving the world to take the habit.[72] It is possible that Burchard did not offer open assistance to the monasteries because he feared that he would lose power over those who had entered the religious life. And it seems that he had encountered some difficulties along these lines during his tenure.[73]

With reference to the collections cited in this chapter, it is to be kept in mind that they did not reflect the exact state of the law, such as pure codifications (e.g., *Hadriana, Hispana, Dacheriana*) or contemporary conciliar legislation would have done. They were rather the collections of those authorities of the past who most forcefully advanced their personal viewpoints. Each editor had set purposes in mind in making his compilation, and selected the texts which most closely corresponded to those ends. Thus one has truly, in most cases, not a picture of the actual law as it existed at the time of the compilations, but rather a reflection of those conciliar decrees which proved acceptable to these authors' views, together with the citations of privileges and of other documents which were intended not to be law, but simply decisions and favors granted in individual cases.

From the foregoing it would be difficult to conclude that the two last works treated, and others similar to it, and published before and during the period here studied—the False Decretals and the work of Regino of Prüm—were the single sources for the legislation of the period. They were probably supplementary to provincial legislation and genuine codification of the

[72] "Vita Burchardi," cap. 17—*MGH, Scriptores*, IV, 840.

[73] Cf. Fournier-LeBras, *op. cit.*, I, 395.

law, and were used as guides, being quoted when material in them concurred with the intentions of the legislating fathers. The very fact that exemptions were appearing in such great numbers, even before the time of Abbo of Fleury, indicated a spirit in opposition certainly to the False Decretals, which exalted the bishops' position against that of the abbots and monks. The privileges even contradicted Regino of Prüm, who made no radical departure from the traditional position of bishop-abbot relations as stemming from Chalcedon, namely, that the abbots were to be subject to the bishops, although he put the monks directly under the abbot rather than under the bishop.

In the collections immediately subsequent to the early 10th century, Abbo of Fleury forcefully defended the cause of monks against that of the bishops, while Burchard, coming later by a few years, cherished opposite views. Although not influencing the first half of the tenth century, they reflected the conflict over monastic independence, which in our period had not as yet erupted. The two authors indicate the approach toward monasticism typified by their separate spheres of interest. What is expressed by them in their period is surely embryonically present in the period immediately prior to them. The Papacy undoubtedly possessed the False Decretals, or portions of them, in the ninth and tenth century. However, the popes either questioned their value or genuinity or felt themselves justifiably above the law, for the papal policy did not adhere to the spurious decretals. The conclusions must therefore be these: the collections were guides to legislation in the 10th century. The main body of legislation actually in operation during that time came through synodal meetings. In the absence of synodal meetings, canon law was formed from the past conciliar decrees and only secondarily from the canonical collections.

APPENDIX I

PAPAL INTERVENTION AND BISHOP-ABBOT RELATIONS

The relationship of monasticism with the papacy is admittedly a topic worthy of separate consideration, and yet a cursory summary of the relations between the papacy and the abbots seems necessary if one is to throw a clearer light upon the bishop-abbot relationships. Papal protection was of the greatest importance in exempting the monasteries from episcopal jurisdiction. Gregory the Great was lavish in his support of monasticism, but from his time until the ninth century the cases of papal intervention were rare.

As has been asserted, this protection was accorded to Bobbio as early as 628, appearing at this early date and demonstrating two facts: 1) that Bobbio was an Irish abbey, and that the monks would have wearied Rome with petitions for exemption if it had not been accorded to them, 2) and that the protection and total exemption granted by Rome would exalt the position of the Holy See as being the first to confer these upon a monastery, indicating its jurisdictional primacy.[1]

According to Bobbio's exemption terms, no prelate could enter the monastery except by invitation of the abbot. Pope Honorius I (625-638), who granted the privilege, took this feature from St. Gregory's letter to Castorius.[2] At the end of the 7th century, the text of Bobbio's privilege became Formula 77 in the *Liber Diurnus*, while another one, n. 32, recounted the same privileges in different words. The formulas made their way even into England, according to Knowles.[3]

In Germany, Fulda became directly attached to Rome

[1] J. F. Lemarignier, "L'Exemption monastique," *A Cluny Congrès Scientifique; Travaux du Congrès*, Publiés par la Société des Amis de Cluny (Dijon, Imprimerie Bernigaud et Privat: 1950), p. 293.

[2] Jaffé, n. 2017; McLaughlin, *Le très ancien droit*, p. 187.

[3] *The Monastic Order in England*, p. 576.

through a litteral reproduction of formula 32, in 751.[4] Saint-Denis of Paris in 757 received exactly the same privilege as Boniface had for Fulda.

The Carolingians did not approve of the Roman exemptions; they believed them too Celtic, and therefore too anarchic. For this reason, from Charlemagne until Louis the Pious, there had been little need for papal protection, since the royalty was considered adequate for guarding the interests of the abbey. The bishop was given more power over the monasteries, and the Holy See is relegated to a secondary place.[5] When the secular arm of royalty weakened, the papal protection stepped in to replace it. One may designate the latter part of the ninth century as the beginning of such assistance from Rome, with Popes Nicholas I (858-867) and John VIII (862-882). In 863 Nicholas I granted a rather unique privilege to Vézelay.[7] In payment for protection the monastery offered yearly dues to Rome, which retracted it from all outside domination, and which alleviated the monastery from having to pay the extremely burdensome taxes associated with the episcopal functions of order.

Lemarignier,[8] and Fabre[9] insist that the distinction between temporal and spiritual jurisdiction must be kept distinct until the time of Urban II (1088-1099), and that until then the diocesan bishop still retained explicitly the power of order, and implicitly that of spiritual jurisdiction. This conflicts with other views on this point, which hold that immunity from the bishops in temporalities implied that the abbot had full responsibility for the monastic discipline, and was accountable to the pope alone.[10] One may trace the nature of exemptions

[4] Jaffé, n. 2293.

[5] Lemarignier, "L'Exemption Monastique," p. 294.

[6] Cf. Lesne, "Nicolas I et les libertés des monastères des Gaules," *Le Moyen Age*, XXIV (1911), 277-306; 333-345; Fabre, *Etude sur le LIBER CENSUUM* (Paris, 1892), pp. 41ff.; Letonnelier, *L'Abbaye Exempt de Cluny et la Saint-Siège* (Ligugé-Paris, 1923), pp. 14-21; 23-26; 35, 37-40; 81-83; 90.

[7] Cf. Daux, "La protection apostolique au Moyen Age," *Revue des Questions Historiques*, LXXII (1902), 24.

[8] "L'Exemption Monastique," p. 296.

[9] *Etude sur le LIBER CENSUUM*, p. 94.

[10] E.g., Amann-Dumas, *L'Eglise au Pouvoir des Laïques*, p. 358.

until this date. The Holy See functioned mostly, but not exclusively, in the manner of confirming privileges received either from the bishops or from the kings. The so-called "papal protection" or "*tuitio,*" which enforced the privileges received from other sources, served to secure them from either ecclesiastical or secular powers. The papacy did not use arms to enforce its protection, since it always possessed the power of excommunication, which could be a more potent support to monasticism than artillery. This is not to say that the monasteries did not also seek protection from other than papal power, for the latter moved more slowly, and with intercommunication as poor as it was the practical monastery would seek a more immediate protection with powers closer to home.[11]

If anything was recommended to the Holy See there was actually reflected a juridic contract, for, as was seen from Vézelay's privilege, in return for protection the monastery was to pay dues to the pope as a sign that the monastery was completely delivered over to him and hence removed from all other powers. The papacy was only protecting what belonged to it, whether as a legal fiction or as an actuality, since the end result was the same. Along with the protection came privileges, many of which have been enumerated earlier. "The Holy See acquired the *dominium directum* of the abbey, the *proprietas rei,* while it left to the abbey the *dominium indirectum, dominium utile,* the *utilitas rei,* that is to say, the possession and the usage." [12]

Cluny imitated Vézelay in its charter, and because of its influential position set a precedent, which was copied by many other abbeys, particularly those which were founded and made directly dependent upon it. Cluny gained by papal exemption the confirmation of all the privileges enumerated—freedom from taxes and dues of any kind to the bishops and nobles; freedom of abbatial election; freedom of the internal regime; freedom from all external powers. New in Cluny's charter was the clause, "*non fastibus regiae magnitudinis subiciantur, nec cujuslibet terrenae potestatis jugo subiciantur.*" William of Aqui-

[11] Cf. Schmitz, *Histoire de l'Ordre,* I, 328.
[12] Schmitz, *op. cit.,* I, 332.

taine took it upon himself to remove Cluny from even the royal powers. In 931, this was confirmed by Pope John XI (931-935), who extended it to Cluny and all its dependencies. With the privilege the Holy See demanded a regular *census* (tax).[13] Repeating these provisions almost verbatim were the charters of Bourgdieu in 917,[14] and St.-Pons-de-Tomiers in 937.[15]

Fulda, Vézelay and Bobbio, according to the terms of the exemption received, seemed to have the full extent of exemption, that is, freedom from outside powers in both the temporal and the spiritual order. Yet, the papal exemptions applied explicitly only to the temporalities of the monasteries, since the Holy See enunciated its purpose as being that of seeing to the continued possession by the abbeys of the goods and donations, for the monastery's spiritual good. There was nothing explicit about the exemption from the spiritual authority of the bishop. The immunity from assault on its temporal possessions carried in its train the germs of exemption in the ecclesiastical order, but did not state this in so many words.[16] However in Fulda's bull of exemption[17] was still retained the dependence upon the episcopal exercise of order in ordinations, consecrations, and benedictions, and hence the necessity of recurring to the diocesan bishop, since the bull explicitly mentioned the diocesan's right of consecrating the altars of Fulda, and implicitly included these other episcopal functions also. However, he could not influence the internal discipline of the abbey except by invitations. This was the condition throughout most of the tenth century, and was not changed by the Cluniac

[13] Jaffé, n. 3584 (2744).

[14] *Gallia Christiana*, II, 43 (Instrumenta); Jaffé, n. 3585.

[15] Cf. Fabre, *Etude sur le LIBER CENSUUM*, p. 56.

[16] Amann-Dumas, *op. cit.*, p. 358; Cf. also Fabre, *op. cit.*, p. 47, "Rien dans les documents ne nous autorise à penser que le monastère de Vézelay ait été, dans une mesure quelconque, soustraite à l'autorité de l'Evêque diocésain."

[17] Jaffé, n. 2293 (Zachary, 751); 3392 (Marin I, 883-884); 3466 (Stephen V, 891); 3596 (Leo VII, 936); *MPL*, LXXXIX, 954; CXXIX, 813; CXXXII, 1065). Formula inserted in *Liber Diurnus*, n. 32. Cf. McLaughlin, *Le trés ancien droit*, p. 188. Cf. also Berlière, "Exemption Monastique," *Dictionnaire de Archéologie Chrétienne et de Liturgie*, V, col. 954.

charter. However, in practice, Cluny *de facto* chose other than the diocesan bishop to perform the ordinations, consecrations and benedictions, not restricting itself to calling upon the bishop of Mâcon. Hence, what was not explicitly contained in the charter and confirmation of Cluny, was superadded by interpretation or practice. The tremendous impact of Cluny could not but set a precedent in this matter. Perhaps it is apropos here to state that the canon law of the period recognized by these charters only the exemption from the diocesan bishops in respect to temporalities, leaving to them the implicit right of spiritual jurisdiction. In practice, Cluny ignored the implicit rights of the diocesan in spiritual things, and by a *fait accompli* made herself free of the diocesan ordinary on both levels.

During the first half of the tenth century, the Holy See issued many bulls relating to monasteries in Europe. Most of these appeared at the instance of the abbots, while some few were gained through the solicitation of the bishops or the kings. Without going too much into detail in the nature of these privileges, since these have already been discussed, suffice it to say that there were recorded in the *Regesta* of Jaffé some fifty-four such bulls extended to the monasteries. Five were sent by bishops or their delegates, or signed by them. The principal abbeys to which these were directed were Fulda,[18] Cluny,[19] Subiaco,[20] Monte Cassino[21] and Vézelay.[22] Fleury, Gorze, St. Mary and St. Martin of Poitiers, St. Vincent in Vulture, St. Gall, Corbie, St. Anthimus, and Dol all received two such privileges, while Nonantola, St. Launomar (Laumer) of Clermont, St. Martin of Rome, St. Stephen in Rome, St. Mary of Brogne, St. Saumay (Psalmodius), Romainmoutier (Romanensis), Sts. Mary and Peter of Rippaldsau (Rivipul-

[18] Jaffé, n. 3525 (2710); n. 3558 (2726); n. 3622 (2775); n. 3633 (2784); n. 3642 (2794); n. 3644 (2795); n. 3650.

[19] Jaffé, n. 3578 (2741); n. 3584 (2744); n. 3588 (2747); n. 3598 (2755); n. 3600 (2764); n. 3605 (2759); n. 3648 (2798).

[20] Jaffé, n. 3569; n. 3597 (2753); n. 3601 (2756); n. 3608 (2761); n. 3615 (2768).

[21] Jaffé, n. 3547 (2720); n. 3624 (2777); n. 3634 (2785); n. 3628 (2780).

[22] Jaffé, n. 3542; n. 3589 (2748); n. 3621 (2774).

lense), St. John Baptist, St. Maximinus, St. Germain and Michael, all received one privilege each.

It may be asserted, therefore, in summary, that the papacy, although during this century steeped in intrigue and corruption, was yet as a spiritual institution able to exert a most important influence on the development of relations between the bishops and abbots, by confirming the privileges possessed and by granting new ones, all of which advanced the autonomy of the monasteries and widened the jurisdictional gap between the bishops and abbots.

APPENDIX II

INFLUENCE OF LAY POWERS IN DETERMINING BISHOP-ABBOT RELATIONS

Secular powers played an important role in determining the relations between the bishops and the abbots. Perhaps the most famous example of this is the charter of privileges granted to the Abbey of Cluny by William of Aquitaine, which became the root of the monastic policy of the abbey itself, and was the proto-charter after which were modeled those of the many foundations and reformed houses branching from Cluny. But even outside of Cluny and the houses dependent upon it the kings and nobles played their part in affecting the monastic status of a large number of monasteries in Europe, hastening their progress toward independence.

The royal power was, to begin with, active in several manners in affecting the relations between the bishops and the abbots. The kings and emperors could be approached by the abbot, or the founder, proprietor or benefactor of an abbey and solicited to grant a privilege or to confirm one already given elsewhere. They could grant privileges outright, whether from altruistic or religious motives, or for purely profane and political ones. They could grant a fiscal immunity to the abbey and by so doing pave the way for the reception of exemptions which flowed from this first freedom.[1]

The secularization of the abbeys had made of them political playthings, and an exemption granted could just as easily be retracted on the morrow. Documents of the grants of exemption were retained in the monastic files, but the king could just as easily as he had granted it, violate it at the slightest pretense.[2] Belonging to the kings, the monasteries passed easily by donation into the hands of their loyal subjects, who in turn could also change the status of the abbey established by its former

[1] Cf. Lafontaine, *L'Evêque d'Ordination des Religieux*, p. 159.

[2] Lesne, *Histoire de la Propriété*, II, II, 132.

royal lord. It was not always advantageous for a monastery to hold the status of a royal abbey, for having been given as a benefice to an underling of the king whether he was a bishop or a noble, the latter was not averse to sacrificing the abbey to the interests of the diocese, of the king, of the royal militia, or to their own selfish interests.

The actual value of an exemption was difficult to determine, and the history of each abbey receiving the exemption had to be investigated if one was to uncover the working value of the privilege received in each case.[3] Taken collectively, however, these exemptions represented a trend toward monastic independence, and so numerous were they that with the precedent once set, it was the function of the king thereafter to determine not whether the monastery should or should not receive exemptions, but rather what exemptions were to be given. At times, privileges were taken for granted and the only reason why the king issued a special writ of privilege was to make it available to the abbey when someone threatened to violate it.[4]

It was often at the insistence of the kings that the monasteries received from another external power the freedom of administering their own temporalities, the choice of their abbot, immunity from fiscal or diocesan taxes, episcopal visits, and other practices which disturbed the monastic tranquility. The confirmation of the privileges already obtained were an added inducement to the bishops or nobles to respect them, even though a powerful noble who felt capable of doing so could well violate such rights if he regarded the royal power not sufficiently strong to invoke the needed sanction in support of his command. On the supposition that the hegemony rested in the hands of the royalty, bishops and counts could be fined or be made subject to other penalties upon any violations perpetrated against one of the privileged abbeys.[5]

During the Carolingian period, until after the reign of Louis the Pious, the monasteries were not only protected by the

[3] Lesne, *Histoire de la Propriété*, II, II, 26.

[4] Schmitz, *Histoire de l'Ordre*, I, 347.

[5] Schmitz, *Histoire de l'Ordre*, I, 342 ff. Cf. also Lesne, *Histoire de la Propriété*, Tom. I; Lévy-Bruhl, *Elections Abbatiales*, Pars I, Ch. I; Pars II, Ch. 2.

kings, but also used as their pawns.[6] Of the secularizations which naturally took place, enough has already been said. After the rule of Louis the Pious the regime began to crumble, and instead of exerting a single universal control over the whole of the land, the king became little more than another feudal lord. In the tenth century the king's position was ameliorated and immunities also began to appear. Outside of his immediate domain, the king was prone to grant immunities if for no other reason than to embarrass his foes.

In the German empire the king was stronger, and royal abbeys were the most numerous.[7] Under the kings of Germany in the first half of the tenth century were some of the most powerful and large abbeys in the kingdom. Among these one may enumerate Fulda, Reichenau, Lorsch, Corvey, Saint-Gall, Altaich, Werden, Kornelimunster, Herford, Prüm, Saint-Maximin, Stavelot, and Malmedy.[8] In France, the opposite was the case, Louis IV (936-954) had possession of only a few abbeys in the east and north of his kingdom. Some of these were Notre-Dame de Laon, Saint-Crepin de Soissons, Homblieres, Saint-Omer, Saint-Vaast d'Arras, Saint-Amand, Saint-Martin d'Autun, Saint- Germain d'Auxerre. Other abbeys such as Fleury, and Saint-Martial of Limoges fell under the domination of nobles. It would be interesting to discuss each one of the exemptions granted by the kings and nobles, but since this would become too lengthy, let it suffice at this time to mention some of the more prominent ones as a sampling of the action of the royalty.

Charles the Simple (899-923) in 912 confirmed possessions of the abbey of St. Maximin of Treves, which had been usurped by impious men and negligent abbots. He returned the goods to them and saw that they were cared for in their basic needs of food, shelter and clothing.[9] In 920, the same king granted the abbey of Prüm the privilege of free abbatial elections, dependent nonetheless on his consent and that of other wise

[6] Lévy-Bruhl, *Elections Abbatiales*, p. 187.

[7] Amann-Dumas, *L'Eglise au Pouvoir des Laïques*, p. 298.

[8] Cf. Lesne, *Histoire de la Propriété*, II, II, 4.

[9] *Gallia Christiana*, XIII, 316 (Instrumenta).

persons, and made the abbey immune from outside agencies both in the administration of its policies and in the matter of fiscal taxation.[10] In 908 he confirmed certain possessions for the abbey of Saint Mary in Carcassone and, adding the usual assertion that the abbey was under his protection, "*sub nostrae tuitionis mundeburdo et nostrae dominationis protectu,*" he granted the right of free election of the abbot.[11] Other charters resembled these in their terms, and were given to abbeys of monks and canons.[12]

From the death of Charles the Simple in 923 until 950 few exemptions were granted, since the country was beset with invasions and many of the monasteries were pillaged. A few do appear during the reign of Rudolph of Burgundy (923-936), who granted the usual privileges to the abbey of St. Martin of Autun in 924.[13] The same king confirmed the possessions of Cluny in 931.[14]

Louis IV (d'Outremer—936-954), although not holding the numerous monasteries that the German emperor did, began to grant privileges when the invaders were at a safe distance from his kingdom. In 939 he confirmed the possession of Cluny, which had previously been granted by William of Aquitaine and been given privileges from Rome. This was recognized also by Bishop Artaldus.[15] In 941 he confirmed the possessions and rights of the monastery of Tournon at the behest of Henry, Bishop of Langres, and Count Rotgerus.[16] In 939, petitioned by Hugo, Marquis of Burgundy, he granted immunity from taxes (*a teloneis*), liberty of the personnel, and a right to the

[10] *Gallia Christiana,* XIII, 319 (Instrumenta).

[11] *Gallia Christiana,* VI, 420 (Instrumenta).

[12] E.g., To the monastery of St. Germain des Prés (Paris) in 903 (*Gallia Christiana,* VII, 15 [Instrumenta]; to St. Pierre of Rébais in 907 (*Gallia Christiana,* VII, 16 [Instrumenta;] to St. Mary of Paris in 911 (*Gallia Christiana,* VII, 39); to Fosses in 920 (*Gallia Christiana,* VII, 286); to Saumay in 909 (*Gallia Christiana,* VI, 171 [Instrumenta]; to St. Martin of Tours in 920 (*Gallia Christiana,* XIV, 55 [Instrumenta]; to Brogne in Tours in 923 (*Gallia Christiana,* XIV, 60 [Instrumenta]; etc.

[13] *Gallia Christiana,* IV, 71 (Instrumenta).

[14] Bruel, *Recueil des Chartes,* I, 396 (p. 379).

[15] Marrier, *Bibliotheca Cluniacensis,* p. 266.

[16] Mabillon, *Annales,* III, 424.

tithes to serve the needs of charity. The charter was recognized by Bishop Artaldus.[17] He confirmed the privileges of the monastery of Dol, granting outside of the rights already given by others the right of electing their own abbot, besides giving a chapel, formerly owned by English monk-refugees.[18] Similar donations and privileges were given to St. Savin in 945.[19]

In the German empire, the ruler had many more abbeys under his protection, and hence the number of privileges inincreased in this sector. Conrad, King of the Saxons (911-918), gave to Corvey in 913 the privileges of free election of the abbot, a right to the tithes, and immunity.[20] To Hersfeld he granted immunity in 913,[21] to Murbach, immunity, free abbatial elections, and tax exemption.[22] To Lorsch he granted confirmation of the prior privileges, and immunity and free abbatial elections. Privileges and donations were given besides to Fulda, Heiligenberg, St. Emmeram, Weilburg, Schwarach.[23]

Conrad's successor, Henry I (919-938), granted immunity, free abbatial elections, and the right to tithes to Fulda in 920,[24] to Corvey in 922,[25] and various other privileges to Hersfeld, St. Gall, St. Alban, St. Maximin, Kempten, Werden, Stavelot (Stablo), Klingenmunster, and Brogne.[26] Under Otto I (936-973) the privileges, confirmations, and donations became commonplace because of their frequency. Suffice it here to enumerate the foundations enriched in this manner from 936-950 by Otto. These include Fulda, Corvey, Hersfeld, Werden, St. Alban, Kempten, St. Gall, St. Emmeram, Moosburg, St. Maximin, Lorsch, Moritzkirche, Magdeburg, Salzburg, Gorze, St.

[17] Mabillon, *Annales*, III, 414.

[18] Mabillon, *Annales*, III, 428.

[19] *Gallia Christiana*, I, 1247.

[20] *MGH*, Diplomatum Regum et Imperatorum Germaniae, Tom. I, (*Conradi I, Heinrici I, Otto I Diplomata*), ed. Societas Aperiendis Fontibus (Hannoverae, 1879-1884), p. 6.

[21] *Ibidem*, p. 13.

[22] *Ibidem*, p. 16.

[23] *Ibidem*, pp. 6, 8, 9, 16-39.

[24] *MGH*, *Diplomata*, I, 39.

[25] *Ibidem*, p. 41.

[26] *MGH*, *Diplomata*, I, 39-77.

Evre's, Echternach, Einsiedeln, St. Gery, Kornelimunster, Sens, St. Arnold, Gembloux, Reichenau, Essen, Chevremont, Gandersheim, Prüm, Hornbach, Stablo-Malmedy, Weissenburg, Engern, and Frohse.[27] There is question here simply of the fact that a large number of privileges and donations did arise from the German royalty, the while one may pass over in silence the motives which at times prompted the granting of such prerogatives.[28] The climax of these liberal donations was reached during Otto's rule in his decree of Frankfort in the year 952, when he stated that no abbey which had received the right of electing its own abbot should be given to any individual as his own property.[29]

In addition to the kings, dukes and counts had possession of abbeys which had been given to them usually by the king, and hence were formerly royal. This was particularly true in France, where the royalty, during this period, was weak. The practice of giving abbeys to the nobles arose during the Carolingian period when certain abbeys were granted to the "honor" of the count. The Abbey of St. Martin d'Ambierle in 902 depended upon the "*comitatus*" of Lyons; in 933 the small Abbey of Saint-Paul became part of the *comitatus* of Sens. Being joined to the title, the abbey was passed on from one holder to the next.[30] Some abbeys were founded, restored and reformed by the counts themselves. Being strong enough to defend them, they retained possession of them and did not cede them to the king for his "*tuitio.*" Such abbeys followed the same lines as the royal abbeys, being considered the property of and hence disposable by the seigneur at his will. In 904, for example, the Abbot of Sorèze sold the monastery of Saramon, a dependent of his, to the Count of Gascogne.[31]

[27] *MGH*, *Diplomata*, I, 89-210.

[28] Schmitz, *Histoire de l'Ordre*, I, 316.

[29] Francofurdensis Conventus Regis Ottonis I (952), Cap. 2: "Inventum est etiam a praefato Rege, ut nulla Abbatia, quae per se electionem habet, ad monasterium nec alicui in proprium dari possit; illae vero quae electione carent, Regis donatione, et privilegio ad illud Monasterium, quod sub ejus Mundiburdio consistit, subrogari posse."—Mansi, XVIII, 435.

[30] Amann-Dumas, *op. cit.*, p. 300.

[31] Amann-Dumas, *op. cit.*, p. 301.

The feudal system with reference to private ownership of the abbeys during this period was especially strong in the west and southwest of France. Strong counts, such as Pontius of Toulouse, could grant privileges outright, such as, e.g., the donations and privileges given by him to the monastery of St. Pontius, a foundation of his in 936,[32] whereas others, perhaps fearing their own inability to protect the abbey, gave them to the king. Richard, Duke of Burgundy, in 900 received the monastery of St. Germain d'Auxerre, and asked and received benefits from Charles the Simple regarding it.[33] Similarly, a later lay abbot of the same monastery, opposed vigorously by the bishops of the territory, received from Louis IV in 937 a series of privileges which entirely exempted the abbey from the jurisdiction of the bishops. Among other things, he received these privileges; 1) No bishops or laymen could exercise judgments (*exercere judicium*) in the abbey; 2) the men and the property of the abbey were free of all taxes; 3) no abbot could usurp the goods of the abbey; and 4) offerings were to go to the abbey and the monks, not to the abbot or any other person.[34]

Regarding the episcopal abbeys, little more need be added, since they fell in a category similar to that of the abbeys of the counts, being attached to the "honor" of the "*episcopatus*," and being used in the same manner as that of the counts. Whereas in the 8th and 9th centuries all the abbeys were either royal or episcopal, during the 10th and 11th centuries there existed four categories: independent monasteries; Roman monasteries; monasteries incorporated in a monastic order of congregation; and monasteries which were the property of the king, the seigneur, or the bishop.[35]

[32] *Gallia Christiana*, VI, 77 (Instrumenta).

[33] *Gallia Christiana*, XII, 375.

[34] *Gallia Christiana*, XII, 375; Cf. also Henry, *Histoire de l'Abbaye de S. Germain d'Auxerre*, p. 124.

[35] Schmitz, *Histoire de l'Ordre*, I, 355.

CONCLUSIONS

1. Through the decisions of the Council of Arles (455), which were influential in the formation of the Western attitude toward bishop-abbot relations, episcopal jurisdiction over abbeys became limited to mere ministerial functions, while the abbot had complete jurisdiction over the internal affairs of the abbey, including authority over the "laica multitudo" and the "clerici."
2. By uniting many monasteries under a single rule in the great reform of the 9th century, St. Benedict of Aniane advanced the monks' position with regard to the diocesan bishop. A "scedula" now lost, extant in the time of the reform, gave privileges to all the monasteries confederated under St. Benedict, including the right of free election of abbots, which was a great step forward for monastic liberty.
3. During the period of the Invasions (9th c.), the abbatial office took on a new importance before secular powers, which carried in its train a new prestige in the ecclesiastical sphere also.
4. With regard to monastic privileges in the early 10th Century:
    a) What was not contained by way of charter privileges in Cluny's independence from the diocesan Bishop, was formed by custom arising uncontested by the bishops of the period.
    b) Where privileges were possessed, the bishops respected them but where they were lacking the bishops still retained and exercised their right of surveillance, and this they did by visitating, approving the choice of abbot, and by controls of other sorts traditionally present in preceding periods.
    c) By granting privileges, and approving those given to their abbeys by others, whether by Pope or bishops, the laity made it possible for the abbeys

to withdraw themselves more and more from episcopal control.

5. The papacy, weak as it was during the early 10th century, was yet able to exert a powerful influence in protecting monastic liberty in its initial stages of development.
6. Particular conciliar legislation must be said to supersede canonical collections in importance for the role played in forming bishop-abbot relations, but the collections form a continuous and steady link with tradition and reassert Chalcedon's legislation in this matter.

BIBLIOGRAPHY

Bernard, A.-Bruel, A., *Recueil des Chartes de l'Abbaye de Cluny*, 6 vols., Paris, 1876-1903.

Blaise, Albert, *Dictionnaire Latin-Francais des Auteurs Chrétiens* (Revu spécialement pour le vocabulaire théologique par Henri Chirat, Paris: Librairie des Méridiens, 1954.

Bouquet, Martin (ed.), *Recueil des historiens des Gaules et de la France*, Nouvelle édition Publiée sous la direction de M. Léopold Delisle, 19 vols., Paris, 1869-1879.

Bruns, Herm. Theod., *Canones Apostolorum et Conciliorum Veterum Selecti*, 2 vols., Berolini, 1839.

D'Achery, Lucas (ed.), *Spicilegium sive collectio Veterum aliquot Scriptorum* (Nova editio—ed. Stephanus Baluze, Edmundus Martène, Ludovicus de la Barre), 3 toms., Parisiis, 1723.

Depoin, J., *Recueil des Chartes et Documents de Saint-Martin-des-Champs*, 3 toms., Ligugé-Paris, 1912.

Du Cange, *Glossarium Mediae et Infimae Latinitatis*, conditum a Carolo du Fresne Domino du Cange auctum a Monachis Ordinis S. Benedicti, editio nova a Leopóld Favre, 10 vols., Paris: Librairie des Sciences et des Arts, 1927-1938.

Ferotin, Marius, *Recueil des Chartes de l'Abbaye de Silos*, Paris, 1897.

Gallia Christiana in provincias ecclesiasticas distributa, ed. Dionysius Sammarthani et monachi; editio altera, labore et curis Pauli Piolin recensita et aucta, 16 vols., Parisiis, 1870-1877.

Haddan, A. W.—Stubbs, W., *Councils and Ecclesiastical Documents Relating to Great Britain and Ireland*, 3 vols. in 4, Oxford, 1869-1878.

Hinschius, Paulus, *Decretales Pseudo-Isidorianae et Capitula Angilramni*, Lipsiae, 1863.

Holy Rule of our Most Holy Father Benedict, translated by Rev. Boniface Verheyen, O.S.B., Atchison: Abbey Student Press, 1949.

Jaffé, Philippus, *Regesta Pontificum Romanorum ab Condita Ecclesia ad Annum Post Christum Natum MCXCVIII*, 2 ed. correctam et auctam auspiciis Gulielmi Wattenbach curaverunt S. Loewenfeld, F. Kaltenbrunner, P. Ewald, 2 vols. in 1, Lipsiae, 1885-1888.

Mabillon, Johannes, *Vetera Analecta*, 3 vols., Parisiis, 1723.

d'Achery, Lucas, collegit et cum eo Johannes Mabillon edidit, *Acta Sanctorum Ordinis S. Benedicti in saeculorum classes distributa*, 9 vols., Venetiis, 1733-1738.

Mabillon, Johannes, *Annales Ordinis S. Benedicti Occidentalium Monachorum Patriarchae*, 6 vols., Lucae, 1739-1745.

Mansi, Joannes Dominicus, *Sacrorum Conciliorum Nova et Amplissima Collectio*, 53 vols. in 60, Parisiis, 1901-1927.

Marrier, Martinus (ed.)—Des Chesne, A., *Bibliotheca Cluniacensis*, Mâcon, 1915.

Monumenta Germaniae Historica, Epistolarum Tomus I et II, *Gregorii I Papae Registrum Epistolarum* (ediderunt Paulus Ewald et Ludovicus Hartmann), Berolini, 1891-1899.

—Epistolarum Tomus III, *Epistolae Merovingici et Karolini Aevi*, Tomus I, Berolini, 1892.

—Epistolarum Tomus VI, *Epistolae Karolini Aevi*, Tomus IV, Berolini, 1925.

—Legum Sectio I, *Leges Nationum Germanicarum*, Tomus I, *Leges Visigothorum* (edidit Karolus Zeumer), Hannoverae et Lipsiae, 1902.

—Legum Sectio II, *Capitularia*, Tomus I, *Capitularia Regum Francorum* (denuo edidit Boretius), Hannoverae, 1883.

—Legum Sectio III, *Concilia*, Tomus I, *Concilia Aevi Merovingici* (recensuit F. Maassen), Hannoverae, 1893.

—Legum Sectio III, *Concilia*, Tomus I, *Concilia Aevi Karolini* (ed. A. Werminghoff), Hannoverae et Lipsiae, 1908.

—*Constitutiones et Acta Publica Imperatorum et Regum*, Tomus I (ed. Ludvicus Weiland), Hannoverae, 1893.

—*Diplomata, Diplomatum Regum et Imperatorum Germaniae*, Tomus I, *Conradi I, Heinrici I, et Ottonis I* (ed. Societas Aperiendis Fontibus), Hannoverae, 1879-1885.

—*Scriptores* (Auspiciis Societatis Aperiendis Fontibus; ed. [orig.] Georgius Pertz), 33 vols., Hannoverae, 1826-1926.

—Jonas, *Jonae Vitae Sanctorum Columbani, Vedastis, Johannis*, ed. Bruno Krusch, [orig.] *Scriptorum Rerum Germ.*, 62 vols., Hannoverae et Lipsiae, 1905.

Sancti Gregorii Papae I. Cognomento Magni Opera Omnia, 17 vols. (ediderunt Benedictini ex Congregatione S. Mauri), Venetiis, 1768-1776.

Schwartz, Eduardus, (ed.), *Acta Conciliorum Oecumenicorum*, 4 toms. in 15, Berolini et Lipsiae, 1914-1927, Vol. II, *Concilium Chalcedonense*, 1927.

Sickel, Th., *Regester der Urkunden der ersten Karolinger* (751-840), 2 vols., Wien, 1867.

AUTHORS

Albers, Bruno, *Consuetudines Monasticae*, 2 vols., Vol. I, *Consuetudines Farfenses*, Stuttgardiae et Vindobonae, 1900; Vol. II, *Consuetudines Cluniacenses Antiquiores*, Typis Montis Cassino, 1905.

Alloing, Louis, *Le Diocèse de Belley*, Belley, 1938.

Allou, Auguste, *Chronique des Evêques de Meaux*, Meaux, 1875.

Arnold, Carl Franklin, *Caesarius von Arelate und die Gallische Kirche seiner Zeit*, Leipzig, 1894.

Baloche, M., *Eglise Saint-Merry de Paris—Histoire de la Paroisse et de la Collégiale*, 700-1910, Paris, 1911.

Beauhaire, Joseph, *Diocèse de Chartres, Chronologie des Evêques, des Curés, des Vicaires*, Paris, 1892.

Un Bénédictin de la Cong. de S. Maur, *Histoire de l'Abbaye Royale de S. Ouen de Rouen*, Rouen, 1662.

Berlière, Ursmer, *L'Ascèse bénédictine des origines à la fin du XII siècle*, Paris, 1927.

Berlière, Ursmer, *L'Ordre monastique des origines au XII siècle*, Abbaye de Maredsous, 1912.

Bernard, Aug., *Cartulaire de l'Abbaye de Savigny*, Paris, 1853.

Bernard, Pierre, *Etude sur les esclaves et les serfs d'Eglise en France du VI au XIII siècles*, Paris, 1919.

Bernois, C., *Histoire de l'Abbaye royale de Sainte-Euverte d'Orléans*, Orleans, 1918.

Besnard, A., *L'Eglise et l'Abbaye Saint-Georges de Boscherville*, Paris, 1899.

Besse, J. M., *Les Moines d'Orient antérieurs au Concile de Chalcedoine*, Poitier, 1900.

Beste, Udalricus, *Introductio in Codicem*, 3 ed., Collegeville: St. John's Abbey Press, 1946.

Biziot, Louis—Claudin, A., *Histoire de l'Abbaye de Caunes au Diocèse de Narbonne*, Paris, 1880.

Bouange, G.M.F., *Histoire de l'Abbaye d'Aurillac* (894-1789), 2 vols., Paris, 1899.

Bouillart, Jacques, *Histoire de l'Abbaye royale de Saint-Germain des Préz*, Paris, 1724.

Bouillet, A., *L'Eglise Sainte-Foy de Conches*, Cain, 1889.

Brennan, Michael, *Ecclesiastical History of Ireland*, Dublin, 1864.

Brullee, A., *Histoire de l'Abbaye royale de Saint-Colombe-les-Sens*, Sens, 1852.

Bulliot, J. Gabriel, *Essai Historique sur l'Abbaye de Saint-Martin d'Autun*, Autun, 1849.

Bury, J. B., *The Life of St. Patrick*, London, 1905.

Butler, Cuthbert, *Benedictine Monachism*, London, 1919.

Cabrol, Fernand—Leclercq, H., *Dictionnaire d'Archéologie Chrétienne et de Liturgie*, 15 vols. in 30, Paris: Librairie Letouzey et Ané, 1907- .

Cambridge Medieval History, under direction of J. B. Bury, edited by H. M. Gwatkin and J. P. Whitney, 8 vols., Cambridge, 1911-1936; Vol. II, *The Rise of the Saracens and the Foundation of the Western Empire*, 1913; Vol. III, *Germany and the Western Empire*, 1922.

Catholic Encyclopedia, The, 15 vols., Index and Supplement, New York, 1907-1922.

Chagny, André, *Cluny et son Empire*, Lyon-Paris: Librairie Emannuel Vitte, 1949.

Champly, Louis, *Histoire de l'Abbaye de Cluny*, Paris, 1930.

Chapman, John, *St. Benedict and the Sixth Century*, London, 1929.

Charmasse, A., de, *Cartulaire de l'Eglise d'Autun*, 3 vols., Autun, 1865.

Charpin-Feugerolles, Comte, de—Giugue, Georges, *Cartulaire de l'Abbaye de l'Ile-Barbe*, 2 toms., Montbrisson, 1923.

Chazaud, M., *Fragments du Cartulaire de la Chapelle-Aude*, Moulins, 1860.

Chevalier, C.V.J., *Cartulaire Municipal de la Ville Montelimar*, Montelimar, 1871.

Cote, Leon, *Histoire du Prieuré Clunisien de Souvigny*, Moulins, 1942.

Creusen, Joseph, *De Juridica Status Regligiosi Evolutione, Synopsis Historica*, Romae: Apud Aedes Pont. Univ. Gregorianae, 1948.

Curtis, Edmund, *A History of Ireland*, London: Methuen & Co., 1950.

David, Pierre, *Les Bénédictins et l'Ordre de Cluny dans la Pologne Médiévale*, Paris: Société d'édition Les Belles Lettres, 1939.

D'Ayzac, Felicie, *Historie de l'Abbaye de Saint Denis*, 2 vols., Paris, 1860.

DeClercq, Carlo, *La Législation Religieuse Franque de Clovis à Charlemagne*, Louvain, Paris: Bureaux du Recueil Bibliothèque de l'Université, 1936.

Deladreue, E., *Histoire de l'Abbaye royale de Notre-Dame de Saint-Paul les Beauvais*, Beauvais, 1867.

De Laplane, Henri, *Les Abbés de Saint-Bertin*, Saint-Omer, 1854.

De Lasteyrie, Charles, *L'Abbaye de Saint-Martial de Limoges*, Paris, 1901.

De Lasteyrie, Robert, *Histoire generale de Paris* (Collection des documents), Tom. I, *528-1180*, Paris, 1887.

Delatte, Paul, *The Rule of St. Benedict*, New York, 1921.

De Montegut, M., *Cartulaire de l'abbaye de Vigeois in Limousin*, Limoges, 1907.

De Moreau, E., *Histoire de l'Eglise en Belgique*, 8 vols., Bruxelles: L'Edition Universelle, S.A., 1945, Tom I., *La formation de la Belgique chrétienne des origines au milieu du X siècle.*

————, *Les Abbayes de Belgique* (VII-XII siècles), Bruxelles: La Renaissance du Livre, 1952.

Depoin, Joseph, *Notre-Dame des Champs, Prieuré Dijonisien d'Essonnes*, Corbeil, 1904.

Deshayes, C. A., *Histoire de l'Abbaye royale de Jumièges*, Rouen, 1829.

de Valous, Guy, *Le Monachisme Clunisien des Origines au XV siècle*, Vol. I, Ligugé, 1935.

De la Ville, Cirot, *Histoire de l'Abbaye et Congrégation de la Grand-Sauve*, 2 toms., Paris, Bordeaux, 1844.

Dewez, Jules, *Histoire de l'Abbaye de St. Pierre d' Hasnon*, Lille, 1890.

Dhetel, Philippe, *L'Abbaye de Notre-Dame-de-Lone*, Dijon, 1864.

Dictionnaire de Droit Canonique, 5 toms. et 4 fascicles (incomp.), Paris: Letouzey et Ané, 1924-

Duchesne, Louis, *L'Eglise au VI Siècle*, Paris, 1925.

Dudden, F. Holmes, *Gregory the Great, His Place in History and Thought*, 2 vols., London, 1905.

Duples-Agier, H., *Chroniques de Saint Martial de Limoges*, Paris, 1874.

Ebrard, Johannes, *Die Iroschottische Missionskirche des 6, 7, und 8 Jahrhunderts*, Gütersloh, 1873.

Eidenschink, John, *The Election of Bishops in the Letters of Gregory the Great with an Appendix on the Pallium*, The Catholic University of America Canon Law Studies, n. 215, Washington, D.C.: The Catholic University of America Press, 1945.

Evans, Joan, *Monastic Life at Cluny*, 910-1157, London, 1931.

Fabre, Paul, *Etude sur le LIBER CENSUUM*, Paris, 1892.

Fallue, Leon, *Histoire de Fécamp*, Rouen, 1841.

de Ferroul-Montgaillard, M. L., *Histoire de l'Abbaye de St. Claude*, 2 vols., Lons-le-Saunier, 1854.

Filibien, Michael, *Histoire de l'Abbaye royale de Saint-Denys*, Paris, 1706.

Fliche, Augustine—Martin, Victor, *Histoire de l'Eglise depuis les origines jusqu'à nos jours*, to be complete in 26 tomes (not yet published, tomes 11, 12 14, 18, 22-26), Paris: Bloud & Gay, 1936-

—Palanque, Jean Remy—Bardy, Gustave—Labriolle, Pierre, *De la Paix Constantinienne a la mort de Théodose*, Tom. III, 1936.

—Labriolle, Pierre—Bardy, Gustave—de Plinval, G.—Brehier, Louis, *De la mort de Theodose à l'élection de Gregoire le Grand*, Tom. IV, 1945.

—Brehier, Louis—Aigrain, René, *Grégoire le Grand, les Etats barbares et la conquête arabe* (590-757), Tom. V, 1938.

—Amann, Emile, *L'époque carolingienne*, Tom. VI, 1937.

—Amann, Emile—Dumas, August, *L'Eglise au pouvoir des Laïques* (888-1057), Tom. VII, 1940.

Fournier, Edouard, *L'Origine du Vicaire Général et des autres membres de la Curie Diocèsaine*, Paris: Séminaire des Missions Etrangères, 1940.

Fournier, Paul—LeBras, Gabriel, *Histoire des Collections Canoniques en Occident depuis les Fausses Décrétales jusqu'au Décret de Gratien*, 2 tomes, Paris, 1931-1932.

Fowler, Joseph Thomas, *Adamnani Vita S. Columbae*, Oxford, 1920.

Fuhrmann, Joseph Paul, *Irish Medieval Monasteries on the Continent*, Washington, D.C., 1927.

Gallagher, Anthony Marie, *Education in Ireland*, Washington, D.C., Catholic University of America Press, 1948.

Galtier, Emile, *Histoire de Saint-Maur-des-Fossés*, 2 vols., Paris, 1913.

Ganshof, F. L., *Wat Warren de Capitularia*, Brussel: Paleis der Academien, 1955.

Gasquet, Francis Aidan, *A Life of Pope St. Gregory the Great, written by a monk of the Monastery of Whitby circa* 713; printed from MS. St. Gallen, 567, Westminster, 1904.

Germain, M., *Histoire de l'Abbaye royale de Notre-Dame de Soissons*, Paris, 1675.

Germer-Durand, Eug., *Cartulaire du Chapitre de l'Eglise Cathédrale Notre-Dame de Nîmes*, Nîmes, 1874.

Gogarty, Oliver St. John, *I Follow Saint Patrick*, London: Constable, 1950.

Gomot, Hippolyte, *Histoire de l'Abbaye royale de Mozat*, Paris, 1872.

Gougaud, Louis, *Christianity in Celtic Lands*, London, 1932.

———, *Gaelic Pioneers of Christianity*, Dublin, 1923.

Gout, Paul, *Le Mont-Saint-Michel*, Paris, 1910.

Goux, Pierre Antoine, *Lérins au Cinquième siècle*, Paris, 1856.

Graham, Rose, *English Ecclesiastical Studies, Being some Essays in Research in Medieval History*, London, 1929.

Guérard, M., *Cartulaire de l'Abbaye de Saint-Bertin*, Paris, 1861.

Hauck, Albert, *Kirchengeschichte Deutschlands*, 2 Bände, Leipzig, 1887.

Hébert, Pierre, *Etudes sur la Ville et Paroisse de Courbevoie*, Paris, 1908.

Hefele, Charles Joseph—Leclercq, H., *Histoire des Conciles*, 11 vols. in 21, Paris: Letouzey et Ané, 1907-1952.

Hefele, Charles Joseph, *A History of the Councils of the Church*, 5 vols., Edinburgh, 1876-1896; Vol. I, 2. ed., 1883.

Heimbucher, Max Joseph, *Die Orden und Kongregationen der katholischen Kirche*, 2 Bände, Paderborn, 1933-1934.

Henry, V. B., *Histoire de l'Abbaye de Saint-Germain d'Auxerre*, Auxerre, 1853.

Herwegen, Ildephonse, *Beiträge zur Geschichte des alten Mönchtums und des Benediktinerordens*, Heft 11-15, Münster in Westf., 1923.

Hilpisch, Stephanus, *Geschichte des Benediktinischen Mönchtums*, Freiburg im Breisgau, 1929.

Hove, Alphonse van, *Prolegomena* (ad Codicem Iuris Canonici), ed. 2, auctior et emendatior, Mechliniae-Romae: H. Dessain, 1945.

Hurry, Jamieson B., *Reading Abbey*, London: Elliot Stock, 1950.

Imbart de la Tour, Pierre, *Les Elections Episcopales dans l'Eglise de France du IX au XII siècles*, Paris, 1890.

———, *Les Paroisses rurales du V au XI siècle*, Paris, 1900.

Kapsner, Oliver, *A Benedictine Bibliography*, Collegeville: St. John's Abbey Press, 1949-1950.

Knowles, David, *The Monastic Order in England, History of its development from the times of St. Dunstan to the 4th Lateran Council*, 943-1216, Cambridge: University Press, 1949.

Kurth, Godefroid Joseph, *Saint Boniface*, Milwaukee, 1935.

Kurtscheid, Bertrandus—Wilches, Felix, *Historia Iuris Canonici*, Tom. I, *Historia Fontium et Scientiae Iuris Canonici*, Romae: Officium Libri Catholici, 1943.

Kurtscheid, Bertrandus, *Historia Iuris Canonici, Historia Institutorum*, Vol. I (ab Ecclesiae Fundatione usque ad Gratianum), 2. ed., Romae: Catholic Book Agency, 1951.

Lacour-Gayet, George, *L'Abbaye Saint-Germain des Prés, et son monastère Bénédictine*, Paris, 1924.

Lafontaine, Paul-Henri, *L'Evêque d'Ordination des Religieux, Etude Historico-Juridique*, Ottawa: Editions de l'Université d'Ottawa, 1951.

Lavisse, Ernest—Rambaud, Alfred, *Histoire Génerâle du IV siècle à nos Jours*, 3 ed., 12 vols., Paris, 1922-1931.

Lebreurier, P. F., *Le mémorial historique des Evêques, Ville et Comte d'Evreux*, Paris-Rouen, 1865.

Lefort, *Les Vies Coptes de Saint Pachôme et de ses Premiers Successeurs*, Louvain, 1943.

Lemarignier, Jean Francois, *Etude sur les privilèges d'Exemption et de juri-*

diction ecclésiastique des abbayes Normandes depuis les origines jusqu'en 1140, Paris: A. Picard, 1937.

Lerosey, A., *Histoire de l'Abbaye Bénédictine de Saint-Sauveur-le-Vicomte*, Abbeville, 1894.

Lesne, Emile, *Histoire de la Propriété Ecclésiastique en France*, 5 vols., (incompl.), Paris, 1910-1940.

Vol. I, *Epoques Romaines et Mérovingienne*, 1910.

Vol. II, *La propriété ecclésiastique et les droits regaliens à l'époque carolingienne*.

Fasc. I, *Les étapes de la Sécularisation des biens d'Eglise du VIII au X siècle*, 1922.

Fasc. II, *Le droit du roi sur les Eglises et les biens d'Eglise, VIII-X siècle*, 1926.

Fasc. III, *La dispersion des droits régaliens à la fin de l'époque carolingienne*, 1928.

Vol. III, *L'inventaire de la propriété. Eglises et trésors des églises*, VIII-XI siècles, 1936.

Letonnelier, Gaston, *L'Abbaye exempt de Cluny et le Saint-Siege*, Ligugé-Paris, 1923.

Levillain, Leon, "Etudes sur l'Abbaye de Saint-Denis à l'époque Mérovingienne," *Bibliotheque de l'Ecole du Chartes*, t. 87, 1926.

Lévy-Bruhl, Henri, *Elections Abbatiales en France*, Paris, 1913.

Lewis, Charlton—Short, Charles, *A Latin Dictionary*, 1951 Impression, Oxford: Clarendon Press, 1951.

Loening, Edgar, *Geschichte des deutschen Kirchenrechts*, 2 vols., Strassburg, 1878.

———, *Kirchenrecht in Gallien von Constantin bis Chlodevech*, Strassburg, 1878.

Lorain, M. P., *Histoire de l'Abbaye de Cluny*, Paris, 1845.

Lot, Ferdinand—Pfister, Christian—Ganshof, Francois, *Histoire du Moyen Age*, 8 vols., Paris: Les Presses Universitaires de France, 1928-1941, Tom. I, *Destinées de l'empire en Occident de* 398 *a* 888, Paris, 1928.

Lot, Ferdinand—Halphen, Louis, *La Règne de Charles le Chauve* (840-877), Paris, 1909.

Loth, Julien, *Histoire de l'Abbaye royale de Saint-Pierre de Jumiège*, 3 toms., Rouen, 1882.

McLaughlin, Terence G., *Le très ancien droit monastique de l'Occident*, Ligugé, 1935.

MacMaught, John Campbell, *The Celtic Church and the See of Peter*, Oxford, 1927.

Malnory, Arthur, *Saint Césaire, Evêque d'Arles*, Paris, 1894.

Marin, Eugène, *Les Moines de Constantinople depuis la fondation de la ville jusqu'à la mort de Photius*, Paris, 1897.

Martin, Eugène, *Saint Columban*, Paris, 1905.

Mehu, Eugène, *Salles en Beaujolais—Le Prieuré des Bénédictins de Cluny*:

Le Chapitre noble des Chanoinesses—Comtesses, Ville-franche-sur-Saône, 1910.
Migne, Jacques Paul, *Patrologiae Cursus Completus, Series Latina*, 221 vols., Parisiis, 1844-1864.
Un Moine de Lérins, *L'Ile et l'Abbaye de Lérins*, Lérins, 1929.
Molitor, Raphael, *Aus der Rechtsgeschichte benediktinischer Verbände, Untersuchungen und Skizzen*, 3 Bände, Münster in Westf., 1928-1931, Band I, *Verbände von Kloster zu Kloster*, 1928.
Montalembert, Count de, *Monks of the West*, 7 vols., Edinburgh, 1861-1879.
Mourret, Fernand—Thompson, Newton, *History of the Catholic Church*, 7 vols., St. Louis, 1930-1955.
Narberhaus, Josef, *Benedikt von Aniane, Werk und Persönlichkeit*, Münster-in-Westf., 1930.
Penjon, Auguste, *Cluny, la Ville et l'Abbaye*, Cluny, 1884.
Pierart, Z. J., *Histoire de Saint-Maur-des Fossés*, Paris, 1886.
Pignot, J. H., *Histoire de l'Ordre de Cluny depuis la fondation jusqu'à la mort de Pierre la Vénerable*, 3 vols., Autun and Paris, 1868.
Porcel, Olegaria M., *La DOCTRINA MONASTICA de San Gregorio Magno y la REGULA MONACHORUM*, The Catholic University of America Studies in Sacred Theology, n. 60, Washington, D.C., The Catholic University of America Press, 1952.
Pöschl, Arnold, *Bischofsgut und MENSA EPISCOPALIS*, 3 vols., Vol. I, Bonn, 1908.
Raby, F. J. E., *A History of Secular Poetry in the Middle Ages*, 2 vols., Oxford, 1934.
Ragut, M. C., *Cartulaire de Saint-Vincent de Mâcon*, Mâcon, 1864.
Reiffenstuel, Anacletus, *Jus Canonicum Universum*, 5 vols. in 7, Parisiis, 1864-1882.
Rocher, M., *Histoire de l'Abbaye royale de Saint-Benoît-sur-Loire*, Orleans, 1865.
Roth, Julien, *Histoire de l'Abbaye royale de Saint-Pierre de Jumièges*, 2 vols., Rouen, 1882.
Roy, Raoul, *Histoire de la Basilique et de l'Abbaye de Saint-Denis*, Lille, 1861.
Ryan, John, *Irish Monasticism, Origins and Early Development*, Dublin and Cork, 1932.
Sackur, E., *Die Cluniacenser in ihrer kirchlichen und allgemeingeschichtlichen Wirksamkeit bis zur Mitte des elften Jahrhunderts*, 2 vols., Halle, 1892.
Schaefer, Timotheus, *De Religiosis*, 4 ed., Romae: Editrice Apostolato Cattolico, 1947.
Schmitz, Philibert, *Histoire de l'Ordre de Saint Benoit*, 7 toms., Tom. I, *Origines, diffusion et constitution jusqu'au XII siècle*, Les Editions de Maredsous, 1942.
Schroeder, Henry J., *Disciplinary Decrees of the General Councils: Text, Translation and Commentary*, St. Louis: Herder Book Co., 1937.
Sickel, Th., *Beiträge zur Diplomatik*, Wien, 1863.

Smith, L. M., *The Early History of the Monastery of Cluny*, London-New York, 1920.

———, *Cluny in the 11th and 12th Century*, London, 1930.

Snow, Terence Benedict, *St. Gregory the Great, his Work and his Spirit*, London, 1892.

Stickler, Alphonsus M., *Historia Iuris Canonici Latini, Institutiones Academicae*, Tom. I, *Historia Fontium*, Taurini: Libreria Pontif. Athenaei Salesiani, 1950.

Stokes, Margaret MacNair, *Three months in the forests of France*, London, 1895.

Symons, Thomas, *REGULARIS CONCORDIA: the Monastic Agreement of the Monks and Nuns of the English Nation*, New York: Oxford University Press, 1953.

Tellenbach, Gerd. (tr. R. F. Bennett) *Church, State, and Christian Society at the Time of the Investiture Contest*, Oxford: Basil Blackwell, 1940.

Thillier, Joseph-Jarry, Eugène, *Cartulaire de Saint-Croix d'Orléans* (814-1300), Paris, 1906.

Thompson, James T., *The Middle Ages*, 300-1500, 2 vols., New York, 1931.

Tresvaux, M., *Histoire de l'Eglise et du Diocèse d'Angers*, 2 toms., Paris-Angers, 1858.

Vacandard, Elphège, *Vie de Saint Ouen, Evêque de Rouen* (641-684), Paris, 1902.

Viollet, Paul Marie, *Histoire des Institutions Politiques et Administratives de la France*, 2 toms., Paris, 1890.

Weigel, Gustave, *Faustus of Riez, an Historical Introduction*, Philadelphia: Dolphin Press, 1938.

Wyard, Robert, *Histoire de l'Abbaye de Saint-Vincent de Laon*, St. Quentin, 1858.

Zeiger, Ivo, *Historia Iuris Canonici*, 2 vols., Romae: Apud Aedes Universitatis Gregorianae, 1947.

ARTICLES

Bacht, Heinrich—Cramer, M., "Die Rolle des Orientalischen Mönchtums in den kirchenpolitischen Auseinandersetzungen um Chalkedon (431-519)" Grillmeier, Aloys—Bacht, Heinrich, *Das Konzil von Chalkedon, Geschichte und Gegenwart*, 3 vols., Würzburg: Echter Verlag, 1951-1954, Vol. II, *Die Entscheidung um Chalkedon*, pp. 193-314.

Berlière, Ursmer, "L'exercice du ministère paroissial par les moines," *Revue Benedictine*, XXXIX (1927), 231-233.

Bishko, Charles J., "Salvus of Albelda and Frontier Monasticism in 10th century Navarre," *Speculum*, XXIII (1948), 559-590.

Bittermann, Helen Robbins, "The Council of Chalcedon and Episcopal Jurisdiction," *Speculum*, XIII (1938), 198-203.

———, "The Influence of Irish Monks on Merovingian Diocesan Organization," *American Historical Review*, XL (1934-1935), 232-245.

Bois, J., "Chalcédoine (concile de)," *Dictionnaire de théologie catholique,* Tom. 26, col. 2192-2208.

Bourbon, Georges, "La license d'enseigner et le rôle de l'écolâtre au Moyen Age," *Revue des Questions Historiques,* XIX (1876), 512-553.

Boutaric, E., "La régime féodal, son origine et son établissement," *Revue des Questions Historiques,* XVIII (1875), 325-373.

Chamard, Francois, "Les Abbés au Moyen Age," *Revue des Questions Historiques,* XXXVIII (1885), 71-108.

———, "De l'immunité ecclésiastique et monastique," *Revue des Questions Historiques,* XII (1877), 428-464.

De Charmasse, A., "L'Ordre de Cluny du X au XII siècle," *Revue des Questions Historiques,* VI (1869), 265-271.

Daux, Camille, "La Protection apostolique au Moyen Age," *Revue des Questions Historiques,* LXXII (1902), 5-60.

Deanesly, Margaret, "Early English and Gallic Minsters," *Transactions of the Royal Historical Society,* 4th series, XXIII (1941), London, pp. 25-69.

DeClercq, Ch., "La législation religieuse franque depuis l'avènement de Louis le Pieux jusqu'aux Fausses Décrétales," (pars 3), *Revue de Droit Canonique,* VI, no. 3 (Sept. 1956), 282 ff.

Deschamps, Paul, "Critique du Privilège Episcopal Accordé par Emmon de Sens à l'Abbaye de Sainte-Colombe," *Le Moyen Age,* XXV (1912), 144-165.

De Valois, Jean, "Sur quelques points d'histoire relatifs à la fondation de Cluny," *Millenaire de Cluny,* Mâcon, 1910.

de Valous, Guy, "Le domaine de l'Abbaye de Cluny aux X et XI siècle," *Annales de l'Académie de Macon,* 3 serie, Mâcon, XXII (1920-1921).

Duby, Georges, "Recherches sur l'évolution des institutions judiciaires pendant le X et le XI siècle dans le sud de la Bourgogne," *Le Moyen Age,* LII (1946), 150-194; LIII (1947) 15-38.

Flach, Jacques, "La royauté et l'Eglise en France du IX au XI siècle," *Revue d' Histoire Ecclésiastique,* IV (1903), 432-447.

Flament, P., "Le premier seigneur de Bourbon et la charte de fondation de Chantelle," *Le Moyen Age,* XXVII (1919), 120-131.

Ganshof, François L., "Charlemagne et l'usage de l'écrit en matière administrative," *Le Moyen Age,* LVII (1951), 1-25.

Gaussin, Roger, "De la seigneurie rurale à la Baronnie: L'Abbaye de Savigny en Lyonnais," *Le Moyen Age,* LXI (1955), 139-177.

Grat, Felix, "La mention "*N. Impetravit*" dans les diplômes carolingiens, *Le Moyen Age,* XL (1930), 8-27.

Grierson, Philip, "Relations between England and Flanders before the Norman Conquest," *Transactions of the Royal Historical Society,* 4th Series, XXIII (1941), London, pp. 22-46.

Heurtebize, B., "Bernon," *Dictionnaire d' Histoire et de Géographie Ecclésiastique,* Paris, 1909-, VIII, 858 ff.

Jourdaine, Charles, "La royauté francaise et le droit populaire," *Revue des Questions Historiques*, XVI (1879), 337-381.

Kuttner, Stephan, "The Scientific Investigation of Medieval Canon Law: The Need and Opportunity," *Speculum*, XXIV (1949), 493-501.

Leclercq, H., "Exemption Monastique," *Dictionnaire d'Archéologie chrétienne et de liturgie*, Tom. V, col. 952 ff.

Lemarignier, J. F., "L'Exemption Monastique," *A Cluny Congrès Scientifique; Travaux du Congres*, Publiés par la Société des Amis de Cluny, Dijon: Imprimerie Bernigaud et Privat, 1950.

Lesne, Emile, "Les Ordonnances Monastiques de Louis le Pieux et la *Notitia de Servitio Monasteriorum*," *Revue d'Histoire de l'Eglise de France*, VI, (1920), 161-180; 321-333; 442-450.

———, "Nicolas I et les libertés des monastères des Gaules," *Le Moyen Age*, XXIV (1911), 277-306; 333-345.

de Leusse, G., "Saint-Remain-des-Iles," *Annales de l'Academie de Mâcon*, 3 serie, XXII (1920-1922).

Levillain, Leon, (Review of Miss Bittermann's article in *American Historical Review*), *Le Moyen Age*, XLV (1935), 236-237.

———, "L'Archechapelain Ebroin, Evêque de Poitier," *Le Moyen Age*, XXIV (1923), 177-215.

———, "Sur deux documents carolingiens de l'Abbaye de Moissac," *Le Moyen Age*, XXVII (1914), 1-35.

———, "Le Formulaire de Marculf et la critique moderne," *Bibliotheque de l'Ecole des Chartes*, LXXXIV (1923), 21-91.

J.A.M., (Monk of Downside), "The Cathedral Priories of Old England," *Downside Review*, XII (1893), 171-191.

Naz, R., "Décrétales (Fausses)," *Dictionnaire de Droit Canonique*, IV, 1062-1064.

Odegaard, Charles E., "The Concept of Royal Power in Carolingian Oaths of Loyalty," *Speculum*, XX (1945), 279-289.

Saxer, V., "Le statut juridique de Vézelay à la fin du XII siècle," *Revue de Droit Canonique*, VI, n. 2 (June, 1956), 145-162; VI, n. 3 (Sept. 1956), 225-261.

Scaduto, Mario, "Bernone," *Enciclopedia Cattolica*, II, 1456.

Schmitz, Philibert, "Benoît d'Aniane," *Dictionnaire d' Histoire et Géographie*, VIII, 177-188.

Symons, Thomas, "The English Monastic Reform of the 15th Century," *Downside Review*, LX-LXI (1940-1941), 1-22; 196-222; 268-279.

Taché, Louis, "Notes sur l'histoire des exemptions monastiques," *Revue de l' Université d'Ottawa*, XI (1941), 5*-31*; 149*-177*.

Ueding, Leo, "Die Kanones von Chalkedon in ihrer Bedeutung für Mönchtum und Klerus,"—Grillmeier, Alois—Bacht, Heinrich, *Das Konzil von Chalkedon, Geschichte und Gegenwart*, 3 vols., Würzburg: Echter Verlag, 1951-1954, Vol. II, *Die Entscheidung um Chalkedon*, pp. 569-676.

Vykoukal, E., "Les Examens du Clergé paroissial à l'époque Carolingienne," *Revue d'Histoire Ecclésiastique*, XIV (1913), 81-96.

Williams, Schaefer, "The Pseudo-Isidorian Problem Today," *Speculum*, XXXIX (Oct., 1954), no. 4, 702-707.

Williams, Watkin, "St. Benedict of Aniane," *Downside Revue*, LIV (1936), 357-374.

PERIODICALS

American Benedictine Review, Newark, 1950—
Benediktinische Monatschrift, Beuron, 1919—
Downside Review, Downside Abbey, Bath, 1880—
Le Moyen Age, Bruxelles, 1888—
Revue Bénédictine, Abbaye de Maredsous, Belgium, 1884—
Revue de Droit Canonique, Strasbourg, 1951—
Revue d'histoire de l'Eglise de France, Paris, 1910—
Revue d'histoire ecclésiastique, Louvain, 1900—
Revue des questions historiques, Paris, 1866—
Speculum, Cambridge, Mass., 1926—
Traditio, New York, 1943—

ABBREVIATIONS

Bouquet	Bouquet, *Recueil des historiens des Gauls et de la France*
Bruel	Bernard—Bruel, *Recueil des Chartes de l'Abbaye de Cluny*
Cap. Reg. Fr.	*Capitularia Regum Francorum*
DACL	*Dictionnaire d'Archéologie chrétienne et de liturgie*
Gallia Christiana	*Gallia Christiana in Provincias Ecclesiasticas distributa*
Lesne	Lesne, *Histoire de la Propriété*
Mansi	Mansi, *Sacrorum Nova et Amplissima Collectio*
MGH	*Monumenta Germaniae Historica*
MPL	Migne, *Patrologiae Cursus Completus, Series Latina*

ALPHABETICAL INDEX

BIOGRAPHICAL NOTE

Charles William Henry was born on July 22, 1923, in St. Cloud, Minnesota. He received his primary training in St. Mary's Parochial School in St. Cloud, and entered Cathedral High School in 1937, graduating in 1941. He attended St. John's University, Collegeville, Minnesota, from the fall of 1941 until the spring of 1943. On February 10th of that year he entered the Armed Forces, and served in the American and Southwest-Pacific Battle Theatres for three years, receiving an honorable discharge on February 28, 1946. Returning to St. John's University, he completed another year and one half of studies there. In 1947 he entered the novitiate of the Order of St. Benedict at St. John's Abbey, and made simple profession of vows in 1948. In 1950 he received the degree of Bachelor of Arts from St. John's University, and was subsequently sent by his Abbot to the International Benedictine Academy, the Pontifical Athenaeum of Sant' Anselmo in Rome, for his course in theology. He was ordained to the priesthood in 1953, and received the degree of Licentiate in Sacred Theology in the following year. On his return to the abbey, his abbot sent him to the Catholic University of America to study Canon Law, in which discipline he received the Baccalaureate degree in 1955, and the Licentiate degree in 1956.

www.ingramcontent.com/pod-product-compliance
Lightning Source LLC
La Vergne TN
LVHW050244080826
844660LV00012B/595

* 9 7 8 0 8 1 3 2 2 5 4 2 5 *